D0985005

THE ANIMALS' WAR

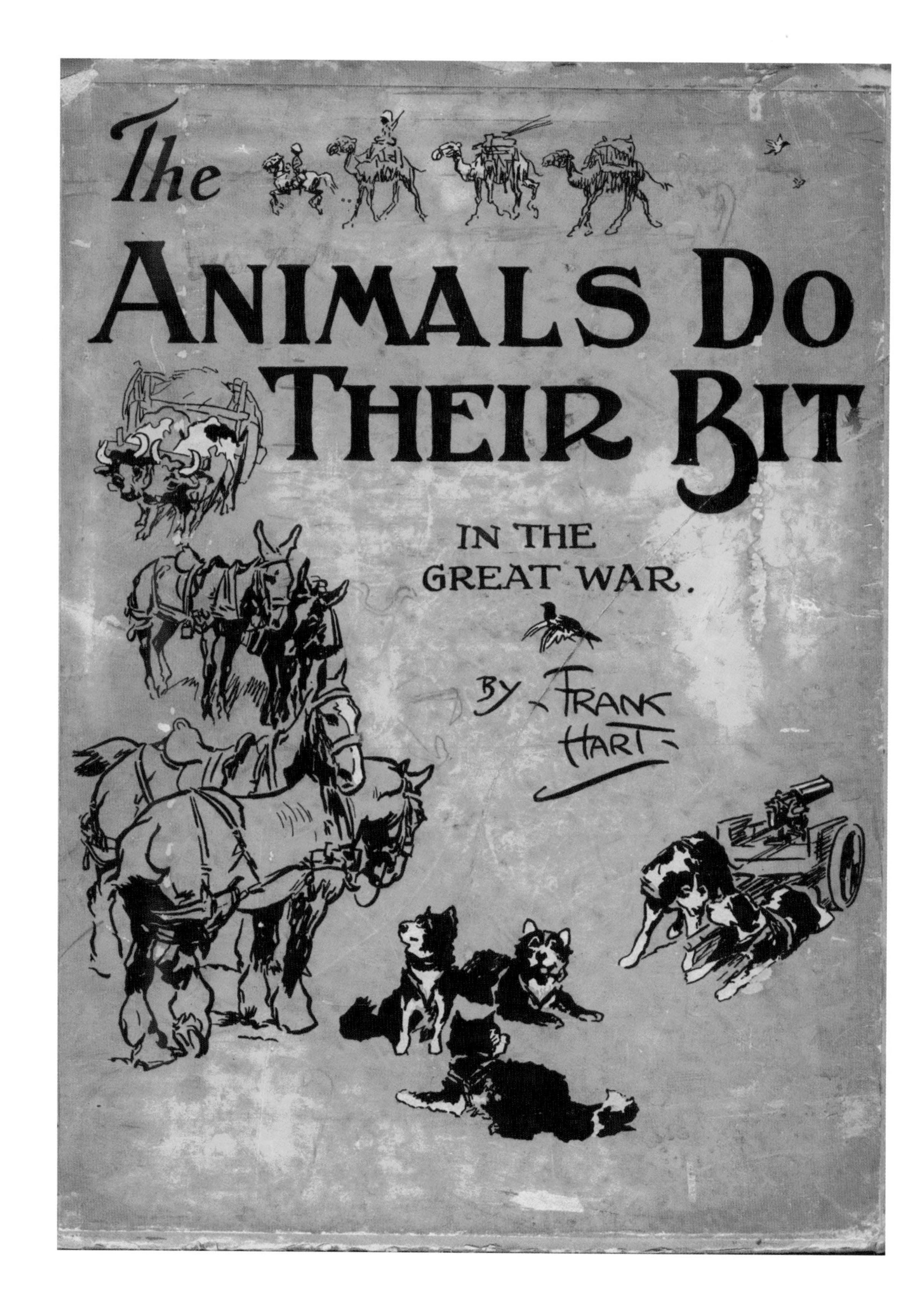
The
ANIMALS DO
THEIR BIT
IN THE
GREAT WAR.
BY FRANK
HART

THE ANIMALS' WAR

Animals in wartime from the First World War to the present day

Juliet Gardiner

in association with the Imperial War Museum

Visit the Portrait website!

Portrait publishes a wide range of non-fiction, including biography, history, science, music, popular culture and sport.

Visit our website to:
- read descriptions of our popular titles
- buy our books over the internet
- take advantage of our special offers
- enter our monthly competition
- learn more about your favourite Portrait authors

VISIT OUR WEBSITE AT: www.portraitbooks.com

Copyright © 2006 by Juliet Gardiner

First published in 2006 by **Portrait**
an imprint of Piatkus Books Ltd
5 Windmill Street
London W1T 2JA
e-mail: info@piatkus.co.uk

In association with the Imperial War Museum
www.iwm.org.uk

Every effort has been made to identify and acknowledge copyright holders. Any errors or omissions will be rectified in future editions provided that written notification is made to the publisher.

The moral right of the author has been asserted

A catalogue record for this book is available from the British Library

ISBN 0 7499 5103 6

Designed and edited by Compendium Publishing Ltd,
First Floor, 43 Frith Street, London W1D 4SA

Set in Adobe Bembo

Printed and bound in Italy by LEGO SpA, Vicenza

Contents

Foreword by Jilly Cooper

It is with great joy that I welcome Juliet Gardiner's wonderful book, *The Animals' War*. Its publication will coincide with what I'm sure will be an equally wonderful second exhibition, staged by the Imperial War Museum, to illustrate the role animals have played in war – a subject with which I have been obsessed for more than 20 years.

May I start by taking you back to 25 May 1983 and the Museum's epic first 'Animals in War' exhibition? This was opened by Barbara Woodhouse at a splendid launch party swarming with military top brass. Glamour was provided by such animal-loving stars as Joanna Lumley, Judy Geeson, Katie Boyle, Selena Scott and the blond, blue-eyed Commanding Officer of the Household Cavalry, Lt-Col Andrew Parker Bowles. I was present because I, like Juliet Gardiner, had written a book to accompany the exhibition, entitled *Animals in War,* which had been published on the same day.

Outside, a hilarious photocall in spring sunshine included such military 'A' list celebs as a ram mascot called Derby XXIII of the Worcestershire and Sherwood Foresters, who was longing to take on Billy the goat mascot of the Royal Welch Fusiliers; Flight Lieutenant Frederick, an insouciant pelican in an RAF tie; Rats, the little terrier mascot, who endeared himself to so many regiments in Northern Ireland; and finally Sefton, at 19 the oldest and most terribly injured horse in the IRA bombing at Hyde Park, who survived and returned to work, a national symbol of heroism.

Both Rats and Sefton were still receiving daily sackfuls of fan mail and with megastar Caprice resisted every attempt by Barbara Woodhouse to discipline them. Rats took refuge on Sefton's back. Sefton refused to 'sit' or 'go walkies' and hampered the photographers by resolutely exposing himself.

It was all terribly funny. I needed to laugh. Not being an academic or a historian, I had been excited and flattered to have been asked to write my book. Nothing, however, had prepared me for the horror and sadness of the subject. I had no idea of the millions and millions of different animals who had served and died alongside our armies, and was absolutely shattered to discover the enormity of their suffering.

Locked away in my study day after day, I despaired I would ever finish on time. The only redeeming feature seemed to be the animals themselves: horses, donkeys, oxen, mules, camels and elephants to mention only a few, who had such idiosyncratic and endearing personalities, and who somehow brought true affection and humour to even the most desperate military situation. The result was a book written in tears and not ink.

I was delighted last year to learn that a second exhibition was planned and a new book would bring fresh recognition for the animals to a new generation; but I trembled for Juliet Gardiner, who I admire and like enormously, and who would now have to immerse herself in such a heartbreaking subject. Happily she has risen magnificently to the occasion. *The Animals' War* is not only beautifully written and intensely moving, but as an historian Juliet has also burrowed like a search and rescue dog to unearth fascinating new material and a host of little details which make her reconstructions of the past so vivid.

Having written so poignantly about evacuees being wrenched from their parents in *The Children's War,* she captures the anguish that members of the public felt when their horses were called up in the First World War and quotes 'the sadness of one rough-looking man who came in with two carthorses and stayed half an hour patting them and giving them sugar'.

Little did these owners appreciate the hellhole – dragging guns and ammunition through miles of foetid mud – to which they were committing their beloved horses, and how few would return home. A dreadful eight million horses are estimated to have died in the First World War; Juliet creates a harrowing picture of the Western Front, where most of the horses and mules perished not from enemy fire but from cold, disease or starvation, so famished that they chewed other horses hairless or ate each other's rugs and choked on buckles.

The Animals' Memorial, Brook Gate, Hyde Park, London.

Here again Juliet leavens the horror with fascinating facts: that grey horses proved far more resilient than black or dark brown ones and that when the army ran out of curry combs, the soldiers used empty bully beef tins to scrape down their mud-caked horses.

One of the only good things about war was the love that grew between the soldiers and their animals. For a man far from home, frightened, lonely, facing death, a horse, an ox, or even a ferret mascot, who could return affection, was an immeasurable comfort.

Animals in addition relieved the isolation of men in high command. General Eisenhower, like President Bush today, adored the cheerful, black Aberdeen terriers known as 'Scotties'. His Scotty accompanied him on campaigns and was the only living thing, Ike claimed, he could talk to that didn't want to discuss the war. Juliet writes of Winston Churchill's passion for animals – dogs, cats, and budgerigars.

During the Second World War, I nightly shared a Morrison shelter in the dining room with Jamie our Scotty until the siren went and my parents would tumble groggily in beside us. I was therefore particularly intrigued by Juliet's evocative chapter on the Home Front, but appalled to learn that pets weren't allowed into public shelters and dogs had to be tethered outside or tied to white posts, with chains and collars attached, which had been hammered in all over Hyde Park. Knowing my own dogs' terror of fireworks, the

poor creatures must have been utterly traumatised. Even more horrific was an RSPCA suggestion that when the family trotted off to the shelter its dog should be left imprisoned in a dustbin, driving it literally 'barking mad'.

Conversely, Juliet cites much press outrage in 1940 when £100 was spent on a shelter for 36 dogs in Kensington Gardens. Why should mere animals be saved when there was a single woman and child unprotected in the land?

Perhaps this disregard for any animal right stems from the fact that, despite the millions of words written over the years to glorify the soldier's courage, little praise was ever given to the horses which bore him. To single out a horse or any other animal for praise was as alien to most military commanders as to suggest a tank or helicopter fought with gallantry.

The 60th anniversary D-Day celebrations in 2004 rightly honoured the valour of human veterans. But no one mentioned Bing, the Alsatian. Dropped into Normandy on D-Day with the 13th Battalion of the Parachute Regiment, this handsome dog landed in a tree and all night endured the terror of enemy shelling. Although badly wounded in the neck and eyes, once cut free of his parachute, Bing stood guard on a vital section of the battalion's front, his presence a huge comfort to the troops, especially at night.

There is also a pernicious school of thought that says animals don't deserve medals for gallantry, because bravery is only the result of instinct or training. But surely bravery was displayed by mules that marched uncomplaining for days with bullets embedded in their spines, or by mine dogs that kept searching when their faces were half blown away or by pigeons that battled through blizzard and shell fire with beaks and claws shot off to save planes and ships in distress?

Think of the police horses in the Blitz that, when the bombs fell showering them with broken glass, carried on calmly setting an example to everyone, as their riders directed the traffic. Think too of the guide dogs on 11 September 2001 that carried on the baton, leading their blind masters down more than 70 flights of stairs out of the blazing, crumbling World Trade Center to safety. How can you not call this courage? By honouring such valour with medals you draw the public's attention to the valour of the animals and, as a result, they may be treated more kindly in peacetime.

My favourite human in *The Animals' War* is Air Force Sergeant Christopher Batta, handler of a Belgian Malinois sniffer dog, Carlo, who on a 60-day tour of Kuwait discovered a phenomenal 167 caches of explosives. On returning to America, Sergeant Batta was awarded with a Bronze Star. But on learning there was no accompanying award for his gallant dog, he whipped off his medal and hung it round Carlo's neck, saying that Carlo worked harder and was always in front.

One of the pleasures of Juliet's extensive research is that she has discovered much more about animals who only had walk-on parts in my book: Rob the 'paradog', for example, a jaunty collie who made 20 drops and was awarded the 'animals' VC', the Dickin Medal, for leading SAS patrols into enemy territory. I was thrilled to learn that Rob made it home after the war, settling happily into farm life, his only condition being that in future he would lead his patrol of sheep from the front instead of herding them from behind!

Animals have been treated so badly in war that one cannot forbear to cheer when they assert themselves like Rob or kick over the traces, like the wilful American sea lions, who, having been extensively and expensively taught to detect enemy submarines, bunked off into the open sea never to return. One of my favourite stories in my book was of the experienced but opinionated Royal Army Veterinary Corps officer who, when put in charge of the Mule School in Hong Kong, decided the mules' fitness might be improved by a little jumping. Alas he left the timber to build the fences in the mules' field overnight. By morning, like beavers, they had eaten the lot.

Few animals in fact inspired more devotion than the mule. One thinks of the Indian muleteers, paid only £1.20 a month, who refused ever to go on leave and be parted from their beloved mules. My father, who was at Dunkirk, said the saddest sight was the mules abandoned on the beaches because there was only room in the little boats back to England for their heartbroken drivers.

Even more dreadful was the fate of the guard and patrol dogs in Vietnam who were estimated to have saved the lives of 10,000 US soldiers. When the army moved out, however, these poor dogs were classed as 'surplus equipment' and left chained to their kennels to the non-existent mercy of the Viet Cong.

Long after my book was finished, I was haunted by the suffering of the animals and bitterly ashamed that we, as an ostensibly animal-loving nation, were one of the few countries in the world not to recognise their heroism with a national monument.

As a result, in 1996 I and a group of friends, including Joanna Lumley, Kate Adie, General Peter Davies, then head of the RSPCA, and Andrew Parker Bowles, now a Brigadier, decided to remedy the situation by founding the Animals in War Memorial Fund.

After the mother of all battles raising the money, our memorial was unveiled at last in November 2004 on a beautiful grassy site in Park Lane. Designed by David Backhouse, it is evocatively described by Juliet on page 187.

From the little glow worms that lit the soldiers' maps to the poor white hens used to detect the presence of chemical attack in Iraq, there is hardly a member of the animal kingdom that hasn't been dragged suffering and uncomprehending into our wars. They had no idea why they were fighting or when the nightmare would end. They gave their service, their lives, and their love without any thought of reward. That is why our memorial is engraved with the words, thought up by my husband, Leo Cooper: 'They had no choice'.

As people pour out of the Imperial War Museum this summer, I urge them to buy *The Animals' War* so that the beautiful pictures and Juliet's inspiring text will constantly remind them of the debt we owe the animals.

I hope the same people will find time to visit our memorial, which I believe will become as much a London landmark as Nelson's Column. As they ponder in sadness on the appalling casualties, pat the wistful dog and the noble horse, and whisper encouragement to the trembling mules, I pray they will be as glad as I am that a terrible injustice has been righted and the animals that fought so bravely have at last been thanked.

The Animals' Memorial, Brook Gate, Hyde Park, London.

INTRODUCTION

The displacements of war. Mary Kessell (1914–78):* 'A Dying Horse Pulling Chattels'*, 1945. Kessell worked as an official war artist in Germany at the end of the war.

Three weeks after Britain declared war on Germany on 4 August 1914, Sir Edward Elgar, the composer of 'Pomp and Circumstance March Number 1' better known as 'Land of Hope and Glory', wrote to a friend. 'Concerning the war I say nothing – the only thing that wrings my heart and soul is the thought of the horses – oh my beloved animals – the men – and women – can go to hell but my horses; I walk round and round the room cursing God for allowing dumb brutes to be tortured – let Him kill the human beings but – how CAN HE? Oh, my horses.'

The conscription of animals to fight man's wars strikes a deep chord: Elgar's anguish resonates throughout books, stories, songs, paintings, photographs, prayers and poems, the words and images paying tribute to the part that animals have played in warfare throughout the centuries. 'They Also Serve', 'Silent Heroes', 'They Had No Choice' are all paeans of praise to the courage of animals caught up in combat, recognition of the vital tasks they have performed – and continue to perform today – in front-line action, transportation, communication, protection and detection, and their contribution to morale. And there is always an undertow of sorrow that the brutality men can inflict – and suffer – is so often shared by animals.

From the horses and elephants of the ancient world carrying soldiers into battle and transporting supplies, to the warrior dolphins of the 21st century, animals – from pigeons to camels, from glow worms to donkeys, from mules to goats, from dogs and cats to canaries – have been indispensable to man's belligerent or defensive activities and thousands upon thousands have perished in the endeavour.

There are countless stories and anecdotes about individual animals in war, about their bravery, loyalty, steadfastness and ingenuity, and these deserve to be retold. And since, tragically, war seems to be a perennial and almost universal part of the human condition, new forms of warfare and modern technologies have added yet more names to the roll call of animal heroes – and heroines – and previously undreamt-of ways in which that status was won.

But *The Animals' War* should be more than a collection of plucky tales, no matter how inspiring, interesting or moving these sometimes funny and often sad tales are. Reading about animals tells us about mankind. Animals are not volunteers. They are conscripted for their qualities and their utility. How and where and when they are employed in situations of combat and how they are treated in those situations – and afterwards – are revelatory about how wars are fought, what their objectives are and, perhaps above all, about humanity in warfare. Faced with the atrocities of war: mass slaughter, the extermination of innocents, mutilation, destruction and waste, it may seem trivial – perverse, even – to be concerned with a canary, to mourn a mule. But animals, too, play a vital part in the prosecution of war, being able and prepared to go where no mechanised vehicle can venture, heave loads beyond the strength of men, carry messages when technologies fail, ferret out the injured, sniff out the lethal, and provide companionship where there is little but danger and grim endurance.

Furthermore, the use of animals in warfare raises difficult issues. The various movements in recognition of animal rights have caused us to think deeply about animals being used in situations that are as dangerous to them as they are to the fighting men alongside them. Animals do not give their consent for war, but then throughout history men have been forced, press ganged or conscripted into wars whose objectives were decided by politicians and by generals and not by those who fought and died. Recent work on animal sentience has shown us how near at least a number of animal – and bird and insect – species are to human consciousness. So how far is the 'bravery' of animals simply an evolutionary instinct, and how far and in what ways is it a conscious and selfless conquering of fear for a perceived objective?

At this stage in our knowledge it is not possible for any book – or exhibition – to answer such questions definitively. But the range of ways, the variety of situations, in which animals go to war and the contributions they have made to the successful prosecution of battles and campaigns, skirmishes and engagements, over the centuries should remind us that our understanding of war is diminished and impoverished if we fail to consider the role that animals play alongside that of the fighting men and women, and the civilians of all ages, in times of conflict.

St George fights his dragon. A recruiting poster, 1915.

1

Front Line

The Great Game. A First World War recruiting poster.

Horses have been in the front line of battle since men realised that, by pulling a rope through the animal's mouth, a horse could be ridden and not just herded like cattle for meat. The speed and fleet-footedness of horses transformed warfare since not only could warriors on horseback mount a surprise attack, they could also retreat at a pace that confounded foot soldiers. Over the centuries, animals were bred to adapt to changing conditions of war and trained to outmanoeuvre new weapons of combat, and chariots were developed that were light and manoeuvrable so that they could be pulled by horses into battle.

The iconic images of warfare down the ages are of horses – the near-nomadic Hyksos tribes on horseback and in chariots bearing down victoriously from the north on the mighty Egyptian armies around 1800BCE; Alexander the Great on his powerful horse Bucephalus ('Ox Head') leading a cavalry of 5,000 to rout the Persian armies in 330 BCE; the Huns on their small stocky ponies challenging the supremacy of the Roman Empire, the chain-mail-clad knight depicted on the Bayeux Tapestry, nimble in battle, dodging the arrows of the bowmen; French *destriers*, heavy shire-like horses, which were so effective in carrying knights wearing armour that could weigh as much as 30lb into battle that from the 12th century their use spread throughout Europe; Prague-born Prince Rupert fighting as a mercenary for the Royalist cause in the English Civil War, scorning to use a musket but charging into battle brandishing his sword; Frederick the Great with his ferociously drilled cavalry flanked by outriders pulling gun carriages; the Scots Greys thundering into battle on their magnificent mounts in the paintings of Lady Elizabeth Butler; horses with their riders senselessly crashing and slithering in the doomed charge of the Light Brigade into the 'jaws of the valley of death' during the Crimean War; the great cavalry charge at the Battle of Omdurman in 1898 when Kitchener led an Anglo-Egyptian army into the Sudan to put down the Khalifa's forces.

During the protracted Boer War fought in South Africa from 1899 to 1902, the horse proved paramount. The British forces, confident of trouncing the Boers within a few weeks, were disconcerted to find themselves facing commandos of 'Bible thumping farmers mounted on scruffy little ponies' who could outgun and outride them and fight a guerrilla campaign on land they knew intimately. The British cavalry tactics of a massed charge were impossible against such a foe; also the horses were exhausted by a gruelling sea voyage round the Cape of Good Hope and most were ill-suited to the climate and conditions of the Transvaal. But Lieutenant-Colonel Miller of the Pembroke Yeomanry, who admired the Boers 'as splendid horse masters', pointed out that those British units 'who always filled their horses' bellies with grass of the *veldt* and who took every opportunity of watering, who never brought their horse into camp hot, but off saddled and let their horses have a roll in the sand or earth, who groomed their horses and looked after them before they looked after themselves; those units could gallop when other units could only raise a jog trot.'

Britain was the eventual victor in the wearisome war through sheer weight of numbers – horses as well as men. But the toll was devastating: 5,774 troops from Britain and her Empire had been killed and 22,289 wounded, some 20,000 more died of disease and other non-combat-related illnesses, and out of the 520,000 remounts (horses held in reserve behind the line for when a cavalryman's horse was killed or injured) supplied, 326,073 – well over half the horses – died. Most died not from enemy fire but from sickness, exhaustion and neglect, and, with scant medical attention in the field, many brought diseases back to Britain that would take years to stamp out.

Thereafter the Edwardian period saw a revolution in transportation and mobility that seemed to render the horse increasingly redundant both for military and civilian purposes. By 1905 there were already 16,000 private cars on the roads of Britain and increasingly vans and buses were powered by internal combustion engines rather than pulled by horses.

The horse was so disregarded in this forward march of progress that on the outbreak of the First World War on 4 August 1914 the British Army had only about 23,000 horses, yet within a fortnight seven times that number had been acquired. Some of these horses were sold to the army by firms such as Thomas Tilling – the London bus company – which was then busily converting its vehicles to horseless carriages. Others were impressed or requisitioned. The order that went out from the Deputy Assistant Director

'Life is real and life is earnest ...'

'This is going to be my war diary,' wrote Ethel Bilbrough, a very comfortably-off woman of strong opinions living in Chislehurst in Kent, on 15 July 1915. 'I don't mean that it is to be political, or literary, or anything of that kind ... it will merely be my own personal impressions ... it seems to me that everyone who happens to be alive in such stirring epoch-making times ought to write *something* of what is going on! Just think how interesting it would be to read years hence!'

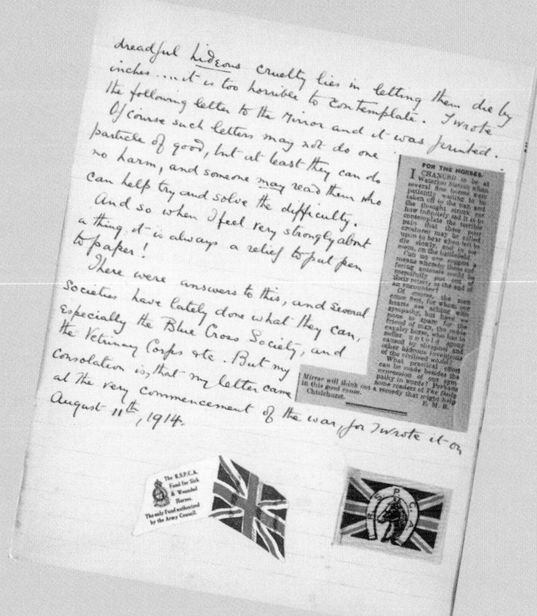

dreadful hideous cruelty lies in letting them die by inches ... it is too horrible to contemplate. I wrote the following letter to the Mirror and it was printed. Of course such letters may not do one particle of good, but at least they can do no harm, and someone may read them who can help try and solve the difficulty. And so when I feel very strongly about a thing it is always a relief to put pen to paper!

There were answers to this, and several Societies have lately done what they can, especially the Blue Cross Society, and the Veterinary Corps etc. But my consolation is, that my letter came at the very commencement of the war, for I wrote it on August 11th, 1914.

FOR THE HORSES.

I CHANCED to be at Waterloo Station when several fine horses were patiently waiting to be taken off to the war, and the thought struck me how infinitely sad it is to contemplate the terrible pain that these poor creatures may be called upon to bear when left to die slowly, and in vain, on the battlefield.

Can no one suggest a means whereby these suffering animals could be mercifully put out of their misery at the end of an encounter?

Of course, the men come first, for whom our hearts are aching with sympathy, but have we none to spare for the friend of man, the noble cavalry horse, who has to suffer untold agony caused by shrapnel and other hideous inventions of the civilised world?

What practical effort can be made besides the expression of our sympathy in words? Perhaps some readers of The Daily Mirror will think out a remedy that might help in this good cause.

E. M. B.
Chislehurst.

'I'm only a cavalry charger/And I'm dying as fast as I can/They've potted both me and my master' – a verse penned to plead to the 'kind folks who work for the Red Cross/Oh please help the Blue one [the animal charity] as well'.

A page from the war diary of Ethel Bilbrough of Chislehurst showing her lively concern for horses. As well as contributing to and collecting for animal charities, the wealthy Mrs Bilbrough frequently wrote to the press, as here, about their plight. 'Of course, the men come first, for whom our hearts are aching in sympathy, but have we none to spare for the friend of man, the noble cavalry horse, who has to suffer untold agony caused by shrapnel and other hideous inventions of the civilised world?' she wrote in a letter to the *Daily Mirror*, published on 11 August 1914.

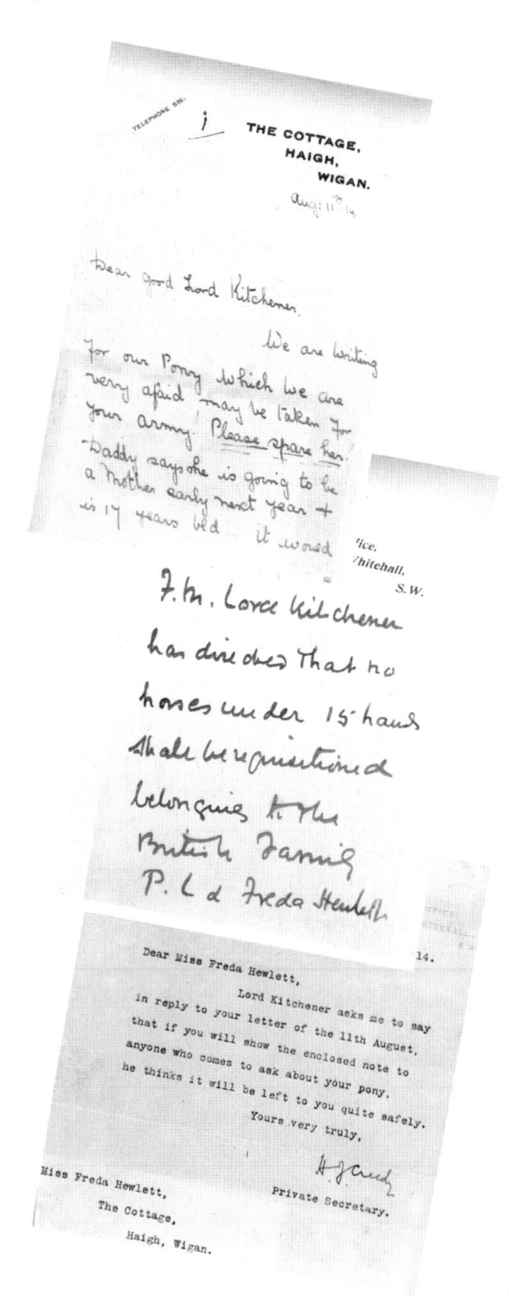

TELEPHONE 515.

THE COTTAGE,
HAIGH,
WIGAN.

Aug: 11th 14

Dear good Lord Kitchener.

We are writing for our Pony which we are very afaid may be taken for your army! Please spare her. Daddy says she is going to be a mother early next year & is 17 years old it would

...fice,
...hitehall,
S.W.

F.M. Lord Kitchener has directed that no horses under 15 hands shall be requisitioned belonging to the British Family P. L & Freda Hewlett

14.

Dear Miss Freda Hewlett,

Lord Kitchener asks me to say in reply to your letter of the 11th August, that if you will show the enclosed note to anyone who comes to ask about your pony, he thinks it will be left to you quite safely.

Yours very truly,

H. J. Creedy

Private Secretary.

Miss Freda Hewlett,
The Cottage,
Haigh, Wigan.

The response Field Marshal Lord Kitchener sent to Poppy, Lionel and Freda Hewlett, three 'troubled little Britishers' who had written from Wigan asking the Secretary of State for War to spare their pony since: 'it would break our hearts to let her go. We have given 2 others and 3 of our family are now fighting for you in the Navy. Mother and all will do anything for you but please let us keep old Betty and send official word quickly before anyone comes.'

of Remounts, Southern Command, stationed at Petersfield in Hampshire on the day that war broke out, was typical. It was headed 'Requisition of Emergency (under the Army Act S115) for the provision of Carriages, Animals and Vessels, for the purpose of completing the War Establishment of His Majesty's Forces', and was signed by the Prime Minister, H. H. Asquith. So thoroughgoing was the exercise that on 20 August 1914 a letter was sent from the War Office on behalf of the Army Council to convey 'their deep appreciation of the services they have rendered to the Army and the Nation … to those gentlemen who have been good enough to carry out the duty of horse purchaser during the period of mobilization. Without these gentlemen's assistance it would have been impossible to carry out the task of providing 14,000 horses in 14 days, and without horses the mobilization of the Army would be incomplete.'

The Army – indeed the country – might well have had reason to be grateful to the horse purchasers. But for those who watched as their horses – either beloved domestic animals or loyal workers, and often both – were summarily examined, commandeered and despatched to war, it was often an anxious and wrenching experience that tested their patriotism and resolve sorely. Mary Coules, who was the daughter of the head of the Reuters Press Agency, kept a journal during the First World War, and on 9 August 1914 she 'went to the Steyne Playing Fields to see the horses that had been commandeered. Poor beasties. Three magnificent hunters came in from Findon and it must have hurt someone to part with them. "Thou'st sold my Arab steed." A rough-looking man came in with two cart horses, and stayed for about half an hour patting them and giving them sugar. It was all very sad. We took a photo …'

A poem in one of the anthologies sold to raise money for wounded horses by the Royal Society for the Prevention of Cruelty to Animals (RSPCA), which was closely involved in the welfare of horses in war, as in peace, summed up the bewilderment of many owners whose horses had gone to war:

'We didn't know much about it.
We thought they'd all come back
But off they were all taken
White and Brown and Black;
Cart and cab and carriage,
Wagon and Break and Dray,
Went out the call of duty.

'And we watched them go away.
All of their grieving owners
Led them along the lane
Down the hill to the station
And saw them on the train.
They must be back by Xmas,
And won't we give them a feed!'

In addition to the horses procured nationally, many thousands more were purchased

Horses disembarking in France are given a cursory veterinary examination before being taken to the Remount Depot. A wash drawing from Captain Sidney Galtrey's 1919 book **The Horse and the War.**

in North America, South America, Australia, New Zealand, India, South Africa, Spain and Portugal. By 1916 there were a total of 103 cavalry divisions (British, German, French, Russian, Austro-Hungarian etc) fighting, comprised of around a million cavalrymen. It was for these men, considered to be the élite of the armies, that such a significant number of horses and remounts were required, since at the start of the Great War most officers and military planners were still confident that wars were won by cavalry attack despite the mechanisation of transport and the increasing power and velocity of the weapons of war. Such officers would have echoed the categorical assertion of the 1907 issue of *Cavalry Training* that 'it must be accepted that the rifle, effective though it is, cannot replace the effect produced by the speed of the horse, the magnetism of the charge, and the terror of cold steel'. And the undoubted glamour of the cavalry lingered on. As a young private watched his comrades preparing to go 'over the top' on the eve of the battle of the Somme which started on 1 July 1916, he noted 'this was to be the big breakthrough to end the stalemate; to end the war … all were intensely alive … a troop of cavalry trotted past them two by two. Sombre enough in their drab khaki, but in the eyes of their trench-dwelling comrades romantic and splendid. A good omen surely!' In fact, the cavalry played virtually no part in the ensuing battle while the infantry fell in their thousands with nearly 60,000 British casualties on the first day alone, of whom a third died.

War Horse

'There were men in khaki uniforms everywhere; and then as Albert's father dismounted and led us past the church towards the green, a military band struck up ... As we approached the flagpole ... an officer pushed towards the crowd towards us. He was tall and elegant in his jodhpurs and Sam Browne belt, with a silver sword at his side ... "Well farmer," said the officer, nodding his appreciation as he looked me over. "I thought you'd be exaggerating when we talked in The George last evening. 'Finest horse in the parish,' you said, but then everyone says that. But this one is different – I can see that ... You're right farmer, he'd make a fine mount for any regiment and we'd be proud to have him – I wouldn't mind using him myself ... Fine looking animal, no question about it."'

An extract from *War Horse* by Michael Morpurgo, erstwhile children's laureate. The book tells the story from the viewpoint of Joey, a horse from a Devon farm, 'and the people whose lives he touches, as they struggle for survival in the blasted wilderness of the Western Front' in the First World War. The book ends as Joey and his master, Albert, come home for Christmas in 1918. 'Both of us were received like conquering heroes, but we both knew that the real heroes had not come home, that they were lying out in France ...'

British cavalry rest in a shell hole on the Arras-Cambrai road in April 1917 during the Battle of Scarpe.

On the Western Front, the Great War would not to be a war of movement, of grand cavalry charges, of thundering hooves in sweeping attack and counter attack with flashing blades ranging over the battlefields of France and Flanders. In this terrain it was to be a war of stasis, of stalemate and desperately slow attrition in which thousands of lives – human and animal – would be lost to bullets and shells to gain a yard or so of muddy ground. And it would not be over by Christmas, as the RSPCA versifier had hoped – a hope shared by those who went off to fight and those who waited at home. Yet, British generals – most of whom were themselves cavalrymen – clung tenaciously to their vision of an ultimate 'cavalry breakthrough'. Field Marshal Sir John French, the first British commander-in-chief, who had won his reputation on the South African *veldt*, deeply regretted the 'tremendous *crust* of defence' the German forces had formed. 'How I should love to have a real good "go" at them in the open with lots of cavalry and horse artillery to run them to earth. Well! It may come,' he wrote longingly. And his successor General Sir Douglas Haig continued to maintain that 'the power of the army as a striking weapon depends on its mobility. Mobility is largely dependent on the suitability and fitness of animals for army work.'

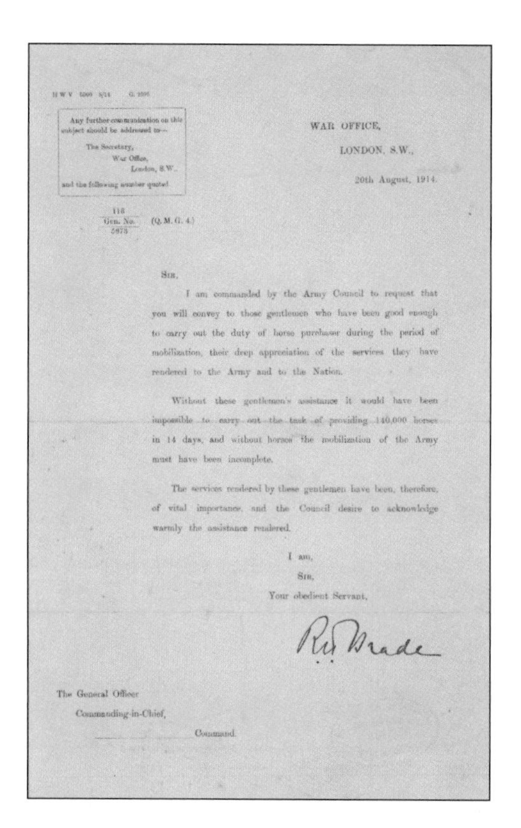

Any further communication on this subject should be addressed to—
The Secretary,
War Office,
London, S.W.,
and the following number quoted.

116
Gen. No.
5878
(Q.M.G. 4.)

WAR OFFICE,
LONDON, S.W.,
20th August, 1914.

SIR,

I am commanded by the Army Council to request that you will convey to those gentlemen who have been good enough to carry out the duty of horse purchaser during the period of mobilization, their deep appreciation of the services they have rendered to the Army and to the Nation.

Without these gentlemen's assistance it would have been impossible to carry out the task of providing 140,000 horses in 14 days, and without horses the mobilization of the Army must have been incomplete.

The services rendered by these gentlemen have been, therefore, of vital importance, and the Council desire to acknowledge warmly the assistance rendered.

I am,
SIR,
Your obedient Servant,

R H Brade

The General Officer
Commanding-in-Chief,
______ Command.

A letter from the War Office ordering that all those who had provided horses for the British Army in 1914 should receive an official letter of thanks.

As a historian of the cavalry observed – somewhat prematurely as it was to turn out – 'the death knell of the horsed cavalry was struck at some unrecorded moment on 13 September 1914.' By that date the German advance on Paris had been temporaily delayed at Le Cateau, some 30 miles south of Mons, on 25 August, a prelude to the Battle of the Marne, in early September, the battle that was to save Paris from rapid conquest. The brave action of the cavalry managed to save vital howitzer guns at a high cost to horses and men. Then, on a September day, a French cavalry corps under General Conneau was poised to strike at the wide-open lines of communication of the 2nd and 3rd German Armies. But Conneau failed to press home his advantage. The Germans 'were given time in which they could dig in their trenches, set up their machine guns, and then wire them in with the deadly barbed wire that was to hog-tie the battle field … Soon every front-line soldier in [Western] Europe was burrowing like a mole, throwing up parapets and paradoses, revetting and wiring, erecting strong points and evacuating dug outs, and abandoning the battlefield to the domination of the machine gun until man's inventive genius thought up the tank.

'Horsed cavalry experienced their moments on the Western Front, but those moments were few and far between – for most of the time they were kept waiting for opportunities that never came … the Great War of 1914–18 … reduced the art of war to a bloody slogging match from trench to trench …'

When the murderous attrition of the deadlocked trenches did finally become one of movement again, it was to a large extent mechanised vehicles, not horses, that charged into combat. Yet even in 1916, when the world's first tanks were deployed on the Western Front, there were still more than a million cavalry horses on all fronts – the greatest number yet assembled for war.

There were, however, moments in the Great War when the cavalry fought in its traditional role: one such occasion was at Moreuil Ridge. The main German offensive had been mounted against the British 5th Army commanded by a cavalryman, General Sir Hubert Gough. The line was vulnerable: depleted by the terrible losses at Passchendaele the previous year, with little time to strengthen the defences. In support of the British, the Canadian Cavalry Brigade, a volunteer force led by Brigadier-General Jack Seely, tirelessly plugged gaps in the Allied lines and then on 30 March 1918 'Galloper Jack', as Seely was known, led his horsemen to retake the captured Moreuil Ridge – 'an insignificant wooded hill in a remote corner of rural France' – that had become key to defending the line from Amiens to Paris. Cavalry soldiers dismounted and fought hand to hand like infantry, while three troops led by Lieutenant Flowerdew charged the German positions holding the ridge, 'killing many enemy with the sword: and wheeling about galloped on them again'. The squadron lost 70 per cent of its members and in the machine gun fire 'horses and men pitched to the ground like rabbits in a farm shoot'. Over 300 men had been killed and wounded and over 800 horses had fallen between 9.30am – when the first squadron of the Royal Canadian Dragoons had charged up the slopes of Moreuil Ridge – and 11am when all German resistance ceased except in the southern corner of the wood. But, aware of the vital strategic significance of the ridge, the German soldiers mounted counter attack after counter attack, and by the early hours of the next morning the Canadians passed the baton to the infantry of

John Singer Sargent RA (1856–1925):* 'Scots Greys 1918'*, horses stabled on the Western Front in the First World War.

the 8th Division who had come to relieve them. As they stumbled back in the dark pounded by the unceasing clamour of the guns, the exhausted men 'passed scores of silent and shadowy figures stretched out in the stubble. For the most part these were dead horses, but here and there a rider lay torn and twisted beside his mount …' The cost of the day's action had been tragically high in men and beasts 'but the German advance had been stemmed'. The charge at Moreuil Ridge, an old-style cavalry action that had 'pitted men on horseback, armed with swords, against men in trenches, armed with machine guns', had, against all the odds, succeeded and has become enshrined in the record of the Canadian cavalry.

If the war in France and Flanders offered only limited opportunities for the horsed cavalry, there were other theatres in the Great War where it played a key role. On the wider plains of the Eastern Front, German and Austrian cavalry skirmished with the Russian Cossacks, but, according to James Lunt, a historian of the cavalry, 'even in Galicia and Poland the machine gun and barbed wire restricted their mobility'. But it was in

The Last Cavalryman

Albert 'Smiler' Marshall was born in 1897 in the garrison town of Colchester in Essex. As a child he had thrilled to the red coats of the soldiers on parade and when Kitchener called for young men to go to fight in the Great War, Marshall lied about his age and enlisted in the Essex Yeomanry. He had learned to ride as a small child when his father put him on a goat and taught him to ride it facing its head and then its tail. Marshall proved to be a natural cavalryman in those days when the commanding generals – Haig included – believed it was cavalry that would win the war. At Cambrai in 1917 the Essex faced the advancing German infantry. 'We drew our swords and cut them down. It was cut and thrust at the gallop. They stood no chance,' Marshall recalled proudly and was to be deeply impressed as he watched the Bengal Lancers riding bareback, lances aloft, rout the enemy. 'It was "a colossal sight"'. But it wasn't the cavalry that won close engagements: high-explosive shells terrified the [horses] and chlorine gas blinded them – as it did the men. And horses were an easy target as they stood corralled behind the lines. Of 800,000 horses used on the Western Front, most of them for transport and hauling artillery, only about half survived.

It was hard to persuade Albert Marshall to go on battlefield pilgrimages since he had 'such terrible memories' of the war: his best friend was killed next to him in the trenches by a sniper; as a 20-year-old he was part of a burial party during the Battle of the Somme, burying in the iron-hard ground dead men that he'd breakfasted with earlier that same day. He was half buried in the mud of no man's land when a shell exploded nearby and he was gassed twice. When he was wounded in the hand, the Army decided that he could no longer handle a horse so 'Smiler' volunteered for the Machine Gun Corps.

Albert Marshall died on 16 May 2005 aged 108. He was the last representative, as one of his obituarists wrote, 'of perhaps the most quixotic part of that doomed enterprise, the cavalry units of the Western Front.'

Albert 'Smiler' Marshall, 1897–2005 on horseback. Marshall's nickname related to a drill sergeant who threatened: 'I'll give you something to smile about' when Marshall hit him with a snowball.

ABOVE: *The long retreat from Mons. A line of British cavalry in late August 1914 after the first engagement between British and German forces on the Western Front in the First World War.*

LEFT: 'Immediate Overseas Service.' *An appeal for 'good' men from Canada to fight with the horse artillery on the Western Front in the First World War.*

Palestine that a campaign for which 'there is no parallel in military history … by such a mass of cavalry against a yet unbroken enemy' took place. The cavalry divisions consisted of regular regiments of the Indian Army, light horse and mounted regiments from Australia and New Zealand, many of whose men were sheep farmers who had ranged across the outback on horseback almost as soon as they could walk, and yeomanry regiments from Britain. Most yeomanry regiments had first been assembled at the end of the 18th century when a French invasion seemed imminent, with country gentlemen and landowners raising their own troops of horsemen, which they mounted, dressed and equipped at their own expense, and fox-hunting farmers flocked to join this almost feudal force. Often the horses that the yeomen rode were their own, and Lunt tells of the Earl of Dudley who took the Worcestershire Yeomanry (The Queen's Own Worcestershire Hussars) to Gallipoli in 1915 and armed the entire regiment at his own expense, furnishing his men with modern swords in place of the sabres provided by the War Office.

At the end of 1916, desperate to break out of the terrible stalemate of the Western Front and with British prestige in the Middle East at rock bottom after the disasters in the

ABOVE: ***British cavalry await orders to move forward during the Battle of Arras, 26 May 1917.***

OPPOSITE: ***A German shell bursting amidst the artillery horse lines near La Basée Canal, Neuve Chapelle, during the Battle of Estaires, 9–11 April 1918. Estaires was retaken by the British on 20 August 1918.***

Gunners watering their horses in the snow near St Pol in February 1917.

Feliks Topolski (1907–1989): **'A Russian Cavalry Horse-drawn Machine-gun',** *1941. The Polish-born artist came to Britain in 1935 and served as an official war artist in the Second World War.*

Dardanelles, the Prime Minister, Lloyd George, ordered that the Allied troops then along the Egyptian border should advance into Palestine. However, two disastrous battles to take Gaza forced the troops back with heavy casualties, so that by the late spring of 1917 it had begun to look as if the trench warfare of the Western Front would be replicated in the Middle East. This time, however, without the mud but with sand storms, an unforgiving heat that could soar to 110° Fahrenheit (41° Centigrade) in the shade, and flies which drove men and their horses alike to near insanity. In June 1917 General Allenby, a cavalryman 'with a reputation for ruthlessness', was appointed to command the Egyptian Expeditionary Force. Charged by the War Office to break the deadlock in Palestine and to capture Jerusalem, Allenby had some 76,000 soldiers, 20,000 of them mounted. His force far outnumbered the Turks but could be effectively deployed only if the Turks could be driven out of their fortifications to fight on the desert plains. And there was the problem of water for the horses, most of which had been without water for between 24 and 60 hours. To secure an adequate supply, Allenby would need to capture the desert settlement of Beersheba with its plentiful wells within 24 hours, or the operation would have to be called off. Riding through the night, the cavalry had covered 35 miles by dawn and was able to take the Turkish defenders by surprise. After a day of fierce fighting, as the desert night was drawing in, the 4th Australian Light Horse Brigade massed for a final assault. Wielding their bayonets like swords, the horsemen galloped furiously towards the Turkish trenches. The horses' hooves kicked up dense clouds of smoke and, reaching the

Cossacks in the front line. The Red Army cavalry charging the enemy in a posed photograph taken* circa *1941/2.

outskirts of the settlement, which they found unprotected by barbed wire, the men dug their spurs deep into the horses' flanks and leapt the obstacles 'like steeplechasers'. Within two hours Beersheba was in British hands, the victory achieved by the speed and daring of the shock action of hundreds of mounted troops, first in attack and then in pursuit. Jerusalem fell in December 1917 and the 5th Cavalry Division ended its 500-mile pursuit of the Turkish armies at Aleppo in October 1918, close to where Alexander the Great had shown 'how battles could be won by bold and well-handled horsemen'.

Lest there is any temptation to thrill to a vision of flying hooves and flashing steel, there was a very heavy price to be paid by men and their mounts in 20th-century cavalry charges which faced not a sea of swords but a barrage of shells and machine gun fire. As a British NCO reflected in the aftermath of such a charge, all he could see was 'Dead 'uns, dead 'orses, shell 'oles, and the 'undred other 'orrors what goes to make up the pageant of war!'

If the cavalry went into battle but rarely on the Western Front in First World War, it might be expected that horses would have been rendered obsolete by the Second, with the development and deployment of tanks – or 'land ships', as they had been called in the First World War – along with motorised vehicles, heavy guns and aircraft, causing them to be replaced by the armoured vehicle with simpler needs and greater resilience. A poem written by Mary E. Dawe saluting this transformation had appeared in the RSPCA magazine *Animal World* in March 1917:

'To a Tank

'How like a dinosaur or mastodon
Some weird survival of the ages gone, Looming before us;

' ... With caterpillar wheels and scaly hide,
Taking the trenches in an easy stride,
Certain to win;
Clearing the course of houses and of trees,
Or armed battalions with consummate ease,
Bound for Berlin ...'

However this was not entirely to be. The French Army, with its great tradition of horsemanship, had dwindled to only three cavalry divisions out of which five light cavalry divisions were formed in 1940 each with a combat strength of around 10,000 men with 2,200 horses. And, all told, two and three-quarter million horses and mules were used by the German Army, twice the number that had been used in the First World War. The majority were, to be sure, used for transport and supply, but the 1st Cavalry Division saw action in eastern Holland and France until on 3 November 1941, the feast day of St Hubertus, the patron saint of the cavalry, the division dismounted for the last time and

James Prinsep Beadle (1863–1946): **'The Breaking of the Hindenburg Line'.** *The line was a series of linked, fortified German defences behind the Western Front under construction from September 1916. Beadle, born into a military family, had depicted military victories since his painting of the Duke of York's Own Loyal Suffolk Hussars was exhibited at the Royal Academy in 1893 to considerable acclaim. His paintings of the Great War included* **'Dawn: Waiting to Go Over'** *and* **'Neuve Chapelle, 10 March 1915'**, *all painted from imagination but sometimes with the help of veterans of the war.*

Horses of the Royal Field Artillery sheltered near a ruined church in Ypres in January 1918.

was finally mechanised during the winter of 1941/2 to become the 24th Panzer Division, part of the 6th Army which fought at Stalingrad. From then on, mounted squadrons were used by the German Army mainly for reconnaissance, until a reserve cavalry force was reformed to be on mobile alert, and this force saw action in densely wooded areas in which it was hard for mechanised vehicles to venture. In addition, the SS Death's Head Mounted Regiment was formed on 21 May 1940 to become part of an SS cavalry division, which fought in the Balkans and on the Eastern Front alongside a Cossack division whose 2,000-odd horsemen controlled their horses with a plaited whip and snaffle. According to a historian of the cavalry of the Second World War, these horses were 'superbly trained. They would obey one rider alone, his voice or his whistle.' During these campaigns the Germans studied their horses closely and discovered that brown horses were more likely to go lame and bruised more easily and black horses were more susceptible to fatigue, while grey horses proved to be the most robust. But during the bitter winter of 1941–2 in Russia, all horses were desperately short of forage and up to 20 per cent of the German horses died of starvation, even though their masters tried to supplement their meagre rations with whatever they could find including potato tops, birch leaves and a type of locally grown bean that sadly proved to be poisonous to the horses. Meanwhile, with a shortage of men for the front, German women were used to

LEFT: ***Shelters erected to protect horses from shellfire on 'W' Beach, Gallipoli,* circa *May/June 1915.***

OPPOSITE: ***Sir Alfred Munnings (1878–1959):* 'Charge of Flowerdew's Squadron', circa *1918. Lieutenant Gordon Flowerdew, commander of C Squadron, Lord Strathcona's Horse, a formation of the Canadian Cavalry Brigade, was awarded a VC for leading a mounted charge at Moreuil Ridge. Munnings, three times rejected for military service as he was blind in one eye, spent much of the war working at the horse remount depot at Calcot near Reading. But in 1918 he was attached to the Canadian Cavalry Brigade as official war artist, and his paintings of the brigade's horses earned him subsequent commissions, fame and fortune.***

break in horses and to train infantrymen to ride – though the cavalry units had their own remount supplies.

In Poland, the largely aristocratic-officered cavalry that went to war in 1939 was in all essentials the same as the élite force that had fought in the 19th century. Though the men carried rifles and bayonets, and cooking utensils as well, the cavalry fought with lances, long tubular steel shafts that were thrust at the enemy, and the officers could be distinguished by their elegant, highly polished hand-made leather riding boots. When Germany invaded Poland on 1 September 1939 (the *casus belli* of the Second World War as far as Britain and France were concerned) almost the entire 70,000 horsemen of the Polish cavalry were deployed in a defensive formation strung out along the 950-mile frontier but were unable to play either a tactical or a strategic role in the bitter fighting that followed. Horses crashed to the ground, hit by hails of bullets, or bolted, dragging their riders with them, as cavalrymen charged the infantry behind the advancing German Panzers with their lances, and soon bodies littered the ground and riderless horses galloped across the battlefield. Throughout September the cavalry counter-attacked whenever and wherever possible with great bravery and élan, and it was not until 6 October 1939 that reluctantly but 'in order to save further bloodshed' the Polish cavalry surrendered.

(John) Edwin Noble (1876–1961): **'An Injured Horse Being Loaded into a Motor Ambulance'.** *Noble served as a sergeant in the Army Veterinary Corps during the First World War where he was employed as an official war artist depicting horses and mules in charcoal and watercolours. He subsequently appears to have worked almost exclusively as an animal artist, illustrating, for example,* **Aesop's Fables.**

At the start of the Second World War, apart from the Poles and Romanians, the Red Army was the only army with large cavalry formations. The Red Cavalry Army had been set up after the revolution of November 1917 by a former Tsarist cavalry NCO, Semyon Mikhailovich Budenny. The force had first conquered the Ukraine and Southern Russia, and then in the 1920 war against Poland nearly managed to reach Warsaw. As late as 1934, the 17th Communist Party Congress was told that 'it is necessary once and for all to put an end to the theory of replacing the horse with the machine'. Cossacks were horsemen from communities that existed on the frontiers of the Russian Empire and who maintained a certain independence when they flocked to the colours in time of war. Each Cossack brought two ponies of his own on the promise that should his mounts be shot from under them, the government would furnish 'as many more as they would live to ride in battle'. Large numbers of Cossacks had been liquidated or deported by Stalin in the years following the Revolution: now that war had come, they were reinstated. They went on to form the core of the mounted troops of the Red Army – a small but highly mobile combat force which although perhaps half the size of an infantry regiment possessed almost the same fire power. The Russian cavalry had been deployed in the invasion of Poland and took a major part in Russia's battles for Moscow and Stalingrad. One of the last full-scale cavalry charges of the war took place in November 1941 when the Red Army's 44th Mongolian Cavalry Division was wiped out near the village of Mussino by a German infantry division. None the less the Russians and the Germans persisted in using cavalry units throughout the war for patrolling and mopping-up operations.

By the outbreak of war, all British cavalry units except one had been mechanised as armoured formations. The 5th Cavalry Brigade consisted of three regiments, and one of these, the Cheshire Yeomanry, was to take part in the last action of a mounted unit of the British Army, against the forces of Vichy France in Syria during the advance on Damascus in 1941. The horses were mainly hunters and the men were armed with sabres and rifles, though each section also had a machine gun section attached. Soon after the successful campaign in Syria, the regiment was dismounted and men and horses were deployed as dispatch riders for the Royal Signals.

OPPOSITE TOP: *Bandaging wounded horses, near Ypres, October 1916.*

OPPOSITE BELOW: *A model of a horse treatment box with restraints.*

By 1941, the only British cavalry still fighting was with the Burmese Frontier Force. Consisting of Burmese troops commanded by British officers from the Indian cavalry, their function was largely reconnaissance. On 18 March 1942 a column of the 2nd Frontier Forces was ambushed by the Japanese. But rather than attempt to escape, their commander, Captain Sandeman, drew his sabre, ordered the bugler to give the signal for attack and galloped towards the enemy, his men following with their battle cry 'Sat, Sri Aka!' It was the final charge in the history of the British cavalry and it ended in death from a barrage of bullets for the commander – still brandishing his sabre – his men and their horses.

By the end of 1941, when America entered the war after the Japanese attack at Pearl Harbor, the United States Army, the first army in the world to become fully motorised, had only one mounted cavalry unit, which was stationed north of Manila in the Philippines. In January 1942 the US Army garrison and the newly-formed Filipino Army withdrew to the Bataan Peninsula 'like a cat into a sack', where, with no fodder for the horses, they were fed on highland rice straw left over from the previous year's harvest. Embattled, with men dying from malnutrition, malaria and dysentery in the humid conditions, with no food for the horses and with the Japanese advancing, a desperate decision was taken. On 15 March 1942 the 250 horses of the 26th Cavalry and 26 baggage mules were slaughtered – and cooked. The resulting stew 'tasted good with curry and rice' though the meat was tough. On the night of 8/9 April, three or four remnants of the 26th Cavalry managed to escape by boat from Bataan along with some 300 US infantrymen and a number of Filipino soldiers.

However, over 60 years later, at the start of the 21st century, the US Army was rumoured to be fighting on horseback again – this time in Afghanistan. In a war in which 'smart bombs' targeted the Taliban insurgents, it was claimed that commandos of the US Special Operation Forces had taken to the saddle and were advising Northern Alliance troops how to 'employ light infantry and horse cavalry in an attack against Taliban T-55s (tanks) mortars, artillery, personnel carriers and machine guns ... We have witnessed the horse cavalry bounding

'Who Dares Wins'

Salvo, the 'paradog' that made a record number of drops, in training in Britain during the Second World War.

'Rob is fit and well and doing a grand job,' read a note from the War Office to the Bayne family on their farm in Shropshire. Rob was the black and white collie that the family had loaned for the war effort. But this cryptic report failed to say that dog 471/322 was by then one of Britain's 'paradogs', working with the SAS (Special Air Service), and he had been dropped in North Africa and then in Italy to assist the small, highly-trained groups operating behind enemy lines.

The training of parachute dogs had started in January 1944. 'It was obvious,' wrote the man charged with the possibilities of parachuting dogs into action along with the parachute troops '... that a dog chosen for this work must have higher qualities than those of an ordinary patrol dog,' and clearly Rob was such a dog, 'of great energy ... and utterly fearless.'

Dogs that fitted this profile and were 'for reasons readily obvious ... if anything of an aggressive nature' were selected from the War Dog School, and training began in a fully equipped but grounded fuselage. They then moved on to an operational Dakota aircraft that was being repaired but in which the animals could get accustomed to the vibrations of the aircraft and the revving of the engines. Canine parachutes were designed with straps looping round the dog's four legs and the 'chute was opened automatically by a static line, on the same principle as the human parachutist's equipment. It was decided that the dog would jump last of the 'stick' (the line of parachutists about to jump) to ensure that there was no risk of it getting entangled in the men's parachutes, with possibly fatal results for both.

The dogs were trained to jump by getting them accustomed both to aircraft noise and the 'pull' of the slip stream with a velocity of 60mph. 'Not being capable of logical reasoning nor gifted with imagination,' they would associate the situation with food and being reunited with their handler rather than the somewhat hazardous operation they were expected to undertake.

After two months' training, it was time for the real thing. On 3 April 1944, an Alsatian bitch Ranee, plus 'a two-pound piece of meat', was taken up in an Albermarle (which had been found a more suitable aircraft for paradogs) and she eagerly watched the line of parachutists jump before doing the same herself. Her 'touch down' was exemplary, she was 'completely relaxed, making no attempt to anticipate or resist the landing, rolled over, and immediately scrambled to her feet and started looking round.' However, a descent of 400 feet in 14 seconds, 'a speed at which a human parachutist would probably break his neck', was considered too fast, so the size of the parachute was increased to 24 feet, rather than the original 18-feet span, to slow the animal's descent.

Building on Ranee's experience, SAS Rob was to complete more than

20 parachute jumps, and, had the authorities not insisted that he comply in full with quarantine regulations on his return from duty overseas, he would have been involved in the parachute drop on Arnhem as part of Operation 'Market Garden', in which so many of the men he had got to know perished.

In February 1945 Rob was awarded the Dickin Medal for his valiant service. In November he was demobbed back to the farm where forever after he refused to round up the cattle from behind, but insisted on leading from the front.

ABOVE: *Salvo, a fox terrier owned by a 2nd Lieutenant in the US Army Air Force, ready to eject. The dog leapt from 1,500 feet and landed without a scratch on Andrewsfield in Essex during the Second World War.*

LEFT: *Rob, a collie awarded the Dickin Medal, the 'animals' VC', along with seven other decorations for his valour as a 'paradog' with the tough SAS in North Africa and Italy during the Second World War.*

RIGHT: ***In Egypt the Desert Mounted Camel Corps used horses and camels to pursue the Turks. The 1st Hertfordshire Yeomanry and Bikanir Camel Corps (in the background) are shown during a desert reconnaissance.***

OPPOSITE: ***Stuart Reid:*** **'Bombing of the Wadi Fara on 20th September 1918',** ***depicting an attack by the Australian Flying Corps (AFC) on the Turkish 7th Army which effectively 'ceased to exist' after the 'massacre' from the air. No 1 Squadron of the AFC went on to assist T. E. Lawrence (Lawrence of Arabia) whose Arab army had been constantly harassed by enemy aircraft.***

BELOW: 'Regimental Band'. ***Design for a poster by Darsie Japp (1883–1973).***

from spur to spur to attack Taliban strong points – the last several miles under mortar, artillery and sniper fire. There is little medical care if injured, only a donkey ride to the aid station which is a dirt hut,' according to a declassified report from the US Defense Department in February 2002. Other military watchers were sceptical. They pointed out that horses are a traditional form of transport and supply in the mountainous terrain, that all troops might resort to horseback on occasions, and that some insurgents carry weapons and fight on horseback. However a planned cavalry charge against tanks and armoured vehicles is a desperate tactic. Though it was one that was on occasions used in the Second World War, as one cavalryman in Germany's 1st Mounted Regiment wrote: 'the horse does what you ask of him' and hundreds of thousands, if not millions, perished in the field, pitted against cold, disease, starvation – and the brutal methods of combat.

STUART REID

2

Beasts of Burden: Horses on the Western Front

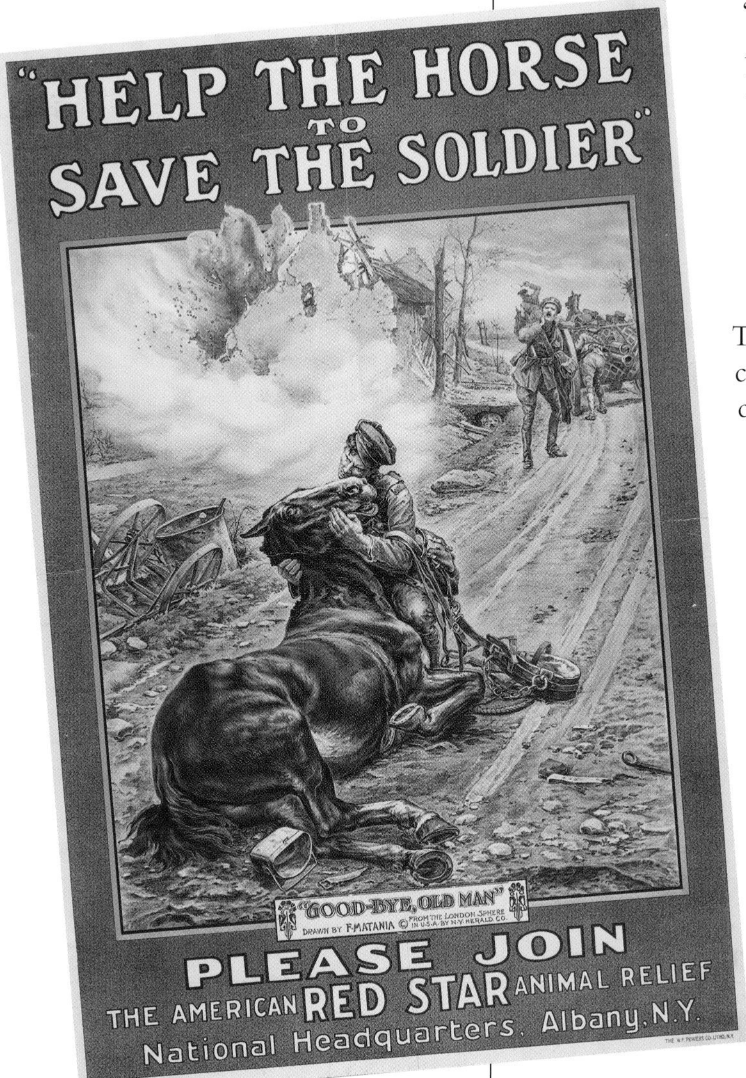

Poster incorporating the painting by Fortunino Matania of* 'Good-bye, Old Man' *used to raise funds for a US animal welfare charity, 1918.

'You're not a cavalry charger,
An officer's pride and delight,
Dashing with comrades around you
Straight into the thick of the fight
You are only a humble servant
Of the tenth divisional train
Just hauling a heavy wagon
Through the ruts of the shell-swept plain …'

This was the lot of most horses in the two world wars and in subsequent conflicts. The poem, published in *The Animal World* in November 1916, continues:

'You can give no grand distinction
Old horse, but you've given your best
With a faithful, dumb submission …'

In the First World War horses – and mules too – were yoked in teams to pull the heavy howitzer guns, some of which discharged shells as heavy as 60lb. They were employed to haul ammunition wagons, to transport shells, food and other supplies needed at the front, and to bring back to the field hospitals the wounded and the bodies of the dead. By November 1917, the number of horses and mules in use in the British Army was 'not less than a million. Their task – the forward movement of supplies and artillery – on ground where motor-traction is impracticable – is an arduous one,' explained an article entitled 'An Impression from the Western Front' in the RSPCA magazine.

'On the way up to the front line one encounters a ceaseless steam of traffic, amidst which horse and mule-drawn vehicles predominate. Intermingled with them are ridden horses, many of which are carrying shells, or returning empty from a trip to the various batteries. In summer the work of our equine friends is less arduous than during the vigorous months of winter, but both horse and mule lead a hard and strenuous existence no matter what the weather conditions may be.

'In summer there are flies and heat to contend with, and in winter the awful mud

William Roberts RA (1895–1980): ' "Feeds* **Round!" Stable-time in the Wagon-lines, France',** *1922. Roberts was a founder member of the short-lived but influential Vorticist group of avant-garde artists founded by Wyndham Lewis in 1914 that celebrated the hard-edged dynamism of the modern world. The First World War effectively brought the movement to an end but Roberts continued to paint geometric, two-dimensional tubular shapes, and this representation of the wagon lines in France is one of his several powerful images of front-line scenes of the war.

tries the powers of the gamest horse. Yawning shell-holes gape to receive the unwary beast which wallows into them … Coming down from the line, one passes horses and mules caked from ears to tail with a thick, adhesive coating [of mud], both the teams and the vehicles behind them looking as if they had wallowed in the yellow filth for weeks. Their work over for the time being, both horses and mules receive attention in their lines, but stables there are none. Cleaned and fed they spend the night standing together in dejected groups, awaiting the time for a return to duty …'

Rowland Luther was a young Welsh coal miner when the First World War broke out, but then he saw a poster depicting 'depleted ranks of soldiers, artillery, gunners and drivers with empty saddles urging *"Here is a place for you. Fill IT"* … I joined up on 9th September 1914' and the young man soon found that he was to be 'known as 28933 Driver RM Luther of the Royal Field Artillery Regiment'. He was sent to a riding school to learn to ride. 'I was given instruction as a rough rider, bare back, and for a week's training practised mounting and dismounting until hard gristle appeared between my legs and I could not sit down. The horses were well trained and would throw their riders quite simply. "Grip with your knees" was the constant instruction … Guns and horses were given to us – the real thing at last. Admittedly it was only one horse per man, but the day

The landscape of war (1). A pack horse loaded with trench boots is led through the mud near Beaumont Hamel on the Western Front.

was not far distant when it would be possible to handle three horses per man … I eventually began to like horses, and became a good rider. We were issued with spurs which we fixed to the heels of our ammunition boots. We were also given bandoliers and were looking more like soldiers every day … Now the real training began: two horses per driver. One day a corporal was dragged a hundred yards. His saddle had slipped through a slack girth. It was horrible to see his head and body being bumped and dragged along the ground. His foot had got caught in the stirrup. That ended his army career …

'We could now trot and canter and drag our guns into almost any position, and we were issued with whips … we learned how to use them, and make them crack to startle the horses, but we were warned never to use them on the animals, unless in real danger, and then only to urge the horses to extra effort in extreme circumstances. This was strictly obeyed … We learned how to use reins with the left hand, and always leave the right hand free for emergencies. Every driver had four reins in his hand at the same time, but used his knees to guide the horse. There were three drivers to each gun … We were taught that after every job was done, the horses must be attended to first; they must be fed and groomed. That was all right on Salisbury Plain where there were plenty of water troughs, but was impossible at the Front. In the Battle of the Somme … we men suffered terribly, but the horses suffered even more.'

The landscape of war (2). The Battle of Arras, April 1917. Mules quartered amid the ruins of Feuchy.

Nineteen-year-old Driver Luther was finally ready to embark for France.

'We led our horses up the gangway and down into the hold of the ship. Some would not budge, and we had to tug at their heads and shove at their flanks, while their hooves were flitting in all directions. The impossible we slung up in a hammock, and dropped in the ship.' After disembarking, the men and their horses marched for five days until they neared 'the firing line, or what was known as the front. We could hear distant gunfire.'

As they drew nearer 'an artillery gun would fire … we now realised that we were actually in the firing line. Horses were rearing up, terrified, and the drivers were having to use every possible effort to control them.'

On 25 September 1915 Luther and his brigade were ordered to prepare to advance.

'The German gunfire had quietened down, but machine guns were active while rifles were whistling all around. We somehow managed to leap from our front line trenches, and got tangled up in the barbed wire. The horses became almost unmanageable, but the orders were to advance. We must have gone forward about two

H. R. Cooke: **'Saving the Horses'.** ***An incident at Ypres. Driver A. Robinson, of Wagon T.4, 250886 49th (West Riding) Divisional Train, was awarded the Military Medal for rescuing his horses on this occasion, 1918.***

miles to the outskirts of Loos, when we were suddenly halted. The Germans were striking back and men and horses were falling right and left. The centre and wheel drivers were ordered to dismount, and the lead drivers were to take the team of six horses to the rear, which was virtually impossible with the terrified animals, some of which had received bullet wounds. Indeed I had never known before that horses can scream, but they can, in such conditions … it was carnage, British and Germans and animals dead or dying lying all around.'

The next day Luther was sent 'with a working party where a group of horses had been killed, and were ordered to take off their equipment – saddles, bridles, traces, for collection. There were dead men lying about in great numbers, chiefly British – legless, armless, headless …'

During the Battle of the Somme, the main Allied offensive of 1916, artillery had to be brought forward to new positions, across mounds of debris and countless shell holes. It was impossible to make use of motorised transport and nearly all the work had to be carried out by horses or pack animals – donkeys or mules. Realising this, the German troops scattered sharp iron spikes to halt the advance by piercing the animals' hooves and rendering them *hors de combat*. All the ground that had been won in the Battle of the Ancre was turned into a vast sea of mud by the latter stages of the battle in the autumn of 1916 in which the limbers of the carts sank up to their axles. 'But the guns could not cease fire. It was necessary at any cost, to place them in the forward position, so as not to give respite to the enemy. When one team of horses fell exhausted in the mire, another took its place' and thus the guns were able to continue battering the enemy's position, while those in the rear were being consolidated.

Sidney Smith, then a private, recalled his experience on the Somme when there was 'nothing the eye could see except waves rippling the mud as the wind blew, I had the terrible experience to witness three horses and six men disappear completely under the mud. It was a sight that will live for ever in my memory, the cries of trapped soldiers were indescribable as they struggled to free themselves. The last horse went to a muddy grave, keeping his nostrils above the slush until the last second. A spurt of mud told me it was all over.'

On the Somme, as 'the German artillery blasted away … we horsemen had to make a bolt, under fire, driving straight to a heavy crater filled with stinking water. Our horses were up to their bellies and even higher in mud, and how we ever got them out was a mystery,' Driver Luther wrote.

Trench Warfare

The War Budget, January 27th, 1916.

Ratting: The New Sport in the Trenches

Of the minor hardships of the trenches, "rats" are so numerous that Tommy's dug-outs are often quite uninhabitable. Terriers have been sent out by trainloads, and our illustration gives a graphic example of their methods of hunting the rodents. To encourage this new sport of rat-catching, rewards are offered. In a single fortnight one army corps alone disposed of 8,000 rats.

331

An illustration from **The War Budget** *of 27 January 1916 illustrating* **'Ratting: The new sport in the trenches'.**

There were lice (or 'chats' as they were often called) in the trenches that drove the soldiers frantic with itching. The men would use a candle or a match to run the flame up the seams of their shirts to get some grim pleasure in the crackling of the incinerated insects, but it was but a temporary respite. Then there were the rats. 'There are millions!!' wrote Major Walter Vignoles. 'Some are huge fellows as big as cats. Several of our men were wakened to find a rat snuggling down in the blanket alongside them!'

Ralph Smith was a private in the 12th Battalion, Gloucestershire Regiment when he was sent to the Somme in 1916. The men, who were in support of the troops on the front line, slept in 'an old shed out of sight of the Germans but quite near in the case of attack. Our beds were bunks of 2-inch wire netting fixed to wooden posts and about 4 feet off the ground. Outside was a pile of discarded Bully Beef tins. At night it was swarming with rats, inside and out. I laid in my bunk with my haversack as a pillow. In the morning I was shocked to find a hole had been bitten through my haversack and most of my hard biscuit eaten, yet I had slept through it all.'

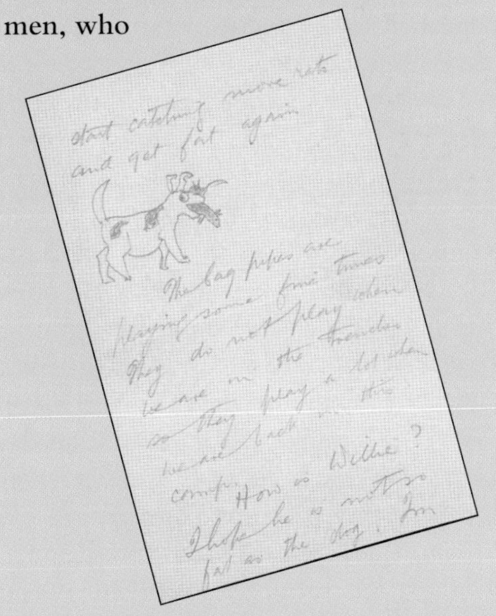

start catching more rats
and get fat again

How is Willie?

An extract from a letter sent from the Western Front by Captain James Foulis, 5th Battalion, Queen's Own Cameron Highlanders (9th Division) to his niece in Scotland.

Later, Private Smith 'was sent ... to Arras where I joined the lads doing another spell in the front line ... We had our amusing incidents such as "rat bashing". At the rear of some of the sheds in the reserve position there were piles of rubbish and tins etc. We would creep out in the dark and surround it while one would go to the centre and switch on a torch while we killed them with pieces of wood and sticks.'

Captain John Cohen who was serving with the BEF in France had a solution of sorts. 'The weather is very hot and sultry,' he wrote home in May 1916. 'We play football in the evenings though – & when the light is too bad for that, I take a ripping little brown dog (partly Irish terrier, partly pug) out ratting. He has a splendid scent for rats & is a good sportsman. I caught four last night, and one this morning just after breakfast on my way out to work. The rats are prolific here, and often their nests are made under a tree or piece of timber lying by the roadside. As the dog passes by, he scents the rat, squeaks and starts scratching away head well down ...

'Sometimes one has to dig a good deal – but often enough the rat gets under any loose pile of stuff & you only have to lift it to make him run out. Very often he gets away to another hiding place too quickly for the dog to catch him, but where he has a clear run the chances are always with the dog ... PS My dog is called Jim.'

The Battle for Pilckem Ridge, July 1917, during the Third Battle of Ypres, best known as Passchendaele from its final phase. Lloyd George called the battle, which lasted until November 1917, 'The Campaign in the Mud' and here one of the pair of horses pulling a water cart stuck in the mud up to its axle has fallen off the edge of the brushwood path at St Eloi and is trapped in deep mud.

'If they had received shell fragments, we cut their traces, and many received a bullet to end their suffering and agony. Here we were stuck until after Christmas 1916. Our poor animals ... were now sinking in mud. True we had been given a coat covering for the animals, but the cold and rain were getting worse. The horses, however thirsty, would not touch shell water. Their rations of oats and hay were very poor, and the poor devils with mud on their legs and bellies now developed balls of mud which froze on their limbs and it was impossible to release them ... In this cold and hunger, the horses now developed a new habit – they started chewing – ropes, leather or even our tunics. While you were attending to one horse the other would be chewing at you. So we reverted to chains, a big steel chain for pinioning down, another from the horses' nose-band, just like a heavy dog chain. The bags from which they fed oats had become sodden with rain, and when a harness man was placing this on his head, the horse would swing it up and sideways. Many a driver was hit senseless with such a blow. No man could feed two horses like this, so it was a case of one man per horse, otherwise the horse not being fed would rear up and plunge in all directions. The horses then turned to chewing at one another, and soon became hairless, and a pitiful sight.'

Lieutenant John Capron, who fought on the Somme, and at Ypres and later battles, noticed that:

(John) Edwin Noble (1876–1961): **'A Horse Ambulance Pulling a Sick Horse Out of a Field'.** *Each mobile veterinary section was supplied with an ambulance for the conveyance of animals. This was paid for mainly by subscriptions raised by the RSPCA.*

A model of a tarpaulin-covered horse-drawn wagon as used for general transport functions on the Western Front in the First World War.

'However careful and watchful one must be in getting the convoy to the guns, there was no need to worry over the journey home! As each wagon shed its load, the only order "Off you go!" was promptly and implicitly obeyed … I often wondered what time [for sleep] the drivers did get. Most nights most of them would be in the saddle, and horses and mules, unlike mechanised transport, had to be watered, groomed and fed – it all took time. The wagon lines were a hive of industry, if the batteries were never to be let down and shell and rations always there on time. Watering alone was time-consuming: rarely was the water point close to the lines – usually there would be a trek of a mile or more to the troughs set up in an unshelled area by the Engineers. Horses must be taken there twice a day: even those who had been up on the line with the night convoys: and around 9 o'clock each morning, the subaltern (or it might be a sergeant) at the wagon line paraded all the horses (and mules) with enough men to ride them bare-back to water – one man might take three horses, but more meant delays at the watering, as uncontrolled horses tended to bunch and jostle and spoil "fair shares for all" … The whole performance to and from the water was repeated in the evening, long before the "details" for the convoys came in … Some are surprised to hear of the horses being groomed [at the front] – but of course they were and daily unless an emergency prevailed, as during a rush to the guns before a "show" … Before the official stable parade [a daily inspection by the Wagon Line Orderly Officer] every driver was at work for about half an hour on his pair [of horses] where they stood,

An improvised horse line near Bazentin on the Western Front, 1916. Horses were tethered some way back from the front line, but could still be vulnerable to shellfire.

tethered on the line. He must go carefully round them, grooming thoroughly, especially under the belly and down the legs and fetlocks where the mud had dried and hardened, and there might be cuts or sores to clean and dress. Curry combs were an Army "issue", but were often lost, and empty bully beef tins were equally effective against dried mud and were in general use. Lynx-eyed Sergeants and other NCOs patrolled and supervised this careful daily all-weathers operation, essential for keeping the unit mobile and always ready for instant action. A check on feet and hooves at least once a day was especially important … All these animals had four feet each, continually on the go and needing constant care and attention … I never remember … any trouble on the move from lost shoes, or indeed from lameness other than from wounding or barbed wire or other injuries … we had our "specialists" in the background – efficient, skilled and dedicated – just as they came from their "trades" in civvy street. In those days blacksmiths (like horses) were two a penny throughout the land: and here they were in France on the work they'd always done. Each battery had its Farrier Sergeant ("Shoey") with his assistant responsible for "feet" and feet alone. Our other specialists included our Saddler Sergeant ("Waxey") … The horses and mules HAD to be kept as fit and well as possibly could be done – their lives and ours depended on it as did the outcome of the War! In fact, in a field battery, life

A mule being laden with rocks and stones required for building new Canadian quarters at Souchez on the Western Front during the First World War.

Lucy Kemp-Welch (1869–1958): **'The Straw Ride: Russley Park Remount Depôt, Wiltshire, 1918'.** *As a young girl Kemp-Welch sketched New Forest ponies on walks near her home, and in 1897 the Tate Gallery bought her painting* **'Colt Hunting in the New Forest'.** *Primarily a painter of horses, she was elected President of the Society of Animal Painters and her depiction of reserve horses waiting to be shipped overseas during the First World War shows her skill.*

revolved round the horses as much as round the guns – useless without mobility, even in trench warfare fairly frequent "moves" were made … or when the Division were moved to another sector and we went with it.'

In fact, although high rates of pay and attractive prospects of promotion were offered to blacksmiths to join the army, 'the motor car, by replacing horses for many purposes, both in town and country, had hit the art of farriery very hard [by 1914] and the village smithy had for sometime fallen off in attractiveness to young men seeking a trade to follow. Obviously, therefore, the thing to do was for the Army to train its own shoeing-smiths …' The cavalry was fairly well provided for as it was able to use older farriers called up from the Reserve to train younger men, so the greatest need was in the Royal Field Artillery and infantry transport. Early in the summer of 1915 the Army Veterinary Department of the War Office established three schools of farriery near remount depots or garrisons, where there was an ample supply of Army horses on which to practice – although initially trainees practised on 'a highly effective apparatus … to which the foot of a dead horse has been attached. The apparatus with foot attached can then be manipulated and moved through varying angles in exactly the same way as a blacksmith manipulates a horse's foot and leg in the course of shoeing. The learner thus begins on a

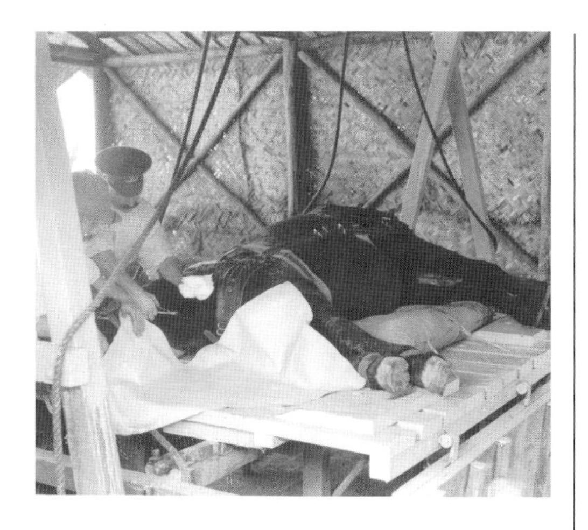

A horse on the operating table at a veterinary hospital in Mesopotamia. The Army Veterinary Corps operated in all theatres of war and in 1918, in recognition of its services, was given the title 'Royal'.

Model of a horse operating table from the First World War.

dummy of infinite patience and insensitivity to pain should the [trainee] be clumsy in his early efforts to nail on a shoe.' These establishments were capable of turning out about 1,000 'cold shoers' every month. (A cold shoer is capable of taking off and nailing on shoes and effecting minor repairs, whereas a shoeing smith is able to make horse shoes as well as adapting them to specific purposes.) A small school was also set up by the BEF on the Western Front. Two months' training enabled a man 'of fair average intelligence and manual dexterity to qualify as a "cold shoer"'. But [it took] 'not less than three additional months of training before a pupil is qualified to pass out as a "shoeing-smith" and then both "useful artificers" could be sent to ply their trades on the battle field'.

Given his concern for his battalion's animals, Lieutenant Capron was appalled during the Battle of the Somme, when:

> 'The weather turned bitterly cold and a further disaster followed, the result of an insane recent Corps Order. By this, our mules and horses had been clipped right out – not just trace high to save the belly sweat – but shorn right over like hunters. And to crown it all, the corn ration (about 12lb of oats) was now cut down to 10lb … I suppose due to short supply. [Previously] they had, like us, been well sheltered, but here they stood in the open, the lines on the higher and bleaker ground to avoid the muddy bottoms. Can it be wondered that before we left this area our horse strength had been terribly reduced by cold and exhaustion? Indeed we left many of our best horses along the Arras-St Pol road, where they would just collapse. Most heart-breaking, worse than losses by shell, and all because of that Corps Order!'

This order was not officially rescinded until the last year of the war though some unit commanders declined to implement it, including a commander of the Royal Horse Artillery who dumped all the grooming kit when the unit arrived in Belgium and so 'the horses' coats grew thick and strong, and were waterproofed by all the grease left in the hair, so that although they stood in the open all that very hard winter [of 1914/5] none died and we had little sickness' as men 'groomed' their mounts by scraping the mud off with their canteen knives and rubbing the beasts down with handfuls of hay or straw.

Before the Battle of Waterloo, the wounded horse had been largely left to its fate: its wounds either healed by themselves or they did not and it died, sometimes an agonising and lingering death unless it was shot by a concerned trooper. But the lack of veterinary care exacted a high price: during the Franco-Prussian War of 1870–71 50,000 horses were killed, and during the Egyptian Campaign of 1882 600 animals died of disease while only 60 were killed on the battlefield. The Boer War proved a catalyst: between October 1899 and May 1902, 326,073 horses and mules died, and by the outbreak of

A First World War postcard showing vets of the Blue Cross (the animal equivalent of the Red Cross) tending wounded animals during the First World War.

the First World War the 'lesson had been learned', primarily for economic, but to a degree for humanitarian, reasons, and every British unit, whether infantry, artillery, or transport, had one or more veterinary officers attached to it. In total, some 18,000 officers and men served in the Army Veterinary Corps (AVC – after the war 'Royal' was added), responsible for around 400,000 horses at any one time. In the case of the infantry of the line the veterinary officer was stationed at the 'horse lines' (tethered at the nearest point to which horses were allowed to approach the firing line) from where he kept an eye not only on all transport and baggage trains moving backwards to the railhead or rendezvous for supplies but also on the pack mules going forward with daily rations to points nearer the trenches. He had a team of his own, corresponding roughly to the stretcher bearers attached to each regimental medical officer and his staff, and he performed much the same service for the horses as the medical officer performed for the men.

The object of the Army Veterinary Corps was 'twofold: first from the combatant point of view to safeguard the animals, to prevent their unnecessary injury, to act quickly when injuries occur, and to restore horses to active service for further combatant purposes: the second is the humane purpose, to be merciful to animals, which, through the contingencies of war, are necessarily used in military operations.'

Veterinary officers nearest to the front of the battle, and their men, were equipped with panniers carrying field-dressings, bandages, splints, antiseptic and other necessities for giving first aid to the horses. They might also run basic small field hospitals for the treatment of

16th June, 1917.
THE WAR Illustrated
No. 148. Vol. 6.
A PICTURE-RECORD of Events by Land, Sea and Air. Edited by J. A. HAMMERTON

AT THE SIGN OF THE CAT AND WHISTLE.—Many British soldiers take back to the trenches canine and feline friends they have found in village rest billets behind the lines. Mr. Stanley L. Wood here depicts a pleasant "off hour" scene at a dug-out entrance, where the men enjoy a comrade's solo on a tin whistle and the company of their pets.

Companionship in the trenches. The cover of **The War Illustrated** *showing the pets the soldiers adopted from their rest billets behind the lines.*

Hayden Reynolds Mackey (1881–1979):* 'Epéhy, 1918'. *The previous spring it had been in the woods around Epéhy that British troops had feared a large contingent of German cavalry lay in waiting to attack: a fear that proved groundless.

minor wounds and sickness. They also carried drugs for minor ailments, and as a last resource they had to hand what a historian of the Great War, Sir John Hammerton, called 'one humane little weapon for putting a painless end to any poor animal so stricken with wounds as to be beyond cure. The instrument was a Greener's cattle-killer. Loaded with a powerful explosive charge, it was capable of penetrating a horse's skull instantly. The weapon was held against the horse's forehead, one tap was given on the cap and the animal lay still, his sufferings over.'

As there were specialist hospitals for the men, so there were for their animals, and the general veterinary hospitals, of which there were a total of 20 by 1918, had separate wards for different conditions, for whether the animal needed surgical or medical treatment or isolation. A horse would arrive usually with a chalk mark on its flanks noting what the problem was, and at the hospital (most of which had been built to cope with upwards of a thousand animals) this would be copied onto a disc tied to the animal's tail before it was taken to the appropriate place for treatment. The surgical wards would deal with bullet wounds, severe lacerations caused by shells and barbed wire and suchlike and if an operation was required a solid leather muzzle containing a wad of cotton soaked in chloroform would enclose the mouth and nostrils, effectively anaesthetising the animal. Staff in the medical wards would minister to horses suffering from pneumonia, catarrh,

From the first day of the Battle of the Somme, 1 July 1916, until the end of the Great War on 11 November 1918 total British horse casualties numbered 140,370: of these 210 horses died from the effects of poison gas. Military police stand at the graveside of one of their horses near Ypres in October 1916.

exhaustion and general debility, while the isolation wards dealt with skin conditions and cases of mange (a parasitic skin disease that caused the animal intense irritation) by dipping the horses in specially constructed plunge baths filled with copper sulphate solution. Over two and a half million admissions to veterinary hospitals occurred between August 1914 and March 1919 – though of course some of these were readmissions, and in addition to the hospitals and mobile veterinary sections, there were four convalescent horse depots for recovering animals.

Despite this attention, the loss of horses due to cold, hunger and disease was about four times more than the 58,000 lost through enemy action – and the most pernicious killer was 'debility', invariably caused by exposure, which lowered the animal's resistance. During the winter of 1916, one veterinary hospital in France was losing on average 50 horses each day from a virulent form of influenza and the Somme offensive that year left the Army with 16,074 debility (poor condition) cases, while the appalling conditions at Arras meant that 20,319 animals were admitted to hospital during April 1917 alone. However, diagnostic medical advances meant that glanders, which had killed off a large number of horses in previous wars, had been largely eradicated by the 1914–18 war.

As an article in the journal of the RSPCA coolly observed: 'at the front … horses fare better than men, in so far as their thicker skin and bulkier tissues offer greater resistance

A poster appealing for funds for the Blue Cross's work with horses during the First World War.

Gas Warfare

'[Gas] produces a flooding of the lungs – it is an equivalent death to drowning only on dry land. The effects are these – a splitting headache and terrific thirst (to drink water is instant death), a knife edge pain in the lungs & the coughing up of a greenish froth off the stomach and the lungs ending finally in insensibility and death. The colour of the skin from white turns a greenish black and yellow, the tongue protrudes & the eyes assume a glassy stare,' wrote Sergeant Elmer Cotton of the effects of chlorine gas in 1915.

Lethal chlorine gas was first used by the Germans during the Second Battle of Ypres in April 1915, and the first British retaliatory attack came during the Artois-Loos offensive in September 1915 – but the wind blew it back in the attackers' faces.

Mustard gas was used from September 1917: its delayed-action symptoms – internal and external bleeding, accompanied by vomiting and frequently death – made it hard to detect. Other gases used in the trenches were bromine, phosgene and chloropicrin, and the French Army occasionally used a nerve gas obtained from prussic acid.

The first gas masks issued to the Allied troops were primitive affairs consisting of cotton pads dipped in bicarbonate of soda and held over the face, but by 1918, troops on both sides were equipped with filter respirators using charcoal or antidote chemicals to neutralise gases. Although gas was never the decisive weapon of war that had been anticipated and only 3 per cent of casualties proved fatal in the short term, the long-term effects for hundreds of thousands of men were devastating, with active lives cut short, diminished or disabled.

The loss of life among the horses was surprisingly low. Between 1916 and 1918 there were only 2,220 equine casualties from gas, and of these only 210 died. Horses proved much more resistant than men to the effects of chlorine and mustard gas. As a Royal Army Veterinary Corps manual pointed out in 1949: 'animals will stand quietly in a concentration of [war gasses] that will close the eyes of men in a few seconds.' However, mustard gas was a severe skin and eye irritant and the effects could take up to six weeks to heal and often the horse's eyes would be permanently scarred. Respirators were provided – in three sizes for horses and mules – as were eye shields, and soldiers carried tins of anti-gas ointment in their haversack to rub into the horse's legs should it traverse contaminated ground. By the Second World War – when thankfully they weren't needed – respirators were sophisticated affairs of rubberised canvas held on by a 'triple suspension harness with adjustable straps ... a steel frame fitted to the interior to prevent collapse ... and a flat metal box containing a gas and toxic smoke filter.' But in the First World War they had been regarded as somewhat risible: 'just a damn great flannel bag tied with tapes behind the horse's ears. The snag was our horses were always fed with nosebags so that anything that looked like a nosebag and pulled over their heads should logically contain oats: horse sense,' wrote an ex-artillery correspondent. 'Bag tied on, down went head, and horse rooted around trying to find oats that weren't there ... life expectancy as a gas mask, three minutes flat.'

ABOVE: ***Gas precautions. A mounted lance corporal of the Household Cavalry wearing a gas mask, Windsor, 1939. His horse is also wearing a gas mask, but thankfully gas was one of the First World War horrors that was not employed in the Second.***

OPPOSITE TOP: ***A dog wearing a gas mask and anti-gas goggles at Rousbrugge military kennels, Belgium, 16 May 1916.***

OPPOSITE BELOW: ***A British messenger dog with injured paws due to crossing ground impregnated with mustard gas at the Army Veterinary Corps headquarters kennels near Nieppe Wood in Flanders.***

Horses belonging to officers of the Northumberland Hussars stabled in wintry conditions in the ruins of a cottage damaged by shellfire at Etricourt. Stabling arrangements on the Western Front were often makeshift and primitive – if they existed at all – and many horses died of exposure.

to projectiles and splinters; but worse than men in that economic considerations and mechanical difficulties often render it necessary to destroy horses for wound conditions which would at most maim a man.' But when a horse was killed, destroyed or died, it could leave the soldier who had ridden him, cared for him, fed and watered him, and sometimes even lain alongside him, feeling bereft at the loss of a companion. The two, were, after all, a fighting unit, and when half of that unit was lost it might not easily be replaced in the eyes of those who must sometimes have felt like a bereaved centaur. In the Battle of the Aisne, Private Arthur Cornfoot, who was himself to die of wounds on 7 October 1917, wrote to his girlfriend in Bristol, expressing the indivisible horror of it all. 'It was proper hell I can tell you. Until at last we were relieved, we lost about 40 men, about 12 killed, the remainder wounded, and about 60 horse killed, so we left the Aisne thankful to get out of it, with faces as white as sheets, and our nerves completely shattered – and sorrowful for our missing comrades which we buried where they fell with a simple wooden cross. I lost one of my best comrades on the Aisne, he was wounded there and died in a French hospital about 2 weeks after. The horse I had killed was my favourite – it was a beauty, the best horse I ever had, and it was patted a good lot in the battery, so you might guess there was an excuse for me when I cried a little over him, for I loved him. We also lost a promising young officer …' And in the Battle of the Somme, where distances 'were measured not in yards but in mud', Captain Harry Yoxall wrote a letter home about 'a heart-breaking horse I saw lying wounded near High Wood. It seems such a shame to drag animals into the mess we've made of things.'

Sefton

On 20 July 1982 Sefton, a gleaming black horse of the Household Cavalry, trotted out of Knightsbridge Barracks, where he was stabled, bound for his regular ceremonial duty on guard in Whitehall, where he would be photographed and patted by admiring tourists. But that summer Tuesday was different. A nail bomb, for which the IRA later claimed responsibility, left in a blue Austin car, was detonated as the cavalry rode through Hyde Park. Two hours later another device exploded under the bandstand in Regent's Park as the Royal Green Jackets played at the first of a season of lunchtime concerts.

Six soldiers were killed instantly in Regent's Park and 24 were injured. In Hyde Park the death toll from the bomb, that had sent a blast of hundreds of four- to six-inch nails at 500mph, was two soldiers killed instantly, with six others – two of whom would die later – and 20 civilians injured.

One of the injured was Sefton's rider, Trooper Michael Pederson, a four-inch nail ripping through his hand. Seven of the 16 horses of the Household Cavalry were so badly maimed that they had to be shot, and blood was spouting from Sefton's neck. The horse suffered 38 wounds, including five four-inch nails buried in his face, his jugular vein pierced by a jagged piece of metal from the Austin car and lacerations across his body. In what was probably the first operation on a cavalry horse in more than half a century, Major Carding, the veterinary officer at Knightsbridge Barracks, managed to save the life of the seriously injured horse. Sefton became a symbol of equine courage, a proud cavalry horse that was a war victim in a very different kind of war.

Sefton (right) during his convalescence from his terrible injuries.

3

Ships of the Desert in the First World War

A fully laden camel supply column travelling through the desert near Shellal near the banks of the Nile in Egypt during the First World War.

During the First World War 484,143 animals in British service lost their lives, including 5,589 lost at sea through enemy action. Of those animals, 120,013 were camels, of which 22, 812 were killed on active service. The mortality among camels was far higher than that among horses, even though horses were exposed to more danger from enemy action. In the last year of the war, for example, 86.53 per cent of the camels used in Mesopotamia died.

In November 1914 the war in Europe was extended to the deserts of the Middle East and North Africa, lands where camels were the graceful, swaying beasts of burden and of rapid movement, the transport – and now the warriors – of a landscape of sand and scrub and rock. The Ottoman Empire, a huge swathe of the Middle East including Syria, Palestine and much of the Arabian Peninsula, with an overall population of some 25 million people, was ruled by the Sultan of Turkey. When Britain declared war on the Ottoman Empire on 5 November 1914 it offered, over the following years, the opportunity to a various and disparate coalition of Arab nationalists to fight for independence from the Ottoman Empire in pursuit of their dream of a single unified Arab state stretching from Aleppo in Syria to Aden in Yemen. Britain agreed to 'recognise and support the independence of the Arabs …' wrote Sir Henry McMahon, the British High Commissioner in Egypt in 1915. The interpretation of this agreement between the British and Sheriff Hussein ibn Ali of Mecca was to cause considerable bitterness and

James McBey (1883–1959):* 'The Camel Corps. A Night March to Beersheba',** ***October 1917. A Scottish etcher, McBey served as an official war artist during the First World War and spent his last years in North Africa. In two years McBey produced nearly 300 images of the war in Palestine and Egypt.

political upheaval after the war, and its effects continue to be a source of great tension in the Middle East today, but from 1916 to 1918 the Arab revolt was an integral part of the Allied war strategy.

It was to be a very different form of warfare for the Europeans – and it would be the camel that would prove to be its conscript warrior, fighting alongside the horses and mechanised transport but also able to venture distances in conditions that no equine could have managed. The Arabian camel, or single-humped dromedary (strictly speaking, this name belongs to a particular species of trotting camel from Upper Egypt and the Sudan) had been the mode of transport in the desert since time immemorial. The camel was first domesticated in Arabia and was later exported to the deserts of North Africa, the Indian subcontinent and Australia. The value of the camel is its fortitude: a camel in good condition can be ridden for 25 or 30 miles a day for weeks on end at a speed of between 4mph and 10mph (depending on conditions) with an average trotting speed of 6mph, carrying a load of up to 450lb, including its rider. A perfect example of design for function, the camel can exist on a limited amount of food and can go without water for as long as five or six days – and when it does finally get to water, a camel is capable of drinking 25 to 30 gallons of water at a time, although it balloons up spectacularly when it does so. Its hump is not a water pouch but a reserve of fat that shrinks noticeably after

A camel submits to the indignity of having its load of branches checked by a mine detector at the Sheikh Othman checkpoint in Aden, March 1967. The soldiers were searching for arms smuggled in from the Yemen.

days of hardship and lack of food, rather like a fuel tank emptying. Camels have thick calloused feet and there are callouses on the other parts of the body that carry the animal's weight as it levers itself from sitting or crouching on the ground. The padded hooves can endure sand scorched by the midday sun, as well as sharp rocks, and prevent the animal from sinking into the sand as a horse would. The camel's film star drooping eyelids and long eyelashes serve a practical purposes too: they protect against blowing sand, as do its slitted nostrils which can be closed at will. Camels have extremely strong and long razor-sharp teeth and a tough protective covering to the roof of their mouths which means that they can feed on practically anything, including the prickly thorn bush, which may be the only vegetation in the desert. The lifespan of a camel is exceptionally long in the animal world, 40 years is not unusual. When selecting 'a ship of the desert' a training manual for the British forces, published in anticipation of a desert war, advised that 'a camel fit for work should be able to rise easily from the ground with the weight of three men on its back. A buyer should test in this manner all animals he proposes to purchase.' And presumably ignore the terrible roars of protest from the camel as it rose to its feet with its heavy human cargo.

What camels do not always have is a docile and tractable nature, particularly during the frequent rutting or syming season. Unusually, the bull camel that is in contact with the nagas (mare) comes on heat during the winter months, and sprays a cud which appears like an extreme form of halitosis. During this time the camel can be ferocious and kick viciously, sideways rather than backwards, which those unaccustomed to its ways find most unnerving – and hazardous. With its massive teeth, a camel bite can be extremely painful and carry a high risk of blood poisoning. 'Nearly every day one or more men went to hospital with a camel bite,' recalled Lieutenant McPherson of the Camel Transport Corps:

> 'And frequently when a camel got loose at night and excited the others, the whole camp was kept awake practically all night … I have yet to meet the hero who will stand up to a really "man-eating" camel … Our OC [Officer Commanding] gave us "useful hints" on how to act. We were to calmly await the onslaught, step aside and smite the brute on the nose with the butt end of a whip that would stop and daze it – then a blow over the knees would bring it down, so its legs might easily be tied … I had never been the definite object of a direct attack until one day when superintending a watering, I noticed a brute giving sidelong glances from bloodshot eyes and warned the Adjutant not to come too near him. I had hardly spoken when he left the water and came for me open-mouthed. As I turned the horse, his jaws met so near my bare knee that he covered it in foam. I was splendidly mounted, but the horse could not get sufficient pace on at once, and the camel, missing me again, fixed his teeth in the pony's flank and hung on, literally the incarnation of grim death. My poor beast reared, tried to bolt and finally foundered in a pool of blood, quite done for: then the camel turned his attention to a native, picked him up by the throat and shook him until his neck broke.'

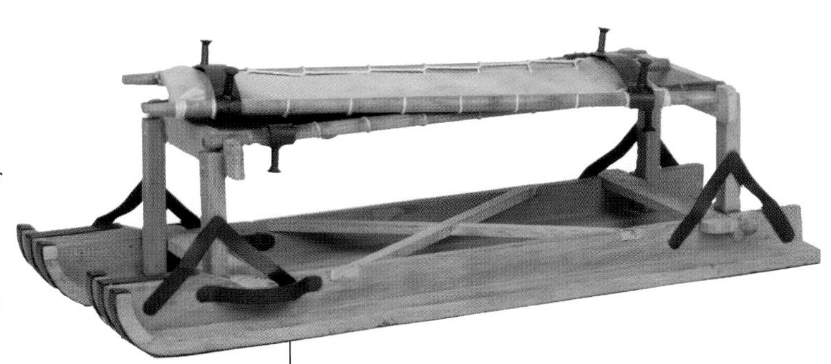

Wooden sand sledge pulled by a camel, fitted with a canvas stretcher and used to transport the wounded.

An Arabian Adventurer

'My day's delight is past. My horse is gone,' Lieutenant Joseph McPherson sorrowfully wrote on a 'little horse shoe of wood' he erected above the grave of his 'flame red Arab pony of singular beauty', Tammuz, named after a Phoenician god. The wilful and spirited pony had carried McPherson, who was camel officer with the 42nd Division, to a number of outpost sections in the Sinai Desert during the First World War. He had rounded up camels that had bolted, carried messages and found his master's way back to camp through the perplexing landscape of endless sand dunes, until, 'after a perfect desert day', the horse was killed as he stood tethered to the horse lines in a bombing raid on the camp in 1917.

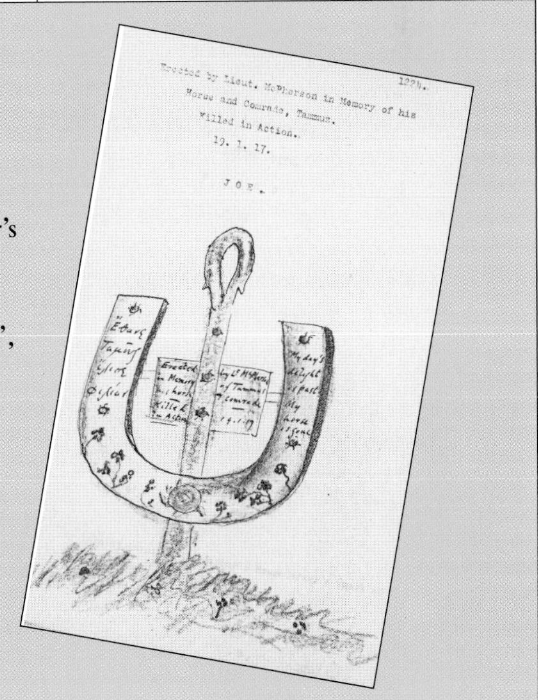

An Australian demonstrates the docility of his camel, Sudan, 1917.

Even if muzzled and unable to bite, a camel could knock over a man and kneel on him, crushing all breath from his body. There was thus a great deal that the British soldiers who were to carry the war into the desert needed to learn about camel management from the life-long experience of their Arab co-fighters.

There had been a Camel Corps, known as the 'Nile Circus', with four camel regiments comprising 1,789 officers and men raised to act as a mounted infantry during the British expedition to rescue General Gordon in the Sudan during the Mahdi's revolt in the 1880s. This 'Circus' became the genesis of the Imperial Camel Corps (ICC), an independent, self-contained fighting force established in the First World War manned by troops who had for the most part served at Gallipoli. The realisation that the Allied troops were going to have to patrol vast tracts of waterless desert during their battles with the Turks, and the unsuitability of the horse cavalry units for this task, was the impetus for this mounted infantry. At first cavalry officers were distinctly sniffy at the idea since for them 'it was almost an insult to mention camels in the same breath with horses, and even when permission was finally obtained and the new corps had come into being ... and already begun to more than justify itself as a fighting force, they persisted in their belief that it was no more than a glorified labour force' explains the historian of the Corps. Operating alongside the Egyptian Camel Corps, the Bikanir Camel Corps, and the Camel Transport Corps, comprising largely Arab soldiers officered by the British, the Imperial Camel Corps was charged with transporting the vast quantities of water and supplies required in the desert field. The Corps, which had its depôt at Abbassia near Cairo, was made up of four battalions, each consisting of four companies. The 1st and 3rd Battalions were mainly from the Australian Light Horse, the 4th was manned by Australians and

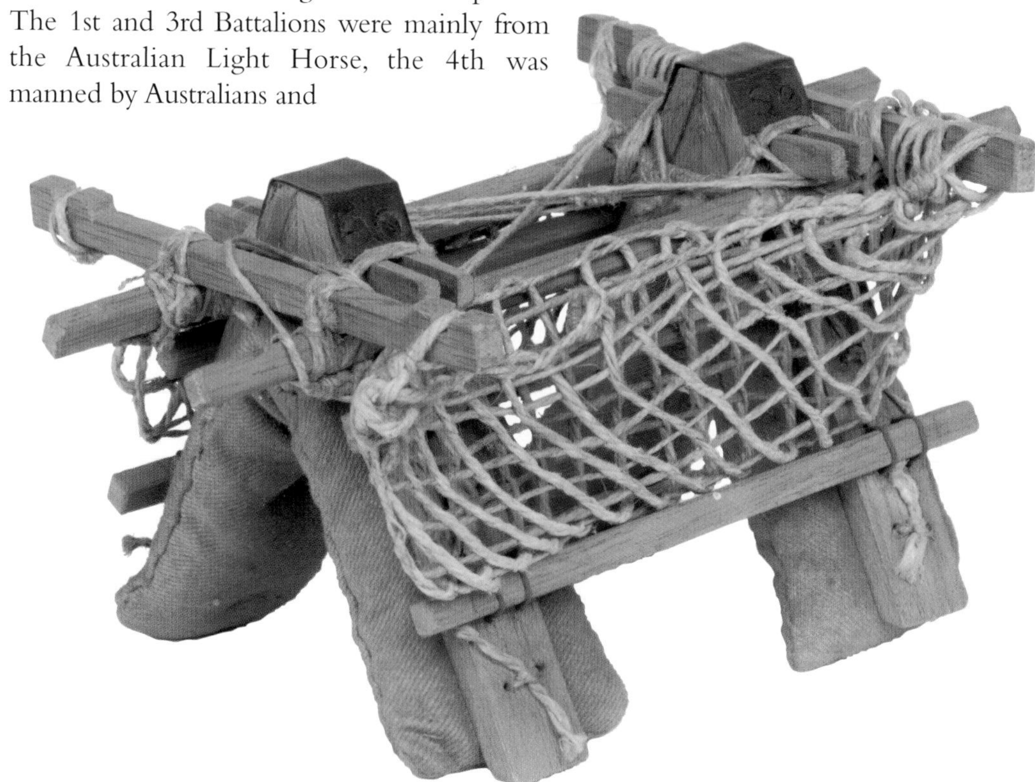

RIGHT: ***A camel saddle with a hole in the centre which fitted over the animal's hump, and a stout wooden peg at the front and rear from which were hung horizontally a bag of durra (a kind of millet) for the camel and a fantassi containing five gallons of water which was supposed to last the trooper for drinking, washing etc for five days. Across it would be hung two stout canvas saddlebags containing the driver's rations of bully beef and army biscuits, his spare clothing and personal equipment. Blankets – often as many as four – would be folded to make a comfortable seat in the hollow of the saddle. A rubber ground sheet covered these, and above all this sat the rider, cross-legged, with his calves resting on a leather apron hung from the front of the saddle over the camel's shoulders.***

The Desert Doggerel of Corporal Cuss

'If you seek for information
On Polo, Maps or Gin,
Beer, Beauty or Ballistics, you can find it all within:
If you seek the heat of battle
Or you're finding life too drear
Go join the "Curse of Egypt"
In the huts of Abbassia.'

[Abbassia was the HQ of the Imperial Camel Corps.]

A poem by 'Corporal Cuss' that appeared in September 1917 in the second issue of *Barrak*, the magazine of the Imperial Camel Corps, describing the more congenial side of desert warfare.

Egg and Spoon Race on Camels.

FINALS.

1 ....

2 ....

EVENT No. 14

MUSICAL CHAIRS ON CAMELS.

Prizes: 1st ₽ 100 — 2nd ₽ 50 — 3rd ₽ 25

1 Heil
2 Woodcock
3 Sutherland
4 Hargreaves
5 Mc Cue
6 Pollock
7 Wheatley
8 Thompson
9 Neilands
10 Foyle
11 Gillett
12 Haworth
13 Phillips
14 Earle
15 Humphreys
18 Sapsad
19 Loughnan
20 Connors
21 Dollin
22 Russell
23 Mc Cail
24 Cail
25 Hardisty
26 Jamieson
27 Bowie
28 Labh Singh
29 Shah Nawaz
30 Kehar Singh
31 Hari Singh
32 Leonard
33 Ovrengton

Souvenir Program of Imperial Camel Brigade SPORTS
Somewhere in Palestine
12th - 13th February 1918.

GREETINGS FROM THE CAMEL CORPS

ABOVE: *'Barrak' – the instruction given to a camel to sink to its knees so it could be mounted – was appropriated for the title of the Camel Corps Review with its mixture of irreverent verse, sketches and anecdotes of life in the desert during the First World War.*

LEFT TOP: *'Cameliers at play'. 'Wrestling on camels ... proved a most popular event, stubbornly contested,' wrote Oliver Hogue, himself an Australian camelier known as 'Trooper Bluegum'. 'As a mirth-provoker, the Egg and Spoon Race on camels was some stunt ... [and] no less diverting was the Musical Chairs ... If camels do think, they must wonder why Allah ever permitted these cameliers to cross the seas and make merry at the expense of the erstwhile dignified dromedaries.'*

LEFT BELOW: *The 1917 Christmas card of the Imperial Camel Corps.*

James McBey (1883–1959): 'Water Transport', 1917. 'It's a sun-scorched earth the East is/So we need you when we trek/... You thirst a week unblinking/And when I see you drinking/You always set me thinking/Lord, I wish I had your neck,' hymned Australian camelier Oliver Hogue.

New Zealanders and the 2nd Battalion, which was formed in early 1916, derived almost entirely from British yeomanry regiments. Artillery was provided by the Hong Kong and Singapore Mountain Battery (composed of Indian troops). The Imperial Camel Corps thus justified its imperial title. In total, the 2nd Battalion comprised some 30 officers and 800 NCOs and other ranks and around 1,000 camels, though the nature of the warfare meant that the battalion rarely operated as a single unit, but was spread out across hundreds of miles of desert.

Despite the camel's supercilious look, sometimes mean temperament and tendency to volatility – running amok when surprised by some small incident such as a tent flapping in the wind or a bagpipe sounding – the men came to admire their mounts for their remarkable powers of endurance and willingness to go on until they dropped. The camels proved brave – or insouciant – under fire, even when suffering minor injuries and dripping blood. The men also found the camels surprisingly comfortable to ride. 'There was no up and down movement, just forward and back' and with their wooden saddles packed around with blankets or sheepskins, the soldiers found they could ride for several hours without discomfort. The camels did not have reins or stirrups: a rope was tied onto the animal's nose and the men guided their camels by pulling on this and digging their boots into the beast's shoulders. One problem was that after a few days' gruelling march with no food or water the camel would become skeletal and the saddle, which had fitted snugly before, would now rub against the poor beast's emaciated frame and cause terrible sores. The problem was finally resolved by attaching webbing girths that contracted and expanded as the camel did.

Conditions in the desert were gruelling when the ICC started its training in spring 1916: that summer was to be the hottest for 40 years with temperatures of anything up to 128° Fahrenheit (53° Centigrade) in the shade – and there was very little shade. Such maps of the desert that had been issued to the 'rookie' British cameliers were virtually useless: thousands of square miles were represented either as a blank space, or by the label 'unexplored'. Some parts of the desert were soft, yielding sand while others were hard gravel on which fast progress could be made. Geoffrey Inchbald, then a 20-year-old volunteer, found that over the 50,000 square miles the corps patrolled 'apart from our little party there was hardly a living creature to be seen. Occasionally one would glimpse the trail of a gazelle or the track of a lizard in the sand ... There was no water and hardly any growth except for the camel thorn which by some miracle of nature contained an element of water. Nor were there any birds and insects were rare though occasionally one came across a praying mantis.' The Corps' most difficult task was finding its way in a featureless landscape when the desert wind could obliterate any track marks in a matter of seconds, and often the troops trekked for days, uncertain if they were going in the right direction. On occasions when they did come to a well they would find either that the water was brackish, polluted by the body of a dead camel, or the well had been filled with sand, a common tactic of desert warfare. The men would suffer from heat stroke, intense thirst, exhaustion and disorientation, and from the plagues of mosquitoes, flies and ticks. The camels suffered all these tribulations too, and frequently went lame, or broke one of their delicate spindly legs and had to be shot. They were frequent victims of the mange that afflicted horses, and they passed the parasite on to the men, causing such intense irritation that the victims would pace around all night in an agony of scratching.

Although bull camels were the mainstay of the camel forces carrying men and

'The Arabs say that at the Creation, when the beasts of the earth were formed, there were left over a lot of remnants out of which was made a camel ... The head of a sheep was placed on the neck of a giraffe, which was attached to the body of a cow, and the neck itself bent in shame at being put to such a use. The tail of an ass was appended and the whole was set on the legs of a horse, which ended in the pads of a dog, on each of which was stuck the claw of an ostrich, and the monstrosity, evidently being considered a failure, was banished to live in the desert where no other quadruped could exist, and where its solitary existence gave it "the hump",' according to an ex-camelier from New Zealand .

LEFT: *A photograph taken by T. E. Lawrence ('Lawrence of Arabia') of the Arab army mounted on camels and Arab ponies (which were renowned for their speed and agility) approaching Yenbo on the banks of the Red Sea in what has been, since 1932, Saudi Arabia.*

OPPOSITE BELOW: *A cacolet, which is a chair, litter, or other contrivance fitted to the back or pack saddle of a mule for carrying travellers in mountainous districts, or for the transportation of the sick and wounded of an army.*

OPPOSITE: ***The dust jacket illustration by M. de V. Lee for* The Boy's Life of Colonel Lawrence*, by Lowell Thomas, published in 1927, the same year as Lawrence's* Revolt in the Desert.**

LEFT: ***Emir Feisal leading his forces from his base at Wejh, Saudi Arabia, during the Guerilla Campaigns in 1917. From the T. E. Lawrence collection.***

supplies in the desert, shortages towards the end of the war meant that 3,000 female camels, most of which seemed to be pregnant, were conscripted. The foals, born en route, were summarily collapsed into nets and carried along with the caravan. The troops took an avuncular interest in the welfare of these endearing 'anthills on sticks' and also benefited themselves from the mobile milk bar since they found camel milk perfectly acceptable in tea!

A number of battles and skirmishes, including Romani and Beersheba, culminated in the largely unsuccessful raid on Amman in the Jordan Valley in the early spring of 1918. The weather was bitterly cold and wet and the camels struggled in unaccustomed mountainous territory, did the splits, never to rise again, plunged down steep ravines, and were in acute danger from bombing raids since several camels were laden with explosives and would detonate if hit. Finally it was decided to disband the main body of the ICC. Most camels went to strengthen the newly arrived Indian cavalry brigades, but some 400 camels and 300 men were seconded to T. E. Lawrence (later to become famous as 'Lawrence of Arabia') to join with the Arab forces in attacking the Hejaz railway, a vital link deep into Arabia. 'It is a most amateurish, Buffalo Billy sort of performance, and the only people who do it well are the Bedouin', Lawrence wrote to a friend about these mounted camel raids.

Lawrence had asked permission to address the men of the Imperial Camel Corps who were to join his guerilla war 'and explain why he had sent for us, a most unusual experience during the First World War, when it was only on very rare occasions for a commander to take the troops into his confidence ...' As described by a former signals officer of the ICC, Lawrence 'had told the Arabs that we were the bravest troops in the world and he begged us to live up to the reputation he had built up for us because ... if

James McBey (1883–1959):* 'Camel Transport Corps'*, 1919, pencil and watercolour.

Captain A. Buchanan's journal recording his service with the 25th Battalion, Royal Fusiliers in German East Africa, May 1915–1917, included many descriptions and sketches of the flora and fauna of the country, like the native ostrich made to resemble crotchets in his sketch.

we did fail in any of our attacks the Arabs might well interfere with our retreat. They would certainly snipe at us from the hilltops and deny us the use of their wells.

'He also begged us, as soon as we captured a Turkish position, to clear out and leave it to the Arabs, whose principal interest in war was loot. We rather chuckled at this because some of the Camel Corps lads were pretty quick and handy with loot themselves, particularly if there was any liquor around, which only occurred if there had been some German officers in position. We were also on the look out for certain articles of equipment such as Zeiss or Goertz binoculars and prismatic compasses, Luger automatic pistols, Mauser telescopic sights and a rather natty line in bivouac sheets, which were very popular with the Turkish officers. The Arabs on the other hand were looking for, in descending

A line of camels of the Camel Transport Corps picketed in Palestine in the summer of 1918. If the entire Corps of over 3,000 animals were mounted, the camels following each other head to tail would make a column eight miles long.

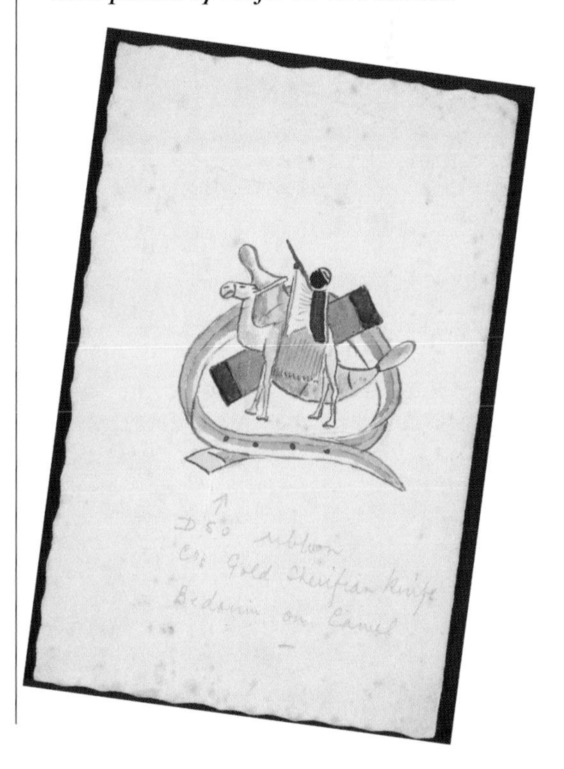

Christmas card of the Imperial Camel Corps hand painted by Major D. G. Pearman.

order, horses – preferably mares, camels, sheep, goats, and failing any of these, women.'

As well as carrying the soldiers on gruelling sorties, usually during the hours of darkness, to blow up railway bridges and tracks, the seconded camels were used in deception operations to fool the Turks into thinking that the opposing forces were much more extensive than they really were. 'Most wars were wars of contact … ours should be a war of detachment. We were to contain the enemy by the silent threat of a vast, unknown desert,' Lawrence was to write in *Seven Pillars of Wisdom*. Bully beef tins were opened, the contents burned and the empty tins strewn around to make it look as if hundreds of men had eaten, rather than a small raiding party. Camel and vehicle tracks criss-crossed the desert in wide arcs in every direction, and piles of camel dung, which

Memories of Sweaty Camels

In 1921 a statue sculpted by Cecil Brown was unveiled in Embankment Gardens in London. Wing Commander Ashlin was one of the cameliers present at the 'simple ceremony and the address by General Chetwode [who was renowned for the part he had played in the Palestine Campaign] which brought back vividly to the minds of those who had been there, the scorching days in the desert, weary forced marches, lack of sleep, food and especially water, sweating smelly camels and the remembrance of those gallant men whose memory was being honoured on that bright, cold November day.'

Camels of the Camel Transport Corps being clipped prior to the application of a dressing for mange, a parasitic disease that afflicted large numbers of camels – particularly in the Libyan desert. If unchecked the disease could destroy a camel force in the field in three to six months.

the men carried to light fires, were added to the usual droppings 'to give the impression that we had with us three or four times the number of camels … meaningless rubbish was scribbled on army signal forms and left scattered around.' Inchbald was confident that when Allenby launched his 'final and overwhelming offensive [a few days later which was to force the Turks to sue for an armistice] it is no exaggeration to say that he was helped by the fact that, because the Turks were misled into thinking that the whole of the Imperial Camel Brigade was present in the Hejaz, they substantially reinforced the Amman-Maan area, thus weakening their main front in Palestine.'

The Hejaz operations brought an end to the activities of the Imperial Camel Corps, although it was not formerly disbanded until the spring of 1919. Its members, who had been on attachment to their regular regiments, reverted to them, and in 1921 a statue was unveiled on London's Victoria Embankment Gardens. Dedicated to the memory of the 346 men of the corps who died in the desert, it shows a soldier of the Imperial Camel Corps astride his camel, but there is no mention of what happened to those 'sweating, smelling' stoical, bad tempered, intrepid beasts once *their* war was over.

4

Beasts of Burden: Lesser Lights and Other Animals

A veterinary surgeon examining a mule at No 4 Remount Depot on 15 February 1918.

'In this war of motor transport, ship, tank and aeroplane.
People "feel" the horse is finished and don't need his work again,
But to utter such a feeling is the action of a fool,
For there's work for him in plenty and his lesser light, the mule.
Taking pack or heavy transport through the mountains and the gorse,
So this time include the two of them in "Gentleman – The Horse!"'

... wrote Private Cartwright of the Royal Army Veterinary Corps from his hospital bed in June 1943.

Every German Panzer (tank) division deployed horses in the Second World War, and also in 1939 a German infantry division required between 4,077 and 6,033 horses for transport and hauling guns. In June 1941 the Germans assembled 625,000 horses for the invasion of the USSR and of these over 180,000 were lost in the first freezing winter. The Russians themselves deployed something like 21 milllion horses on the Eastern Front and probably at least two-thirds perished. It was not until after the German invasion that the Soviet Union was included in the US Lend Lease programme under the terms of which America could supply whatever goods President Roosevelt certified as being 'in the interest of national defense' to those countries fighting against Germany, Italy and eventually Japan. Subsequently, equine losses began to be staunched as the Red Army started to use trucks whereas previously it had relied very heavily on horses.

But when it came to the 'lesser light', the mule, there were some campaigns of the Second World War, particularly in Burma and other Far Eastern theatres, that many commanders were prepared to admit could not have been won without the stamina, fortitude, nimble-footedness and tenacity of this hybrid animal, the offspring – or mésalliance – of a horse or pony mated with a donkey.

'Without pride of ancestry or hope of posterity' the mule was easy game for jeers and contempt, work-a-day and bad tempered rather than well bred and noble like the horse, a beast of burden trudging heavy laden rather than a war mount in full charge. Nevertheless, mules have faithfully served in war for centuries, but it was only in the 20th century that their worth was fully appreciated in European warfare though British soldiers on the North West Frontier of India had long waxed lyrical about their 'long-eared darlin's' ability to go further, carry more, venture sure-footedly into more treacherous terrain with fewer rations than any horse could.

The first mule was imported to Britain from America in 1912: by the end of the First World War 250,000 had been brought over from North and South America. Such was the animal's general stamina and proven record of resistance to disease and cold that

Mulish Behaviour

Suggestions from Captain Galtrey in 1919 about the best way to lead a mule that prefers to see the back of the soldier leading him.

Writing at the end of the Great War, Captain Sidney Galtrey was confident that almost every 'gentlemen in khaki ... has a slight nodding acquaintance with his mule *confrère* in the Army [since] they are both battling in the same cause, both living on army rations, and both, no doubt, longing for victory and the end of war. The difficulty is to know how to treat him. As a beast of burden and haulage which has assisted enormously the Allies' waging of war and will continue to do ... Or as an animal with more eccentricities of character and undeniable virtues than any other creature on God's earth – as, in fact, just a mule? ... Often and often he has done what the horse failed to do. He has survived and outlasted him, and maybe, has shown his perversity by apparent enjoyment of the awful din of battles, the deep mud and piercing cold of France, or the heat and flies of the East. His temper and constitution have remained whole, while the specimens of his mother's branch of the species [the horse] have cracked and fallen by the wayside ... it takes a lot to put the mule out of action. He has even kindled enthusiasm among ardent horse-lovers who were once prejudiced against him and despised the donkey in his outline and demeanour. So in time they have come to say: "Give us mules for this job of war rather than horses."'

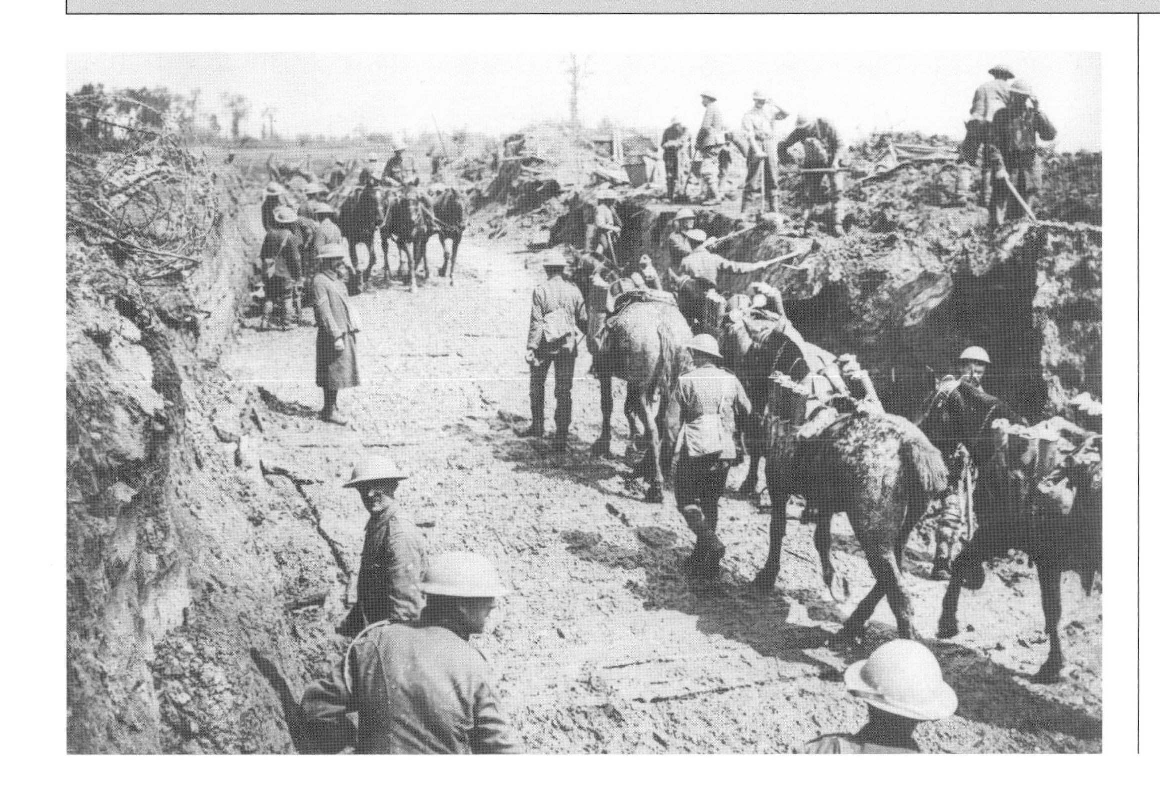

Pack mules carrying shells along a newly built road on 3 August 1917 during the Battle of Pilckem Ridge in the Third Battle of Ypres.

The Third Battle of Ypres. Two pack mules carrying shells struggle out of the mud on the Western Front.

three-quarters of the ammunition delivered to the front line at Passchendaele was carried by mules.

The famed obstinacy of mules could be exacerbated by being tended by men who did not understand their needs. 'The tragedy is that with the increased use of machinery in industry, agriculture and war, there are very few men who know anything about us,' wrote 'Mulus' in a supposed 'first-animal reflection' in the *British Army Journal* on his First World War service. 'And we go through a pretty awful time while they are learning … unfortunately we cannot talk to teach them what to do, we can only remonstrate when they do the wrong thing,' 'Mulus' continued. 'I like to be handled firmly and quietly … My mouth is tender and I only get more excited if men jerk on my reins. I like affection. I like people to encourage the horse in me rather than the donkey.'

'You wait until you have to shoe mules,' a shoeing smith was warned as he left for France in 1917. Claude Sisley 'thought a great deal about these animals during my time

A pack mule fully laden with trenching equipment including picks and shovels, northern Russia, **circa** *1919.*

[at Neufchâtel]. It always seemed odd that such ill-shaped creatures, too long in the leg and with sickle hocks, should in fact be such excellent workers ... Mules, I am persuaded, are more sensible, or more sensitive than horses. They suspect that anyone who comes near them means them some sort of harm, and not unnaturally they try to get their blow in first. Because of their reputation, a great many men, aware of this feeling on the part of the mule, decide to get *their* blow in first, and so trouble develops. Certain vivid memories of mules remain in my mind. There was the mule that had to be dragged from its stable to the forge [to be shod], securely lashed between the heavy horses that worked in our dung carts, and was the devil to shoe when it got there ... [that day] I learned my lesson about which was the safe end of a mule.

'But is there a safe end? Mules have brought cow-kicking to a fine art ... nine out of ten of our mules had to be shod from behind with the aid of a side-line. This meant that there was the tiresome performance of inducing the animal to step into the loop of rope that was later to haul up the leg and after that there was the awkward task of nailing on a shoe the wrong way round with upward strokes of the hammer that were difficult to control.' Mules would bite through ropes so they were usually tethered by chains and grooming a mule entailed the services of two soldiers, one to groom and one to watch out for the animal's flying hooves – and bite.

During the Second World War mules were used by the German and French armies to pull guns and many mules from the Indian Mule Transport Companies and the Cypriot

A mule confined in wooden stocks waiting to be shod near Frise in March 1917 on the Somme.

Simpson and his Donkey

A donkey mascot adopted by the 26th Divisional Train (ASC). They found it dying on the roadside in Salonika, Greece during the First World War.

'The donkeys are the favourites among the men on account of their temper,' reported a soldier, and in the First World War the ass of biblical times was truly a humble beast of burden. It was small enough to be led along the trenches to distribute rations, sensitive enough to be used to test for bad or poisoned water, strong enough to haul bulky loads – panniers of water, food or supplies of as much as 200lb – to the front. Donkeys were also gentle enough to act as stretcher bearers during the Gallipoli campaign where some were trained to carry a wounded man up to the operating table and then 'back pedal' out of the tent again.

Small donkeys carried men so large that their feet almost trailed along the ground. Thousands of donkeys died from tsetse flies in East Africa – or were killed by the arsenic 'cure'. As many as 100,000 donkeys requisitioned from peasant farmers picked their way along mountain paths in Italy. Donkeys carried essential supplies of ammunition and food over 40 miles to besieged troops in Palestine in May 1918. In 1973 donkeys were recalled to service in the guerrilla war in Oman when, with their hooves muffled in hessian, they were transported into the mountains to carry vital supplies over vertiginous mountain tracks. And a donkey became an Australian icon of war.

John Simpson, an Englishman who had emigrated to Australia and served with the Australian Field Ambulance Corps, had a way with animals – dogs, possums and particularly donkeys. With many of his fellow stretcher bearers killed on landing at Gallipoli, Simpson, with a donkey – or maybe a series of donkeys that may have been called Murphy, or perhaps Duffy – worked day and night to carry first aid to the wounded, or bring them back to the field hospital if they could be moved, or bring succour to the dying amidst shells and bullets and sniper fire. Finally, on 19 May 1915, a shell killed Simpson. The donkey – which in legend became 'not much over 30 inches high' – brought the patient it had been transporting back to the dressing station before leading a rescue party back to Simpson's body: an Australian war hero.

Pack Transport (Mule) Company that had been working in France carrying supplies were either 'disposed of' or abandoned on the beaches at Dunkirk when the British Expeditionary Force was evacuated. However, their greatest value proved to be as pack animals in mountainous regions that were all but impassable by motorised transport and too rocky for horses to be able to negotiate safely, in the deserts of North Africa and the dense jungles of the Far East.

An ammunition chest carried by mules during the Italian campaign in 1944–5.

The transport of animals from their place of origin or from one theatre of war to another posed difficulties. Great care was taken in selecting the consignment for shipping by a veterinary officer to ensure that, as far, as possible, only animals in good condition were transported, and no cases of contagious diseases or obviously sick animals were embarked. Forage had to be loaded and the animals were led up the gangplank singly. It was found that most mules would follow a lead pony but those that wouldn't had to be unceremoniously bundled up from behind. Donkeys proved the most difficult to load with their persistent refusal to proceed in any direction except backwards, and various ruses were tried, such as blindfolding them, backing them up, using a lead animal or tying their ears together, but with little success and in the end most were tied up with rope which resulted in some being injured and an entire contingent of affronted animals being hauled aboard. Later, boxes in which four donkeys could be swung into the hold were used. On SS *Mount Everest*, which brought troops and soldiers from Tunis to Italy, a net was spread on the floor, a donkey would waddle into the centre of the net, an NCO at each corner would swiftly attach his corner to the hook of a crane and the animals would be swung aloft and onto the ship. So dextrous did the men get at this that it was soon possible to load two or three donkeys every minute.

An exhausted and mud-caked mule being fed by the roadside on the Western Front during the First World War.

Once aboard, the mules (and horses and donkeys) were restrained in individual stalls of regulation size with a platform on which the tethered animals stood, and coir matting was laid on all the decks to prevent the unshod animals from slipping. Hay was put out as soon as the animals were in their stalls, with the idea that this would make them settle more quickly, though again donkeys proved the most recalcitrant. There was no space for exercise on a voyage that might last several weeks, but

ABOVE: ***Indian mule transport marching along the road to Baghdad through the Jebel Hamrin mountains on the Mesopotamian Front in the winter of 1916–17.***

the animals were fed, watered and groomed with great care, and moved around so none spent the entire voyage next to the boiler room, for instance. There were losses from sickness, heat stroke, enemy action, or, in the case of some equines being transported from Marseilles to Palestine in December 1939, the collapse of the stalls during a storm at sea which was largely because nails rather than bolts had been used to secure fittings, but also because the mules had gnawed away at the partitions.

Mules were used extensively during the Italian and Sicilian campaigns, with the US 5th Army employing 15 Italian pack trains totalling nearly 4,000 mules in the Apennines in the final winter of the war. The French Expeditionary Corps, whose North African *Goums* (small groups of irregulars recruited from the indigenous population of French Morocco) were highly skilled in mountain warfare, relied almost entirely on mules for its logistics. During the attack on the Gothic Line, a series of German defences in the Apennines which ran from north of Lucca to Pesaro on the Adriatic coast, fully-laden mules picked their way more than 20 miles a day in the spring of 1944 over rough mountain tracks, as each troop's 'liberator squad' called at remote farmhouses to barter for provisions. Each battalion was accompanied by 36 mules carrying ammunition, arms, food – and the men's greatcoats. As they approached the enemy lines the going over the mountains got noticeably more difficult and the mules were obliged to carry their heavy loads for nearly 12 hours a day for five continuous days. Without the mules it would not have been possible to cross the steep-sided, fast-flowing River Metauro prior to the attack, but during the battle for Monte Calvo some mules, returning from taking ammunition to the front line, were carelessly marched through a well-marked minefield and 12 were blown up which caused great grief to their Arab and Gurkha drivers who had given each animal a name, cared for it devotedly and 'the loss of a mule caused [them] nearly as much grief as the loss of a man'. As at Monte Cassino, it became obvious as the Allied troops broke the line that 'mules dislike dead bodies as much as we do, and frequently tracks had to be cleared before the mule train would move forward. This was not as easy as it sounds, as frequently bodies were booby-trapped and often were found to be in minefields, just outside the tapes that lined the tracks.' Conditions could be dreadful and the driving rain and sea of mud from broken river banks in which

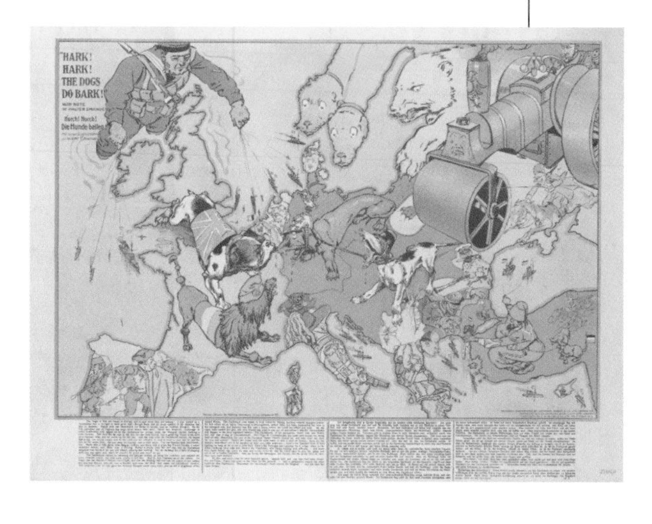

much of the battle for Monte Cassino was fought, up narrow gorges with precipitous mountains on either side, was almost reminiscent of conditions that the pack animals had encountered on the Western Front in the First World War. Jeeps pushed the mud along like snow ploughs, and, as winter approached, the mules trudged along with their tails a solid block of ice and icicles hanging from their noses.

Since the tortuous advance was overlooked by the enemy, it was decided to dye all the grey mules with permanganate of potash so that they blended into the landscape as they made their precarious way up the mountainside. Nevertheless, within three weeks only 16 of one troop's 75 mules were left alive, and among the many terrible sights of human bodies littering the mountainside, corpses still sitting in burnt-out tanks and lorries, a poignant one was of lines of Italian mules still tied to their tethering bar, all dead.

ABOVE: ***Monte Cassino, Italy, 1944. A string of mules being led by men of a newly-formed mule company through the ruins of the small village of San Clemente. By the end of the Italian campaign, Allied troops were using some 30,000 animals. Casualties among the mules were high: in three weeks 59 out of a total of 75 mules with B Troop of the 24th Guards Brigade had been killed.***

OPPOSITE BELOW: 'Hark! Hark! The Dogs Do Bark!' ***A map of Europe in 1914 by the German artist E. Zimmermann in which the combatant nations in the Great War are represented by dogs. Britain is epitomised by a bulldog held on a leash by a sailor; France by a poodle; Germany by a dachshund; Austria-Hungary by a mongrel – and Serbia not by a dog but by a wasp. The bulldog can be seen to be biting the dachshund on the nose.***

In the Sudan the mule proved indefatigable. On some occasions mule trains marched for 14 hours, covering 35 miles under full loads – rations, water, ammunition, mortars, machine guns, hot tea, and, on occasions, live sheep for the Indian troops – and carrying loads up precipitous hills, some of which were 6,000 feet above sea level. Narrow winding tracks had been prepared by sappers if none had previously existed, and the mules did two or three journeys a day, each journey taking from two to three hours up, and rather less down. The noise of battle reverberating round the valley was deafening and on several occasions the mules came under heavy shell attack and increasingly the hazardous journeys were undertaken at night.

In the Balkans, mules were supplied to the partisan forces of Marshal Tito. These were delivered to join the 500 largely Bosnian-bred mules already resident on the small, rocky island of Vis off the coast of Yugoslavia where partisans were training for an assault on the mainland. The mules were conveyed across the Adriatic in holiday passenger boats, with the deckchairs removed and special pens built to restrain the animals. Eventually it was planned that 900 mules would be sent, and when men and animals were fully trained for guerrilla warfare they would be air lifted by the Balkan Air Force to Yugoslavia to act as bearers for the resistance fighters. Four mules, accompanied by a member of the Royal Army Veterinary Corps (RAVC), were packed into each C-47 aircraft and the mules were jumped out onto the runways under cover of darkness.

In the mountains of Greece and Crete mules and donkeys were again the pack animals of troops fighting in the hills. Tragically, a ship in which a number of men and mules were

Model of a mule transporting a dismembered gun during the Second World War.

being evacuated as German troops advanced, was sunk, and practically all the mules drowned, though a few in the unsubmerged stern of the vessel were thrown overboard and managed to swim ashore.

During the North African campaign the Royal Army Service Corps formed animal transport companies each comprising 308 load-carrying mules each, and as every mule could carry 72kg (160lb) that meant that each company could transport about 22 tons of supplies. But it was in the Far East that mules earned their greatest accolades. During the Burma campaign from December 1941 until August 1945, the longest campaign in which the British Army fought during the Second World War, mules were used extensively, exhaustively and often hazardously. Under the command of General Sir William Slim, the 14th Army comprised men of a number of diverse nationalities – including Burmese, Chinese, Gurkhas, as well as troops from East and West Africa. In March 1942 Rangoon was lost and the Burma army began its 600-mile retreat to the Indian frontier. There was a shortage of mules, particularly the larger type of equipment-carrying animals, which made the decision to leave the roads and move through the jungle and mountain paths hard to implement. Rail and road communications were disrupted, so sick animals could not be moved and the long and arduous marches, shortage of forage, saddle galls and injuries from sharp bamboo stumps, poisonous plants and bombing raids took a heavy toll. In addition, leeches, mosquitoes and other insects made conditions very unpleasant and when the men and animals reached the frontier monsoon conditions and the spread of tropical diseases such as malaria, dysentery and surra meant that in 1943 the 14th Army suffered a total of 12,130 animal casualties.

A donkey being winched by means of a harness and cable across the unbridged Ruwu River in German East Africa during the First World War.

In the spring of 1943 Chindits began penetrating behind the Japanese lines to carry on the battle by cutting the main railway line that ran from Mandalay to Myitkyina and generally sabotaging supply and communication lines. The Chindits were long range penetration groups, made up mainly of men trained in jungle warfare under the command of Brigadier Orde Wingate. Their name was a corruption of the Burmese word *chinthe*, the winged stone lions that guard Buddhist temples. This became the force's insignia, since in Wingate's eyes they symbolised the close co-operation between ground strength and air strength that was the basic requirement 'for successful guerrilla fighting of the kind we were pioneering'. The Chindits were accompanied by 547 horses and 3,134 mules, each loaded with heavy equipment, including mortars, flame throwers, wireless sets and rubber boats for river crossings – plus about 250 bullocks which were regarded as 'meat on the hoof'. In order to ensure that the same surprise tactics could not be used against the Chindits, they had no lines of supply: almost everything was supplied from Assam by air – including a total of around 2,000 mules which travelled in specially adapted gliders and landed on narrow, sometimes treacherous, air strips. Supplies followed and the mules had to trek an average of 200 miles from the airbase to reach the fighting columns.

The Chindits were fighting campaigns in which mobility and surprise were the keys to success, so there was an urgent need for wireless equipment in remote areas to ensure that the various groups could keep in close contact. The mules had to carry such

US Marines assist an ox in pulling a heavy load at Saipan in the Marianas Islands in the Pacific theatre during the Second World War.

equipment in areas where the attrition rate for the animals was likely to be high. The dense jungle made it almost impossible to construct landing strips and, to overcome this difficulty and save time and resources, it was decided to investigate the possibility of paradropping mules. Experts who were conversant with the problems of parachuting in jeeps and anti-tank guns were consulted to devise a system of 'packaging' the animals in ways that caused a minimum of damage to the aircraft coupled with minimum distress to the mules. It was estimated that the rate of drop would be in the region of 16 to 18 feet per second and it was clear that a mule could not just be pushed out of the plane with just its vulnerable parts protected. There would be danger from cross winds and, of course, from the impact of landing. A 6ft 5in by 4ft wooden platform was constructed and this was covered with a US-issue collapsible pontoon used for ferrying casualties across rivers. An old mule was selected for the first drop and was sedated, lashed to the platform in an upright position and the boats were inflated to form a snug, protective covering. The animal was ejected – munching grass – at 600 feet altitude from a plane flying at 130mph. With the stiffness of the more geriatric, it was a good 10 minutes after landing before the mule was able to pull itself upright, but subsequently when younger beasts were dropped it was found that these more sprightly creatures sprang straight up and were capable of carrying a full load within 15 to 20 minutes of being dropped.

Mules might offer every advantage when it came to fortitude and nimble-footedness, but when it came to discretion they were worse than useless. The sound of mules braying when they were hungry or lonely carried great distances and could reveal to the Japanese forces the presence of troops who might otherwise have been comparatively safe from discovery in jungle country. In night operations the mules would as good as advertise an

Serbian troops loading shells on ox-drawn wagons, October 1916. Oxen were to prove to be useful military draught animals in both world wars, although they were slow and required large quantities of food.

advance, and a solution was obviously urgently needed to silence the mules without putting them out of action for long periods. It was decided to experiment with removing the animals' vocal chords under a local anaesthetic, and the experiments showed that as the mules 'recovered from the anaesthetic, all were in an excited condition and all vigorously attempted to bray. It was reassuring that despite their best efforts, none succeed in making more than a hoarse wheeze.' Colonel Stewart of the RAVC, who had been charged with this organising this task, summed up the 'conditions under which these operations on 111th Brigade animals were done [as] indescribable. Animals were cast in a jungle clearing on large tarpaulins spread on a bed of grass. As long as the weather remained dry, this was all right, but when the rain came down in torrents we had to drag the animals to a hastily erected tarpaulin shelter with which our main concern was to prevent sufficient rain collecting on top to cause collapse of the overhead structure. When the rain was not too heavy, operations were done with waterproof coats or capes held over the four operators … [who] were able to maintain a steady figure of around 70 to 90 operations a day.'

First World War poster by Harold C. Earnshaw.

The operations were considered a great success: it was concluded that if an animal was mute for six weeks, it stayed mute. Of the 5,563 mules operated on, there were only 53 casualties and the mules were considered sufficiently fit to be exercised with pack saddles within 10 days of the operation and to carry full loads as soon as their external wound had healed. Moreover, it made training mules a lot less fraught as they could be encouraged to swim across a river when a whistle was blown to indicate that there was a meal waiting on the other side 'without the usual terrific outburst of braying'.

As they had served and died in the First World War, so camels were again pressed into service in the Second World War and thousands were used for transportation in Eritrea and British Somaliland, with many dying. 'The lightly armed' undermanned British Somaliland Camel Corps had fought in the First World War, and when mobilised for the next war had been reinforced by a small number of men and animals from Southern Rhodesia. The corps provided 'a thin advance screen for observing and delaying the enemy' on the parched and arid plateaux of British Somaliland. Aided by patrols of Illanos, a small force of tribal levies whose normal task was as a rudimentary police force on the frontier areas, the camel-mounted troops made 'several bold and successful raids against enemy detachments' according to the official history of the against-the-odds campaign. Indeed, so gallantly did the small British Somaliland Camel Corps temporarily keep at bay an Italian invading force of 26 battalions, artillery and tanks, (some nine to ten thousand men) that, 'for extreme gallantry in defence' of the Tug Argan Gap, a member of the East Surrey Regiment attached to the corps, Captain Eric Wilson, was awarded the Victoria Cross.

As General Sir William Slim, commander of the 14th Army in Burma, pointed out, in wartime pigeons, dogs, ponies, mules, horses, bulls, and buffaloes 'served well and faithfully. There were true bonds of affection between men and all these beasts, but the elephant held a special place in our esteem. It was not,

I think, a matter of size and strength. It was the elephant's dignity and intelligence that gained our real respect. To watch an elephant building a bridge, to see the skill with which the great beast lifted the huge logs and the accuracy with which they were coaxed into position, was to realise that the trained elephant was no mere transport animal, but indeed a skilled sapper.'

In Burma the elephant was the backbone of the prosperous teak industry and used by the Bombay Burma Trading Company to haul teak logs cut from the trees that grew high up in the deciduous forests. Some of these animals had been originally imported from Siam and India but many had been bred in captivity from those animals that had first been acquired as a result of *kheddaring* (breaking in) wild animals. Prior to the Japanese invasion probably 6,000 elephants were working in the deciduous forests of Burma, and of those 70 per cent had been born in captivity.

With the outbreak of war in 1939, teak became a valuable munition of war and demand for it was insatiable. After Japan entered the war in December 1941 elephants were used to transport the belongings of families escaping from the Japanese advance or were deployed in the retreat to carry the sick and to transport rations, while others stayed to work long hours with their *oozies* (riders), who rode and cared for them, hauling timber to build roads that would assist any Allied counter attack.

In 1942 'Elephant Bill', the name by which J. H. Williams was to be known throughout Burma, was invited to become Elephant Adviser to what would become the 14th Army 'though at that time the Army had no actual elephants for me to advise on'. But in 1942 a number of *oozies* disobeyed a Burmese defector's order to hand their elephants over to the Japanese and instead delivered them to the Allied forces at Tamu, and these animals would form the No 1 Elephant Company, Royal Indian Engineers. Williams experimented with breaking up anti-aircraft Bofors guns so that the component parts could be transported by

An elephant pulls an aircraft into position on a Fleet Air Arm air station in India during the Second World War.

An elephant using chains to pull tree trunks to build a bridge. The skill and strength of elephants in manoeuvring a diverse number of heavy objects proved invaluable in parts of India and other areas of Asia where there were often few roads capable of taking motorised vehicles.

elephants and found that a section of eight elephants 'could take one gun, with spare barrel, reserve ammunition, and all the kit of the British gun crew without difficulty'. To 'Elephant Bill's' regret, 'these experiments were not followed up. Had the necessity arisen, the elephants would have provided invaluable transport, for they would have negotiated the most precipitous forest tracks over the hills, where no mechanical transport could be taken. The elephants used in the experiment remained quite unperturbed 75 yards from where the Bofors gun was firing' which gave rise to the rumour that there were plans to have elephants in close support of the infantry, each with a gun fired off its back.

Throughout the Burma campaign 'Elephant Bill' was frustrated by the perennial military question of whether elephants were a branch of transport or more of use to the sappers building 'elephant bridges' across rivers, formed with logs which the elephants would carry in their trunks and carefully lay in place. When they were used for transport 'sticky bombs, boxes of grenades, and other heavy equipment would be tied on anyhow with a rope' and, in one instance, Williams swam the animals across a wide river 'with their full loads on. One badly loaded animal overturned in deep water and was lost.'

When the monsoon season came early in 1943 'all motor transport was bogged down. There was a small break in the rain, and then the vehicles were able to start crawling back. But they could never have done it except for my elephants,' claimed Williams. 'All along the road there were urgent requests for help and the elephants were pulling the lorries out of the mud like champagne corks out of bottles. Two or three lorries were wrecked owing to drivers starting up their engines, by spinning the back wheels. But they found themselves and their lorry being taken for a 50-yard stampede into the jungle, ending up with the lorry hitting a tree, or overturning, or the elephant's chains snapping and releasing him from the jungle devil he was towing.'

A line of loaded elephants carrying supplies to Allied forces in the front line during the Second World War in the Far East.

Elephant Bill

Bandoola was a male elephant born in captivity in Burma in November 1897. Full grown, he stood 7ft 4in, and had a 'good temper', according to his record with the timber hauling company for which the 'tusker' laboured. However, Bandoola (named after a famous Burmese general) soon gained a bad reputation since he had apparently killed his *oozie* (rider) in an unprovoked and vicious attack. But in April 1944, Bandoola was one of the elephants on a hazardous march to evacuate supplies and refugees as the Japanese attempted an invasion of India. The elephants were already '5,000 feet up, which is high above any normal "elephant line". In fact we were as high as Hannibal was when he crossed the [Alps]' when they came to 'a sheer rock face escarpment 300 to 400 feet high' according to Colonel J. H. Williams, an experienced elephant hand known as 'Elephant Bill' who was in charge of the expedition. To traverse the cliff it would be necessary for the elephants to climb along an impossibly narrow ledge that in some places 'was so steep that the elephants would almost be standing on their hind legs'. Bandoola's *oozie*, Po Toke, volunteered 'Bandoola will lead [the 45 other elephants] and if he won't face it, no other elephant will.' The track was only about three feet wide in places with 'a wall above and a sheer drop on the outside ... all our chances of success depended on Bandoola'. Colonel Williams stopped just 200 yards above 'the most dangerous spot, at which we had actually cut a series of steps in the sandstone, each just big enough to take an elephant's foot ... Bandoola's head and tusks suddenly came round the corner below me. It was almost as if he were standing on his hind legs. Then up came his hindquarters as though in a slow motion picture. The *oozie* was sitting on his head, looking down, and seemed to be directing the elephant where to place his feet ... It was more than two hours before I saw Bandoola again, and then he was practically at the top ... He was up, at all events, and my relief and excitement cannot be expressed in words ... Po Toke ... gave me a queer fleeting look, that was as good as saying, "Don't you worry. They'll all follow now." He was right. They all did.'

A British officer with his sledge and team of reindeer used for transporting supplies through the snow at Alexandrovsk, Russia, during the War of Intervention, 1918–1920.

Besides pulling lorries out of tight places, the elephants laid causeways of logs in the mud in amazingly quick time, while whole convoys waited to pass over them. Elephants could not be hurried in their work, but they could, and did, work overtime until the job was finished.

It was not just brute strength that was needed in these vital engineering tasks: heavy logs often had to be tossed up five or six feet when a bridge was under construction. In manipulating the wood back with his trunk, the elephant could lose control of it and it could roll back and crush the *oozie* perched high astride the elephant's head, directing operations. To the amazement of watching British officers, the animals were aware of the problem and worked out a way in which the log could be balanced on their trunk and held by a wedge of wood the elephant had jammed between his trunk and his tusk, so stopping it from rolling back over his forehead onto his rider – a 'skilled sapper' indeed.

Despite the pivotal role the elephants played in the Burma campaign, their human advocate 'found it rather a heartbreaking job at times trying to teach not only Indian soldiers but also English officers that an elephant is an animal which needs quite as much care as a mule. It was far more valuable at that time, as mules would have got bogged down at once in a quagmire of mud.'

Belgian dog carts carrying machine guns leave for the front line on 25 October 1914.

The Bulldog Spirit.

At last, in desperation, 'Elephant Bill' issued 'general notes on elephant management. In spite of that, elephants were still kept tied to trees for hours on end, waiting at rendezvous points for patrols instead of being allowed to graze on the necessary fodder. As a result their digestions were upset for no good reason. Animals were also loaded in any fashion, with no attempt at balancing loads. The Gurkha, who is a jolly little man, thought it very funny to be riding an elephant, and it was quite common for me to catch as many as six of them on the back of one animal, with their rifle-slings looped round the animal's ears, as though on a hat-stand. On several occasions when I caught them doing this they would slide off the hindquarters *en masse* and bolt into the jungle to hide from me, like school children climbing apple trees.' Williams finally 'got my way, by a resolute refusal to supply elephants to any troops who would not co-operate in treating them properly.'

During their invasion of Burma in 1942, the Japanese also made use of elephants, mainly to transport mortars and ammunition from Siam. The major Japanese offensive to break into India was also heavily dependent on elephant

Six-week-old Siberian huskies bred for pulling dog sleds over the snow and ice.

Transport old and new. An RAF Morris Light Armoured Car stands next to a bullock cart and its driver on a military airfield in the Azores in January 1944.

Mark, an Alsatian trained to carry ammunition, was donated to the British Expeditionary Force by the French 1st Army and was on active service from November 1939 until June 1940. In this photograph a Lewis gun drum is being attached to the dog's harness.

transport. A column of 350 animals marched through the Chin Hills to link up with motor transport and bullock carts, and when the 14th Army started its rout of Japanese forces, capturing elephants as it went, or having them returned by defecting *oozies*, it was found that most of the elephants' tusks had been sawed off, perhaps to make them less dangerous but also to satisfy the Japanese craving for ivory. In all 1,652 elephants were captured from the Japanese between November 1942 and their surrender in August 1945. Most went back to their work of timber extraction for the teak industry but, of the alleged nearly 4,000 that were lost in the jungle, some may have been killed and others died of untreated wounds, but 'Elephant Bill' was optimistic that many had simply rejoined their kinsfolk in the wild after giving matchless wartime service.

A Siberian husky trained by the US Army to carry a machine gun on its back.

5

Despatches from the Front

'Cheerio! I've joined up', ***etching by George Soper during the First World War.***

OPPOSITE: ***'The Wanderer Sprang Towards His Master with Delight', a 1915 painting from*** **Great Deeds of the Great War** ***(1916) illustrating the story of a terrier which escaped from home in Hammersmith, west London, and ran through the streets, allegedly peering into the faces of men in army uniform. When he saw a draft of soldiers marching to Victoria Station, the dog followed them, jumping into a train compartment with the men, as if he knew they were going to the place where his master was, and travelled with the soldiers to France.***

In time this almost preternaturally clever dog reached the trenches, actually found where the 1st North Staffordshire Regiment was stationed, and eventually located his master, Private Brown. As depicted, man and dog were delighted to be reunited.

Dogs were the first animals to be domesticated. The bond between a dog and its master has been documented for thousands of years with cave paintings showing dogs hunting with men or guarding human settlements against marauders, and the sight of so many tombs in British churches with an effigy of a dog lying prone at the feet of its once master bears eloquent witness to this attachment. As James Serpell, a pioneer in the study of human–dog relationships at Cambridge University, put it: 'the average dog behaves as if it is literally "attached" to its owner by an invisible cord. Given the opportunity, it will follow him everywhere, sit or lie down beside him, and exhibit clear signs of distress if the owner goes out and leaves it behind, or shuts it out of the room unexpectedly.'

In wartime this 'invisible cord', this interconnectedness, was put to use time and again and would save lives, and on several occasions would prove decisive for the survival of a whole fighting unit. The 'invisible cord' would turn out to have an elasticity that could be awe inspiring as dogs, far from their masters, would overcome fearsome obstacles to return to their side. Dogs worked – and still work – as messengers, as guides, in rescue operations and as guards; they sniffed out mines, followed tracks, and fulfilled a vital role as morale boosters and companions, prepared to follow their owners, or handlers, into situations of the gravest danger.

The earliest known dog of war was a type of mastiff from Tibet that was domesticated during the Stone Age. Persians, Greeks, Assyrians and Babylonians all deployed dogs in great numbers in battle. During the Peloponnesian War (431–404BCE) one of the 50 dogs guarding the Corinthian citadel deserted his post to alert the Corinthians to the arrival of the Greek invaders. During the Roman conquest of Britain in 55BCE, Julius Caesar was impressed by the courage of the English mastiffs that harried the invaders. Attila the Hun fought with dogs in the 5th century. Canine armour was developed in the Middle Ages, with dogs wearing spiked collars – as they had in ancient Sparta – being unleashed against the oncoming cavalry, the spikes playing havoc with the horses' legs. Dogs would frequently accompany their masters on a crusade, and in the 19th century Napoleon's dog Moustache was as good as mentioned in despatches for his valiant work at the Battle of Austerlitz. However, with the development of gunpowder, dogs largely relinquished their role as front-line combatants and became an essential auxiliary for the soldiers in the field.

Since so much of the First World War on the Western Front was spent in trench dug outs with the battle lines static, communication between the men and their commanders was vital and it was here that dogs played a crucial role. When wireless or telephone links went down, dogs were often used to carry messages back to base, where they would wait before returning with the response: a double jeopardy with death.

Dogs had the advantage over human messengers in that they could move four or five

Étaples, 28 August 1918. An engineer fits a message into the metal cylinder attached to the dog's collar in which the message was carried.

Trench messenger dog attached to the 5th Manchesters at Cuinchy on 26 January 1918.

times faster than most foot soldiers, with several messages in a metal canister attached to their collar or even a pannier of pigeon messengers on their back. Dogs were easier to camouflage – grey or dark-coloured dogs were selected so they blended in with the mud – and as they were closer to the ground they were harder to see and thus harder to take aim at. Dogs were able to circumnavigate the plethora of shell holes on the Western Front more easily than a man could, and if they did fall in could usually swim through the icy, filthy water to safety. At the battle of Verdun 17 soldiers were killed trying to deliver messages, but when a dog was despatched it managed seven round trips before succumbing to enemy fire. It was not just the dog's speed that was so impressive, it was its instinctive ability to find its way through the honeycomb of trenches that riddled

A Heroine's Pet

Locked in her cell, condemned to death, Edith Cavell's thoughts were for her dog. 'My dear old Jack,' she wrote to the sister in charge of the Brussels hospital where she had been matron. 'Please brush him sometimes and look after him. I am quite well – more worried about the School than my own fate.'

In the grey early dawn of 12 October 1915, Nurse Cavell was taken out and shot by German firing squad.

Her crime had been to help Allied soldiers escape from German-occupied Belgium during the First World War. As well as directing a Red Cross hospital, training nurses and treating the casualties of war, Edith Cavell provided Allied soldiers with civilian clothing, money, forged documents and a guide to smuggle them to the frontier with Holland – and freedom. On 5 August 1915 German police, who had had the hospital under surveillance for some time, burst in and arrested Miss Cavell. At her trial she and some of her helpers were found guilty of a capital offence and while some had their sentences commuted to life imprisonment, Nurse Cavell was not reprieved.

After her arrest, no one wanted to take Cavell's shaggy little dog and he was either kept in a damp stable or chained to a small kennel before being rescued by one of the matron's friends, the Dowager Duchess de Croÿ.

Eventually Jack, 'of no breed, but must have had some ancestor of the shepherd breed', was brought back to England where he worked tirelessly for charities in tribute to the brave mistress to whom he had been such a companion during harrowing, dangerous times.

Sheet music commemorating the courage of Edith Cavell, shown with Jack (right).

Feeding time for the dogs at the Messenger Dog Service kennels at Étaples on 6 September 1918. As part of their training for duty under gunfire, explosions were let off close to the kennels as the animals were feeding.

France and Flanders and unerringly return to the handler who had sent it, bringing information, orders or reassurance that reinforcements were on their way.

Major Edwin Hautenville Richardson, the son of a gentleman farmer, had grown up in a family that had 'a way with dogs' and as a young boy had started to read about dogs trained for military purposes. After Sandhurst and a brief military career, Richardson and his wife acquired a large estate in Scotland where the couple were able to pursue their interest in dog training. One day, in 1895, while shooting on a friend's moor, he noticed 'a foreigner' buying a sheepdog from a shepherd. The man turned out to be an agent purchasing British dogs on behalf of the German government. Perceptively realising that 'we may find our own dogs of service for *our* country, *our* soldiers', the Richardsons started training dogs in earnest, and the Major both visited dog training schools in Germany and was allowed to take his dogs along to British Army summer training camps so he could judge 'where there were weak spots in my training and make alterations'.

In 1905 the Russian Embassy wired to Richardson asking him to supply dogs for their troops fighting in the Russo-Japanese War, and so well did the Airedales he sent perform in the field that the Tsar sent their trainer a gold and diamond watch and chain for his services. For the next few years requests for war dogs came in regularly and Richardson supplied animals to Turkey, Spain, the Balkans and India – and police forces throughout Britain.

On the outbreak of the First World War, Richardson offered his dogs to the British Army. It refused his offer, though the Red Cross was pleased to accept a number of the dogs that he had trained to accompany field ambulances, and though the trade was not officially sanctioned many officers at the front wrote requesting dogs for messenger,

A messenger dog leaping a trench as it carries a message back to the German line near Sedan in May 1917. The canister containing the message attached to the dog's collar is clearly visible.

sentry and guard duties. An official trial was carried out in France in 1916 with two Airedales, Wolf and Prince, who carried messages 4,000 yards over ground they had never previously traversed to the Royal Artillery Brigade HQ. All previous attempts had failed and as a result of this success the War Office contacted Richardson, asking him to set up an official training school for war dogs. This he and his wife did at Shoeburyness on the Thames Estuary in Essex, whence the distant sound of gunfire on the Western Front eerily echoed when the wind was in the right direction.

In order to provide enough dogs for training, the police were ordered to hand over any strays they found. Battersea Dogs Home was combed for likely candidates – as were similar institutions throughout the country. Large numbers were found since wartime food shortages had led many people to surrender their pets, and the government issued an appeal for the public to 'volunteer' their pets and working dogs for the nation's fight. The response was overwhelming. Over 7,000 dogs were offered by their owners for war service, often accompanied by letters such as the one from a child who wrote: 'We have let Daddy go to fight the Kaiser and now we are sending Jack to do his bit.'

The dogs were trained under battle conditions. 'There were all the sounds of war. Shells from batteries at practice were screaming overhead, and army motor lorries passed to and fro. The dogs are trained to the constant sound of the guns and very soon learn to take no heed of them,' reported a journalist who visited the school. 'Many breeds were represented. Sheep dogs, lurchers, collies, retrievers, drovers dogs, but no terriers smaller than Airedales. The breed does not matter much,' he was told and indeed 'cross breeds – mongrels – were often found to be most effective, though apparently not

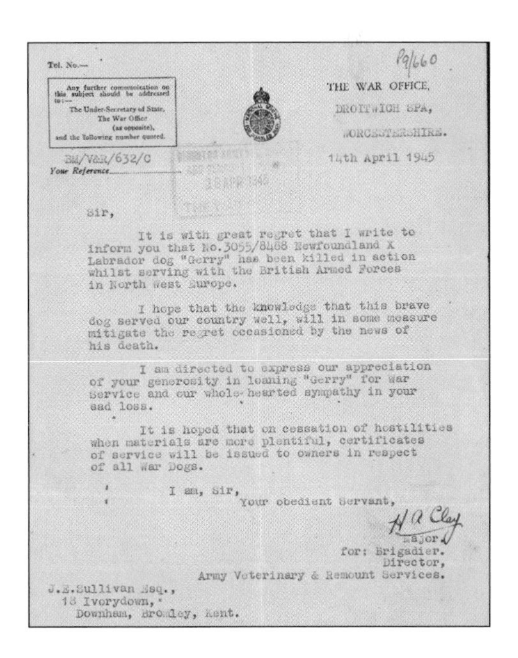

Tel. No.—

P9/660

Any further communication on this subject should be addressed to:—
The Under-Secretary of State,
The War Office
(as opposite),
and the following number quoted.

THE WAR OFFICE,
DROITWICH SPA,
WORCESTERSHIRE.

BM/V&R/632/C
Your Reference

14th April 1945

Sir,

It is with great regret that I write to inform you that No.3055/8488 Newfoundland X Labrador dog "Gerry" has been killed in action whilst serving with the British Armed Forces in North West Europe.

I hope that the knowledge that this brave dog served our country well, will in some measure mitigate the regret occasioned by the news of his death.

I am directed to express our appreciation of your generosity in loaning "Gerry" for War Service and our whole-hearted sympathy in your sad loss.

It is hoped that on cessation of hostilities when materials are more plentiful, certificates of service will be issued to owners in respect of all War Dogs.

I am, Sir,
Your obedient Servant,

H A Clay
Major
for: Brigadier.
Director,
Army Veterinary & Remount Services.

J.E.Sullivan Esq.,
18 Ivorydown,
Downham, Bromley, Kent.

A letter of condolence from the War Office to a Mr Sullivan whose pet dog Gerry had been killed on active service in April 1945.

Three dogs, each with messenger cylinders attached to their collars, stand with their handlers outside the Central Kennel of the Messenger Dog Service GHQ at Étaples.

A dog collar with message canister from the First World War.

retrievers or setters which were 'apt to forget their duty when a rabbit starts up, or a hare.' Hounds were considered to be too independent, fox terriers too frivolous, and Richardson observed that he had 'rarely found a dog with a gay tail which curled over its back or sideways of any use. It seems to indicate a certain levity of character, quite at variance with the serious duties required … It is brains that we want. Sheep dogs, any cross of sheep dogs or lurchers are perhaps the best, but we want all kinds of open air dogs … most recruits pass the test …' 'The drill began with an obstacle race by a squad well advanced in its training,' reported the observer. 'Across the road was placed a barbed wire fence and a few yards further on a hurdle, and beyond that a barrier made of branches of trees. The dogs were taken about a mile up the road and then released. There was a great race for home. The bigger dogs leapt clear of all the obstructions; the smaller ones wriggled their way through; but two wily sheep dogs, strictly in accordance with the rules of the game, preferred to leap a ditch and make a detour, arriving home as quickly as the others.

'Novices who go astray in these and other tests are never ever punished. They are caught by the keepers and gently led back for another try.

'After a month of this simulation, the dogs were considered ready … the next test for the dogs was passing through a thick cloud of smoke. They were released only a few yards from a burning heap of straw, and all, without a pause, dashed straight through the smoke and reached their destination with much barking and tail wagging.

A messenger dog returns to the German lines on the Western Front in the First World War.

'And so most of the effects of the battlefield were produced. The most trying test of all was running towards a number of infantry lying on the ground, who fired blank cartridges at point blank range.

'When the signal was given the ... dogs charged straight at the fire and in a flash were through the ranks of the "enemy". There was a great outburst of applause ... The dogs are trained to ignore the fire of guns of all calibres, and they are accustomed to the explosion of hand grenades near them.' Major Richardson explains that there are many reasons why these animals are indispensable at the front in the present conditions of warfare. 'Once a dog knows his destination he will get there at all costs ... Dogs will go in all weathers and at all times – day or night. After a month of this battle simulation, the dogs were considered to be ready for the front line.' It was an awesome task, as Major Richardson explained: 'the dog has to work entirely on its own initiative and be miles away from its keeper. It has to know what to do ... The highest qualities of mind – love and duty – have to be appealed to and cultivated.'

At first, a number of commanding officers were sceptical about the use of dogs and ignored them, or set them impossible tasks, but gradually 'respect was inculcated and retained when it was discovered what could be accomplished by their aid.'

By 1917 France and Britain had nearly 20,000 dogs working for the war effort, while Germany's canine belligerents totalled nearly 30,000 – many of which had been acquired in Britain before the war. Major Richardson made a trip to France to see how his dogs were doing. 'The two dogs I took out are doing well, I should say exceptionally well,'

A messenger dog carrying the equipment to lay telephone wire on the Western Front in September 1917.

Poster for the Blue Cross Fund designed by John Hassall (1868–1948), an illustrator and poster artist. In the early years of the Blue Cross the charity was particularly concerned with welfare problems faced by the many working horses in London. Then, in the Great War, the Blue Cross helped to relieve the suffering of the horses used at the front, and, during the Second World War, it provided refuge to animals made homeless by the Blitz.

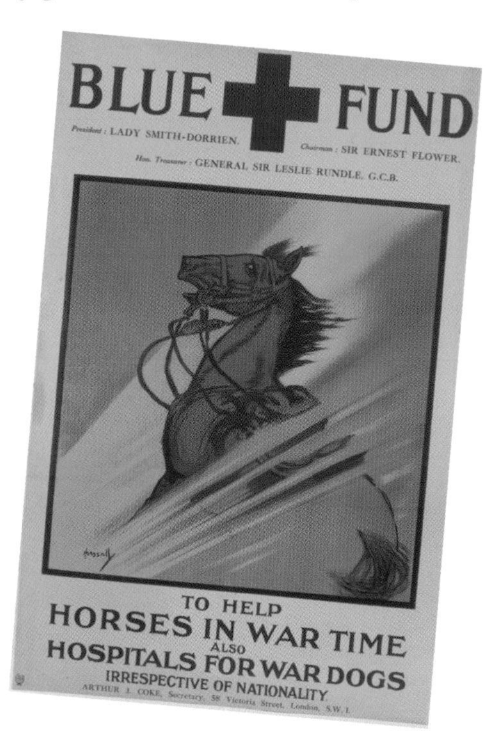

reported a keeper. 'I have not the least hesitation in saying that there is not a brace of better dogs in this or any other country as messenger dogs. Boxer, the Airedale, is running like an engine ... staunch, reliable dog, ran steadily, never let me down. Best time, three miles in ten minutes. On one occasion, he went over the top with the Kents. Released at 5am with important message. He jumped on me at 5.25am. A tip-top performance. A great dog!'

A Major Waley was appointed to superintend the use of dogs in the field and a central kennel was established at Étaples in France. Dogs would be received there, and despatched, with one keeper to every three dogs, to those parts of the line where an attack was impending.

Messenger dogs would have a coloured flash attached to their message cylinder to distinguish which unit they were with so everyone would know that they were 'on duty' and it was an offence punishable by court martial to impede a dog on a mission. The main problem was the troops' kindness towards the dogs – hardly surprising in the trenches where there were few opportunities for sentiment or affection. Men would pet the dogs and feed them titbits, which tended to dilute the single-mindedness of purpose which a dog needed in battle, and it might feel less compulsion to head straight for its keeper and a waiting dinner if it was spoiled elsewhere.

As it has never been possible to know precisely how many men perished on all fronts in the First World War, so it is with the animals. In 1919 it was estimated that 7,000 dogs had been killed, but this is probably a considerable underestimate given the number of animals used by belligerents of both sides. Indeed, there were reports of 7,000 German canine losses alone. And rather than being returned to their original owners as had been eagerly anticipated, the form that the demobilisation of thousands of dogs that survived the battlefield took was slaughter as the war machine was dismantled on all fronts.

As well as carrying messages, dogs were trained to carry a small cable dispenser on their backs and to lay the cable for the transmission of telegraph messages as they went. Cable is heavy, so dogs could carry only sufficient to connect short distances, from one front line position to another, for example. Cable wagons pulled by a team of six horses were able to cover far greater distances, the line could be laid quickly and it was possible to provide down-the-line communication for a division even as it was on the move, but by the end of the Great War horses had largely ceded to the 30cwt lorry in cable laying, though they continued to do service in Mesopotamia, with wagons being pulled by horses and linesmen riding at the rear, manned by teams from the Indian Signals. The work of the Royal Engineer Signal Service during the war had proved so vital that a separate corps was established to provide communications within the Army. The Royal Corps of Signals continued to train linesmen and horses until 1937, when the cable wagons and the out-riding horses were finally replaced by mechanised transport.

Although by 1914, horses no longer had a role in Europe in the wireless section of the Signal Service, they were extensively used overseas, particularly in India – as were mules and camels. The beasts carried not only the sets but also the generator. Mules often required additional training since the wireless equipment was fragile and a kicking, bucking mule could irreparably damage vital equipment, so every afternoon mules were induced to be patient by being led round and round the parade ground in the heat of the day laden with sand bags as substitute wireless equipment. It was said that it took only two days of such training to subdue the most recalcitrant mule – and wear out its handler.

Elephants, which had been extensively used in earlier wars to transport telegraph poles on their backs and cable reels mounted on a howdah, were loaded with more modern technology in Burma during the Second World War in addition to their other transport and bridge-building tasks.

Camels, too, were loaded with telephone poles in the Somaliland campaign in 1903, though this did not prove easy with the type of saddle Somali camels wore, and the poles had to be cut in half and wound around with strong wire. The camel's ability to go long distances without water meant that, unlike the mule, it did not have to be hung around with water containers and could therefore carry more communication equipment. In all subsequent wars in desert regions, including the Gulf War of 1990–91 and the Iraq War of 2003, camels have proved invaluable for carrying radio equipment and batteries in specially adapted harnesses and thus mobile sets can be used to establish communication in remote areas which no other form of transport would find accessible.

A model of a horse-drawn cable cart from the First World War.

Perhaps surprisingly considering their proven worth, the British and the French (one of the first nations to recognise the military value of dogs) disbanded their dog training schools at the end of the First World War, but in 1939 an appeal was again made to the British public to volunteer their dogs for war. A War Dog Training School on the line of Richardson's was reactivated in 1942 and the greyhound racing kennels in Potters Bar near London were used for the purpose of training dogs for patrol work, carrying messages, search, rescue and detection. Just before VE Day, 8 May 1945, the school moved to liberated Belgium and later, Germany. Again, there was an appeal to the public at the start of the war and some 7,000 pets and working animals were 'volunteered'. The owners of those dogs selected were sent a collar, chain, muzzle, label and travel warrant and requested to take their dog to their local railway station for transit to the nearest dog training school – and a number of strays joined the cohorts. All sorts of breeds were enlisted: Alsatians – which proved the most successful dogs in the Second World War, as Airedales had been in the First – Labradors, elkhounds, spaniels, Dobermans, huskies, mastiffs, Great Danes and a full complement of mongrels – or 'non pedigree dogs' as they were more tactfully called.

On arrival the dogs were taken to a holding wing where they were looked after by women from the ATS (Auxiliary Territorial Service, the female branch of the Army) and subjected to a 'gun shy' test. Those who repeatedly baulked at the 'thunder flashes' were offered to the Ministry of Aircraft Production or the RAF for patrol duties, or returned to their owners. Each dog retained was given an official War Office number and a sheet detailing owner, breed, age, distinguishing marks etc. Lessons had been learned and in this war dogs would be tracked and owners informed of the fate of their animal if it was

Six 'priority' pigeon messages despatched from tanks and logged on the Western Front on 5 September 1916.

OPPOSITE: *Canadian soldiers release a carrier pigeon on the Western Front during the First World War, probably in the aftermath of the Battle of Vimy Ridge, May/June 1917.*

killed, seriously injured or for some other reason could not be sent back home at the end of hostilities.

In fact, Hitler's war in Europe gave few opportunities for using messenger dogs, but in the Far East the Japanese used many thousands of dogs in their campaigns and it was falsely rumoured that something approaching 25,000 dogs were shipped from Germany to Japan prior to the Japanese attack on Pearl Harbor in December 1941. The US authorities had been as dismissive of the utility of dogs in war as the British had been in the First World War and on the 'day of infamy' the only US military working dogs were some 50 sledge-pulling dogs in Alaska and some others requisitioned from an Antarctic expedition, which were used in Newfoundland to locate and rescue crashed pilots. It was not until 1942 that the Dogs for Defense (DFD) organisation which had been started by a handful of civilian dog lovers was authorised to start recruiting and training dogs for military service. This body was named unofficially by some wit the K-9 (canine) Corps, and the Army adopted this nomenclature. Dog reception and training centres were set up at various places throughout the US and sought British help in training messenger dogs. Under what might be (and has been) called a sort of 'Lend Leash' arrangement Captain John P. Garle, a peacetime Master of Foxhounds and the Chief Instructor at the War Dog Training School, was sent to America to advise on training, particularly the problem of the dogs proving to be terrified when faced with a full artillery barrage, as they were trained only around small arms fire, and failing utterly to complete their tasks. Until it asked to be relieved of the task in March 1945, the DFD procured some 18,000 dogs through donation, and with the 2,000 that had been bought by the Army for sledge pulling and pack transport it meant that around 20,000 dogs were acquired during the Second World War for the US forces. However, only 10,000 actually finished training for some sort of war work, the other half being disqualified for reasons of disease, inferior olfactory powers, character defects, undersize, or being of an over excitable temperament in the face of gunfire – the most usual reason for rejection. Loyalty was the quality most looked for in a messenger dog: it had to be motivated by the desire to please the two masters between whom it carried messages. This was fostered by each man taking turns to feed and train the dog. The two masters alternated their positions and frequently hid themselves, never using the same hiding place twice so the dog learned to locate them by body scent.

The US dogs of war had their first test in New Guinea where the humidity caused the dogs' feet to swell and the leather pouches the messenger dogs carried to rot rapidly so these were replaced with metal canisters. The marines tested the comparative speed of a man and a dog in heavy jungle and found that it took the man over a quarter of an hour to emerge from the dense undergrowth, compared to the dog's four and a half minutes. In these conditions dogs proved of particular worth as the intense heat, high humidity and tropical downpours caused a number of failures with the communication equipment so dogs became an essential fall back when messages urgently required delivering. On Morotai in the Dutch East Indies messenger dogs were used so that the soldiers could go on patrol unburdened by radios or the need to lay telegraph wires. However, by 1944, following the lengthy but ultimately successful US retaking of Guam which involved some 350 dogs, it was decided that technological communications systems were now sufficiently reliable to obviate the

A double-decker bus converted into a mobile pigeon loft on the Western Front during the First World War.

need for messenger dogs which were mainly redeployed in surveillance or retrained as scout dogs.

In peacetime pigeons tend to have a bad press: seen by those who are not pigeon fanciers as vermin that cause nuisance in cities and defile public buildings with their droppings. But in war the birds played a crucial role as messengers and in November 2000 this was acknowledged when former members of the Pigeon Section were among those who had served their country in war invited to attend the Remembrance Day ceremony at the Cenotaph in London's Whitehall.

Their legacy is long: pigeons are recorded as having relayed the news of Caesar's conquest of Gaul; Genghis Khan organised a pigeon service across Asia and most of Europe in the 13th century; news of Wellington's victory at Waterloo was first relayed by a pigeon and, during the Franco-Prussian War of 1870–1, messages were sent in and out of the besieged city of Paris by pigeon post.

In the Boer War pigeons were used to carry plans and messages in and out of the garrison during the siege of Ladysmith, and in the spring of 1915 pigeons brought situation reports from the front line during the Second Battle of Ypres. Messages from the trenches would reach the Brigade HQ in between 10 and 20 minutes, depending on how great the distance, and shell fire and bullets whistled past the birds as they flew to get their message through, some clipping their wings, shattering a leg, or even downing a bird. Pigeons were more reliable than some of what were at the time distinctly infant communication technologies, and it is easier to tap into wireless communications than it is to stop a pigeon. Pigeons did not get bogged down in the mud as dogs did, and they were capable of flying long distances without a break. Since they flew so fast they were hard, though of course not impossible, for marksmen to hit, but they were vulnerable to predatory hawks or falcons, and could get buffeted off course by gale force winds. It was not advised to release birds in foggy weather as they could lose their sense of direction and they should not be sent off after sunset as they were liable to roost and resume their flight the next day.

Although the Admiralty opined that the invention of wireless had made pigeons redundant, it was wrong. What Major Richardson had done in respect of dogs, Captain A. H. Osman did for pigeons: he persuaded the British authorities of their usefulness and

Plucky Pigeons

'It's not the size of your wingspan that counts. It's the size of your spirit!' A still from the animated film **Valiant** *(2005) with the voices of Ewan McGregor, Ricky Gervais, John Cleese and others.*

A war memorial in Brussels pays tribute to the pigeons and their fanciers who died in wartime, and a similar one in Lille in France reminds those who pass of the 20,000 pigeons killed in the line of duty during the First World War.

Some pigeons were even fitted with miniature cameras to take reconnaissance photographs over enemy or occupied territory, but their most usual role was to carry important messages. When a commander in the field needed to send such a message, he wrote it out on paper, trying to be both brief and yet as detailed as possible. Then he called for a Royal Engineers Signal Service officer, who would bring one of the pigeons that accompanied the soldiers into battle. The message would be put into a capsule on the bird's leg, and the bird would be tossed high into the air to fly home.

The carrier pigeon would fly back to his home coop behind the lines. When he landed, the wires in the coop would sound a bell or a buzzer, and another soldier of the Signal Service would know a message had arrived. He would go to the coop, remove the message from the canister and then pass it on by telegraph, field phone or personal messenger to the person who needed the information.

Cher Ami ('Dear Friend') was one of the most famous pigeons-at-war of all time. On 3 October 1918 Major Charles Whittlesey, the commander of a battalion of the US 77th Infantry Division, was trapped with more than 500 of his men in a small depression in a hillside near Argonne in France. The attrition rate was such that within 24 hours there were fewer than 200 soldiers still alive. That afternoon, US artillery fired barrages of shells into the ravine, unaware that some of its own men were trapped there.

In despair, Whittlesey called for Cher Ami, the battalion's last pigeon, and scribbled a hurried note to put in its canister. 'We are along road parallel to 276.4. Our own artillery is dropping a barrage directly on us. For heaven's sake stop it.' Somehow, despite intense German fire, Cher Ami managed to fly the 25 miles to the artillery site in 25 minutes and thus saved many American lives. For this and 11 other missions completed against the odds, Cher Ami was awarded the French *Croix de Guerre* but no American decoration, since the US military does not honour its war animals in this way.

Today the exploits of plucky pigeons during the Second World War have inspired an animated cartoon film. *Valiant* tells the story of 'a lowly wood pigeon' (voiced by Ewan McGregor) that flees his rural nest to join the Royal Homing Pigeon Service and carry vital messages across the Channel (an echo of Gustav which brought news of the D-Day landings, perhaps). A flea-bitten Trafalgar Square pigeon, with the voice of Ricky Gervais, joins Valiant to survive shell fire and falcon attacks (Sir Ben Kingsley's voice here) to pay a modern, if slightly oblique, tribute to those pigeons that did it for real in both world wars.

A model of a wooden horse-drawn mobile pigeon loft used on the Western Front during the First World War.

persuaded the pigeon fanciers of Britain to volunteer their birds. 'We have got some carrier pigeons, which live in a dug out all for themselves,' wrote Captain James (Jim) Foulis from France (where he was serving with the Queen's Own Cameron Highlanders) to his young niece back in Scotland. 'They are to carry messages for us in case the telephone wires get broken. When the Germans send over poisonous gas the pigeons are put in a bag so they will not be killed by the gas.'

'Killing, wounding or molesting' a 'homer' (homing pigeon) was an offence under Defence of the Realm Act regulations punishable by six months imprisonment or a £100 fine during the First World War. At this time the pigeon service was streamlined and became part of Britain's war effort. Two Pigeon Service Corps were established; soldiers were trained as 'pigeoneers' to handle the birds, feed them and protect them from the predatory rats that infested the trenches. By December 1915 15 pigeon stations had been established on the Western Front, each equipped with a basket containing four birds, a specially-trained handler and other baskets which were kept in reserve – a total of 202 birds. There had been, however, a tragedy in Antwerp on 18 October 1914. As the German forces advanced, the head of the Belgian Pigeon Service 'with tears streaming down his face', according to a historian of pigeons, Garry McGafferty, burned alive 2,500 of his potential messengers rather than let them fall into the hands of the Kaiser's advancing troops.

During the Somme offensive, messages flew backwards and forward. 'Just about to advance to Blue at proper time. Artillery fire a bit short. Shovels wanted,' read one. 'Message from Welsh Guards report enemy are turning their left flank which is not in touch with the 21st division, a battalion urgently wanted to fill the gap,' read another. 'Am trying to establish defensive flank on the left of the Grenadiers of the 4th. All the officers of the 4th Grenadiers appear to be casualties,' communicated a third. The French alone used 5,000 pigeons during the battle and of these only 2 per cent of the birds released with messages failed to get through – and even when this happened it did not mean that vital information or life-saving requests were lost as all essential messages were sent in duplicate carried by different birds 'released at intervals of one minute. Birds are marked on the back: Cock birds RED, hen birds BLUE. Cock and hen birds NOT to be released together' instructed the Director of Army Signals, or heaven knows what they might get up to and completely forget their crucial military mission.

The Somme showed how vital it was that the pigeon service was able to respond quickly and 'mobile lofts' – many of which in the early days were converted omnibuses – were introduced which could be moved from place to place as the need arose, and this added nearly 5,000 birds to the service. Amazingly, as the French found during the Battle of the Marne, the homing instinct of pigeons did not desert them, and even when their lofts were moved they seemed to be able instinctively to find their way home.

The service proved such a success, with several hundred messages being passed

A pigeon being released from a porthole on the side of a tank, near Albert in France during the First World War.

First World War poster warning of the penalties extracted for shooting homing pigeons since they were 'doing valuable work for the government'.

between the trenches and the battalion HQ in each battle, that the number of horse-drawn lofts was increased to 120, and pigeons were being used by artillery officers on forward observation duties to report their sightings. Tank crews also often had to rely on pigeons as their only form of communication with their base. It could be particularly distressing for a pigeon to be released from a tank and they often took a few minutes to recover from the fumes before setting off.

Captain Edward (Ted) R. Pennell of the Royal Flying Corps was detailed to use pigeons for espionage purposes by dropping them behind enemy lines to help British agents relay messages home. 'The idea was that [pigeons] would pull against each other and gradually drop to the ground. In practice it was found that after a few drops, the birds became tangled up and were killed … I taxied out onto the aerodrome, taking off in the wind and climbing steadily to 5,000 feet towards our lines. My particular target was … four miles to the south. I was to look out for six large hay or straw stacks in a field which also contained a herd of black and white cows … a prearranged spot agreed upon by our spies working behind the trenches … My instructions were to drop my pigeons as low as I felt was safe … and

A pigeon parachute used in the First World War. The bird would need to be released from its harness on landing.

avoid anti-aircraft fire. Cruising around for a while, I waited until the clouds opened up. Now was the time to go into action. I must admit that by now I had got the wind up pretty badly. I imagined the whole of the German Air Force would be waiting to pounce on me as soon as I emerged ... Through a gap in the clouds I dived ... circling around 1,000 feet I searched for some stacks but they were nowhere to be seen. Easy enough in theory perhaps, but in practice ...

'On my way back, steadily climbing to get above the clouds, I looked over the side. There, below me was a marvellous enemy dump. There was timber, wire, field services etc and all I had was a box of pigeons. Oh, if only I had had a few bombs!' When Pennell finally landed he was met 'by my Flight Commander and an Army Sergeant, both eager to know how I had got on. When I told my dismal story the sergeant proceeded to unload the pigeons, only to find about half of them were dead. This, it was decided, was perhaps due to the fact that that the birds had been taken too high and remained in the cold too long.

'... A week later another of our pilots carried out a "Pigeon Mission", but it was not a real success for the pigeons were mostly killed in their attempt to reach the ground ... Further drops were later carried out, the pigeons being fitted with small parachutes. But this proved no more successful and as far as is known, this was the end of Pigeon Dropping' – at least in that war.

By the end of the Great War there were 22,000 pigeons in service with British forces, looked after by 400 pigeoneers, and they were providing crucial communication services throughout the whole theatre of war, in Salonika, Egypt and Mesopotamia as well as Europe.

In 1920 the Royal Corps of Signals was established and immediately took over responsibility for the Pigeon Corps with pigeoneers being transformed into loftsmen, a trade within the Corps.

In May–June 1940 pigeon sporting facilities again began to be harnessed for the war effort. With Britain 'standing alone', its army driven out of continental Europe after Dunkirk, pigeons became a way of carrying on the fight in occupied Europe. Birds would be dropped by aircraft in the hope that they would be picked up by a resident of Western Europe and thus vital intelligence about the enemy could be sent back to Britain. Soon over 13,000 birds in pigeon fanciers' lofts all over southern and eastern England had been volunteered and trained for this service to the resistance. The enterprise was co-ordinated by the National Pigeon Service which supplied birds to the Armed Forces and the Home Guard. The pigeons would be collected from their loft owners – some 300 crates a night was usual – transported to an airfield, fitted with a message container and packed into single bird boxes with parachutes attached along with food supplies to last for up to 10 days. The boxes would also contain questionnaires and instructions and the idea was that whoever found the bird would transmit information via the pigeon, which would be released to fly home – a round trip of up to 300 miles. This was a hazardous occupation for all concerned: no one knows how many pigeons reached their destination, or how many were captured or handed over to the Germans or their collaborators. Anyone found harbouring or despatching such an infiltrator in occupied Europe stood him or herself in the gravest risk of reprisal. Of the 16,544 birds parachuted into occupied countries only 1,842 ever returned. Some were felled by German-organised 'squadrons of hawks' posted

Two Canadian soldiers attach a wicker basket containing carrier pigeons to an Airedale messenger dog during a training exercise 'somewhere in Britain' during the Second World War.

across the Pas de Calais but one arrived back at its loft with a message of over 5,000 words plus 15 sketch maps giving invaluable information about the strength and movement of enemy forces, while others brought back evidence of the exact position of the V1 flying bomb experimental station at Peenemünde in Germany.

In total, something like a quarter of a million messenger pigeons were active in the Second World War. Pigeons were used in the Western Desert, where they conveyed messages from headquarters to troops in the line and also from raiding and reconnaissance parties when it was not possible to use radio communication for fear of revealing their presence to the enemy. Pigeons accompanied the Canadian troops to Dieppe in 1942, and returned with the first intimations that the raid had been a disaster, and conversely brought back news that Allied troops had successfully landed on the Normandy beaches on D-Day, 6 June 1944. They were used by the Home Guard – a number of whom were pigeon fanciers themselves – to convey messages, and, had Hitler's Operation 'Sealion' been mounted in 1940 and German troops invaded Britain by sea or air, the service of pigeon-messengers might have been pivotal to co-ordinating the counter-measures.

During the Battle of Arnhem, launched on 17 September 1944 to outflank the German defensive line by establishing a bridgehead across the Rhine at the Dutch town and, it was hoped, bring the war to a speedy

Pigeons that had lost a leg in the course of wartime service in pens at Sorrus near Étaples on the Western Front during the First World War. Carrier pigeons were frequently injured by gunfire but, with careful nursing, many recovered.

A message written on rice paper is rolled up into a container attached to the leg of a carrier pigeon by members of the 61st Divisional Signals, Ballymena, Northern Ireland, 3 July 1941.

conclusion, Allied forces were hopelessly outnumbered. At the time Captain Joseph Hardy was Signals Officer of the 1st Battalion, Border Regiment, part of the 1st Airborne Division. 'I had, as part of my load into Battle, taken two homing pigeons with me. I had not had very much faith in them, but taking them was a way of ensuring that I was carrying as heavy a load as any of my men, and there was always a chance that they could be useful ... after a couple of days later I ran out of pigeon food and realised that if the [remaining] bird was weakened through being starved, it would stand no chance of getting home at all. I requested permission to release it, permission granted, and the CO said he had no message to send. I explained that I would have to send a message of some sort, or they would not know why the bird had been released without a message. His answer was that I should scribble something on a message pad and get the bird away. I sent the following message, which really amounted to a load of nonsense.

'From Lieut. [as he then was] J. S. D. Hardy.

1. I have to release birds owing to shortage of food and water.
2. About eight tanks lying about in sub unit area, very untidy but not causing us any trouble.
3. Now using as many German weapons as we have British. MGS most effective when aiming towards Germany.
4. Dutch people grand but Dutch tobacco rather stringy.
5. Great beard growing competition in our unit, but no time to check up on the winner.'

'The bird miraculously arrived back at Corps HQ and the men got hold of the message, it made headlines in the English papers the next day, and was given such a degree of importance that it ended up in the British War Museum, classified as one of the epic messages from a field of battle. It was absolute nonsense.'

The War Office did not conscript pigeons, nor did it requisition pigeon lofts. However, those owners who declined to provide birds to the National Pigeon Service during the Second World War received no corn ration, and those who did allow their birds to be sent on missions received no compensation for the loss of the pigeons they had nurtured and trained. The fanciers' reward was the knowledge of the significant contribution their birds had made to the nation's war effort.

BELOW: ***Guy Burn:*** **'Divisional Pigeon Loft, Italy, 1944'.**

LEFT: ***The Canadian wireless operator of an Avro Lancaster bomber operating from RAF Waddington in Lincolnshire, carrying two boxes containing homing pigeons. They were to be used to carry messages in the event of a crash, ditching or radio failure, October 1942.***

6 Seek and Find

During the First World War it was proposed to employ sea lions in the fight against German submarines that posed such a deadly threat to British shipping.

The First World War was not only fought in the trenches of France and Flanders: it was fought on the high seas, too. Between 1914 and 1918 34,642 British lives had been lost at sea, and 4,510 men had been wounded and one ship in four that left Britain never returned. Desperate times called for desperate measures and 'every newspaper, every magazine, every public man, and every gentleman at his club had a favourite scheme for defeating the U-boat campaign'. These included allowing a psychic into the Admiralty's tracking room to dangle her threaded needle over charts of the Atlantic; pouring green paint on the sea; dropping barrels of Eno's Fruit Salts at strategic places on the bed of the North Sea so that, when activated by a remote control, the salts would effervesce; arming swimmers with a black bag and a hammer to cover up and then shatter a submarine's periscope as it surfaced; and training seagulls to defecate on periscopes.

None of these seemed particularly convincing solutions, but a notion that the Admiralty *did* pursue for a time was training sea lions to track underwater submarines. Hydrophones (underwater sound projectors) were being developed that could detect the sound of a submarine, but their range was limited to one or two miles and at first they could not tell the direction from which the sound was coming. Sea lions were known to have highly sensitive hearing and were co-operative – as long as they were rewarded with plenty of fish. It was intended to train the sea lion by what were then called Pavlovian methods. As David A. H. Wilson explains, the animal would be hungry but muzzled and would be taught to ignore the fish alongside them in a tank in favour of an artificial underwater sound, and for doing this it would be rewarded by a generous fish supper.

OPPOSITE: *Sergeant Andrew Garrett watches K-Dog, a bottlenose dolphin attached to the Commander Task Unit 55.4.3., leap out of the water near USS* **Gunston Hall**, *in the Persian Gulf, 18 March 2003. The Commander Task Unit is a multinational team from the US, Britain and Australia conducting deep and shallow mine-clearing operations in the Gulf.*

Bobs, a Labrador serving with No 1 Dog Platoon of the Royal Engineers, locates a mine near Bayeux in France as Allied troops fight through France, July 1944.

Gradually the tank would be replaced by open water 'using the submarine as sound and food source'. The sea lion on manoeuvres would be spotted each time it surfaced for air and possibly a way could be devised so that if the aquatic creature could 'be taught to bark [on command], namely by way of inviting the submarine to come up and feed him, so much the better' since that would make it even easier to locate the enemy submarine. The sea lion was also to be taught to leap onto a raft pulled by the ship that was directing operations, before the submarine was blasted out of the water.

The services of a 'Captain' Joseph Woodward, who had a well-known troupe of performing music hall sea lions, were secured and training began in Glasgow Municipal Baths. The 'Captain' succeeded in training three sea lions to respond to faint underwater sounds, and trials moved outdoors to Lake Bala in Wales. Again the auguries were good. Now it was time to test them in the open sea. The idea was mooted of tying coloured floats to the sea lions to make them more visible, but this seemed to slow them down, so it was suggested that they might be painted with vermilion greasepaint by day and luminous paint by night. Unfortunately, the sea lions proved less than satisfactory in the actual conditions in which they would have to operate. Their performance was highly inconsistent, the greatest distance from which they managed to track a submarine was a mere 200 yards and, given the delights of the open sea rather than a glass tank, they had a tendency to abscond. The trials were abandoned: it was recommended that the sea lions should 'return to their legitimate business' (which Wilson surmises seems to have been considered to be the music hall rather than their natural habitat), and the most successful way of protecting shipping was found not to be sea lions but convoys of other ships.

However, what seemed like a wacky clutching at straws idea became almost standard practice later in the century in the US Navy. Experiments with marine mammals started in the late 1950s when the Navy began to study such unique characteristics as the hydrodynamics of the dolphin. By understanding how the dolphin moved, it might be possible to improve the design of torpedoes and submarines. But it was soon apparent that dolphins could be of more direct use in wartime. Unlike human divers, who are susceptible to experiencing the bends or decompression sickness, dolphins are believed to be able to make repeated deep dives untroubled by such difficulties.

Men of the Royal Engineers No 1 Dog Platoon with their sniffer dogs and some of the mines the dogs located in Normandy, July 1944.

Dolphins echo-locate – that is, they use a form of biological sonar to locate objects under water by emitting sound waves and detecting the returning wave reflected off the object. They use their remarkably sensitive echo-location abilities to find food in deep and murky water; they emit sounds in the form of a series of clicks that are all but inaudible to the human ear and the time between the emission of the pulse and the receipt of its echo tells how far way an object is and its direction. This innate facility can be harnessed for mine detection since the dolphin can be trained to 'report back' to its handler.

The dolphin is controlled by having an Anti-Foraging Device, a strip of orange Velcro, attached round its snout to prevent it from catching fish, as it can't open its mouth, or by a sound-transmitting neck harness. It is recalled by the use of a 'recall pinger' that the mammal can hear from a great distance. If the dolphin responds by returning to its handler, it is fed as a 'reward'. This can be dangerous work, since the dolphin can be at risk from the mine it has located – though this is denied by the US authorities – and it can be threatened by the indigenous dolphin population of the area. If it is operating in enemy waters it is likely to be regarded as a combatant and captured or shot – as happened in the first Gulf War in 1990–1 for example. But since mines have been responsible for 14 of the 19 US Navy ships destroyed or damaged at sea since 1950, the Navy is likely to continue its programme, albeit in a supposedly attenuated form.

During the Cold War, both superpowers admitted to using dolphins to guard naval installations but the Soviet Navy was also alleged to have deployed its guard dolphins as killers, both by using them to stick limpet mines onto warships and also to attach lethal devices to enemy divers. The dolphins were fitted with a titanium ball containing carbon dioxide at a very high pressure, which would clamp onto the diver on impact. This would be activated remotely to inject the gas into his body, which would literally blow him up, bringing him to the surface 'with his guts spewing out at both ends' according to a campaigner with the Whale and Dolphin Conservation Society. The US was extremely cagey about its use of dolphins until 1988, when trainers who worked with the dolphins finally went public, and has never admitted to *its* 'swimmer nullification program', in which a long hypodermic needle filled with carbonic dioxide was allegedly attached to a dolphin's snout to be shot into enemy frogmen.

Since the cessation of the Cold War there has been a reduction in the Marine Mammal Program with the US Navy retiring 30 of its 100 dolphins to dolphinariums and leisure parks. But two bottle-nosed dolphins, Makai and Tacoma, were used in the 2003 Iraq War for detecting mines in the approaches to the port of Umm Qasr. And when Hurricane Katrina struck New Orleans in summer 2005 it was alleged that military-trained dolphins were at loose in the Gulf of Mexico. It appears that they were penned up in training pools in Louisiana close to Lake Pontchartrain, and when its banks burst the dolphins were swept out to sea by the floodwater.

Whales at Risk?

An Orca whale.

There is concern voiced by animal protection groups and environmentalists in the USA and elsewhere about the harm that the extensive use of mid-frequency sonar waves – which can be as loud as 240 decibels – to reflect off enemy submarines, could have on cetaceans. Since whales and dolphins rely on sound to guide them, as other species rely on sight, a prolonged and dramatic disruption of sound waves could disturb and disorientate them, and even cause death. This is believed to have happened in the Bahamas during sea tests using mid-frequency sonar devices which resulted, according to the director of the US Center for Whale Research there, in 'an acoustic holocaust that can be likened to fishing with dynamite.'

Like human divers, whales can suffer from the bends (nitrogen squeezed out of the lungs and into the blood stream, which may erupt like carbon and rupture tissue or block blood vessels when they rise to the surface too quickly) and it is possible, according to some scientists who studied beached sperm whales on beaches on Fuerteventura and Lanzarote, that this condition could have been caused by military exercises using sonar waves. However, the US government has recently 'reauthorised' sonar experiments in the oceans for military purposes.

Sea lions, a species turned down for active service in the First World War, have been used by the US military in Bahrain in a SWIDS (Shallow Water Intruder Detection System) programme that utilises their ability to dive to great depths with no apparent ill effects to locate waterborne intruders and suspicious objects around piers and ships. Sea lions have also been used to recover objects from the seabed such as practice mines, many of which are fitted with a device that emits a bleeping noise to help the sea lions detect them.

As dolphins and sea lions are now used to detect mines at sea, other animals were trained to do so on land. Dogs' uncanny ability to scratch up a dry bone that they may have buried months ago was harnessed to a military purpose. In the spring of 1943 the Allied advance in the Western Desert was being seriously impeded by strategically placed German mines. These were encased in glass, plastic or wood so the usual metal detectors were ineffectual, whereas it was found that dogs could be trained to sniff out such mines.

Dogs were trained to search an area where it was expected that land mines might have been laid, and, once they came near to one, to 'freeze' and summon their handler by barking. In Britain the dogs were usually trained by being rewarded when they made a discovery, whereas in the US the 'repulsion' method was used and the dog would receive an electric shock when it happened on a 'mine' in training, so that it would learn to distrust anything buried in the ground and not go near it.

Four platoons of mine-detecting dogs were included in the British invasion force in the aftermath of D-Day, 6 June 1944. Each platoon consisted of 29 dogs that checked the ground inch by inch as the troops advanced across the Normandy countryside and, by the early spring of 1945, were ready to cross the Rhine into Germany.

One particularly adroit mine detector was a Welsh sheepdog called Ricky. His handler had been a circus performer in civilian life and the rapport between the two was immediate. On 3 December 1944 Ricky and his trainer, Maurice Yelding, were instructed to clear the canal banks at Nederdeent in Holland, which was not easy as mines had been hidden amongst the loose shingle. As the dog went about the task, finding three mines in quick succession, one only three feet away was triggered. The section commander was

Colin Self (1941–): **'Guard Dog on a Missile Site'**, *1966. A pioneer of the Pop Art movement in Britain in the 1960s, Self is one of the few British artists to engage with the threat of nuclear war in his paintings. 'It turned my guts and floored me, destroyed my sensibility and understanding of the world,' said the Norfolk-born painter.*

Muzzled sentry dogs and their handlers ride in a truck back to their barracks and kennels after patrolling a US supply and communications centre outpost during the Vietnam War, 1969.

James McBey (1883–1959): **'The Long Patrol: tracks discovered'**, *1917.*

killed and Ricky was wounded in the head by shrapnel. The dog did not panic and managed to lead his handler safely out of the minefield. 'Ricky' was awarded the Dickin Medal, the 'animals' VC', for his courage and the Army was so anxious to retain the services of this ace detector after the war that it offered the maximum sum allowed to its owner, but he declined, insisting it was his dog he wanted back, not money.

Large numbers of dogs were used by the Red Army to detect mines – it is claimed that during the course of the war they unearthed well over a million mines, 529,000 in 1943 alone. A hero of the Russian campaign was Zhucha, a mongrel, which was claimed to have unearthed 2,000 mines in less than three weeks and was employed to clear aerodromes prior to aircraft landing and taking off.

But as well as detecting mines, the Red Army used dogs to plant them. Following the Nazi invasion of the Soviet Union in June 1941, the Russians began training dogs to run under German tanks with bundles of TNT strapped onto their backs. The dogs were kept hungry and trained by only being fed underneath running tanks, so when the dog 'seized' its food on the battlefield it would blow up the enemy tank – and itself. At least that was the theory. But since the dogs had been fed under Soviet tanks, when they encountered the real thing at the front, instead of making for the German tanks, they rushed for the Soviet ones, and an entire Russian tank division had to withdraw until its anti-tank dogs – which were only doing what they had been trained to do – had been shot.

So vivid is the public imagination when it comes to training small animals to undermine great military designs that an elaborate spoof report gained sufficient credibility to start turning up in books and articles as 'fact'. Allegedly, Soviet scientists recognised the potential of using mice in anti-tank warfare. A scientist at the University of Smolensk was supposed to have had the idea that mice could be used to disable the wiring system of tanks, and in April 1942 low-flying Soviet aircraft were reported to have dropped mice onto a German Panzer division near Kirov and another mouse attack was mounted on 22nd Panzer Division in November the same year. A mouse's body was supposedly subsequently discovered inside one of the disabled German tanks, and Mikhail (the mouse's name) was honoured with a special 'Hero of the Soviet Union' award. The whole situation, however, escalated into a farce when it was reported that the Wehrmacht was dropping cats to catch the mice and that the Russians then retaliated by dropping dogs to see off the cats!

However, petrol fumes from the newer models of tanks killed the mice before they could do their dastardly work, and soon tank wires were coated in a plastic so that rodents could not gnaw through them.

BELOW: ***The Dickin Medal-winning Welsh sheepdog, Ricky, rewarded for his bravery in clearing mines in Holland in the Second World War.***

Those who believed in the USSR belligerent mice programme might seem less credulous when one discovers that another rodent, this time the winged bat, was genuinely considered for the role of deadly weapon in the Second World War. In 1940 a Harvard chemist began experimenting with equipping bats with tiny incendiary bombs. After Pearl Harbor, swarms of these bats would be dropped over Japanese cities where they would lodge in crevices and eaves and chew the string of their 'parachutes', causing the bombs to explode and create a firestorm. Tests in New Mexico showed how unlikely this project was to succeed and the experiment was abandoned.

The US Army also experimented with using dogs as combat animals, fixing a pouch with explosives and a timer onto the dog. The argument was that although this was in effect a kamikaze role for the dog, it would save men's lives. Again, it was not an idea that had much success in practice. When sent off towards the bunker they were supposed to blow up, the dogs tended to turn round and head back to their masters – who would be less than keen to see them since they were carrying live ammunition, and it would not be clear to a dog which was an enemy-occupied bunker or which one contained men from its own 'side'.

Altogether dogs were used for seven distinct roles in wartime: as pack animals; as sentries guarding coastlines where invasion might be expected, military installations, equipment and ammunition dumps etc; as messengers; for anti-mine detection; for tracking; for finding casualties and as scout or patrol dogs. The training for each function was different, though obedience was a critical common denominator.

The military dogs that had considerable success in the Second World War – particularly in the Far East – were scout dogs, which played a similar role to those canines doing sentry duty, but they had to be accustomed to heavy gunfire, and were mobile. The dogs were trained to give early warning of the approach of the enemy, but in war conditions this had to be done silently so the dogs learned to alert their handlers by stopping and going rigid when they detected an unknown person in the vicinity, with hackles raised, ears pricked and tail rigid.

In the combat zones in the islands off Japan, in Burma, and in the Philippines, the dogs suffered considerably from heat, from parasites, lack of proper food and sufficient water – much as their handlers did – and the sound of heavy gunfire could make a dog forget its silence training and bark and yelp as it rushed forward. But the dogs proved their worth in situations of near guerrilla warfare in which several US Marine War Dog Platoons were engaged, despite the fact that in some conditions it was impossible to give the dogs the exercise they needed and they had to be massaged instead. On occasions the animals were required to go long distances over very rough ground, including coral reefs that tore at their paws. Leather boots were designed but these were not popular with the dogs, which pulled them off at any opportunity. It was found that even in dense jungle dogs would alert their handler within 70 yards of the enemy and could often pick up a

OPPOSITE: ***Two German soldiers standing on the backs of their horses to get a better view of the surrounding countryside. The men are engaged in a reconnaissance exercise, though there was much more mobility on the Eastern Front during the First World War than the Western, where 'recces' were how the cavalry spent much of its time.***

BELOW: ***Geva Zin, a 26-year-old Israeli mine-clearing expert, training Soda, a year-old miniature pig, to locate anti-personnel mines in Kibbutz Lahav in southern Israel, photographed on 30 September 2003. The French used pigs as primitive mine detectors between the Maginot and Siegfried Lines during the Phoney War (1939–40). Zin maintains that pigs have a superior sense of smell to dogs, are more intelligent and easier and cheaper to train.***

Rescue equipment used by the 3rd Australian Tunnelling Company during the First World War. The cages of canaries and mice used to detect gas can be seen in the foreground.

scent more than 200 yards away. In July 1944 the US War Department received a request from an infantry division operating in the Pacific theatre that 'patrol leaders in our area of operations state that they would like to have Scout War Dogs to use on *all* patrols in enemy territory.'

In the European theatre, dogs were used for sentry duties, guarding railways, bridges, airfields, searchlight batteries and other vulnerable installations. In May 1944 the War Office issued an appeal for more canine recruits to guard secret military installations in the build up to D-Day, and dogs were also used as guards for captured POWs. However, the prevailing circumstances of rapid forward troop movements, often in open territory, and also the use of heavy artillery were not conducive to their deployment as scouts with patrols. Scout dogs were used in the mountains during the Italian campaign, sniffing out ambushes and enemy encampments. And Bob, a white mongrel attached to the Queen's Own Royal West Kents, an infantry outfit fighting in North Africa, was awarded the Dickin Medal for alerting his patrol to the unexpected presence of a German unit.

The use of dogs mapped the evolution of varying forms of warfare in the turbulent postwar world, too. In Palestine in 1946, they were used to assist in anti-terrorist activities by uncovering arms caches; in Korea the first contingent of dogs arrived in 1951 and they were put to work mainly proving and clearing derelict minefields, and patrol dogs were used very successfully by the Commonwealth Division to warn patrols of impending ambushes. In Malaya their main task was tracking down insurgents in territory that was similar to that of the Far Eastern theatre in the Second World War. So successful had the 'recce' patrols been then in mopping up pockets of Japanese soldiers hiding in caves and tunnels in the numerous Pacific islands, that a Jungle Warfare School (JWS) was established in Johore Bahru in Malaya. Using tracker dogs as well as local civilians with a knowledge of the country, the same success was achieved in similar wars in Malaya, Kenya, Cyprus and Borneo.

In such conditions tracker dogs worked off the lead since in dense jungle it was impossible for a dog to 'point' at its quarry from a long distance. The Labrador proved the most successful dog, capable of tracking a scent more than two hours old over several

For Loyal and Faithful Service
1939 – 1945
This Certificate is awarded to R.A.F. Police Patrol Dog
No. 248. Don
in grateful recognition of tireless effort and constant devotion to duty willingly rendered to Britain and all the free peoples of the World in time of War.

Provost Marshal
Chief of Royal Air Force Police

A certificate presented to its owner in recognition of Don's 'loyal and faithful service' as an RAF Police Patrol Dog in the Second World War.

miles. Gyp, a light golden Labrador, was sent to track down a wounded terrorist in the Malayan jungle in June 1954. It was already 14 hours after the terrorist had been shot, and there had been a tropical rain storm, when the dog and his handler reached the spot. Nevertheless, Gyp managed to pick up the scent and tracked down the man, who had concealed himself with grass and branches, lying among the overgrown rubber over 100 yards away in an area where visibility was only a few yards. Although in ideal conditions a tracker dog can pick up a scent at a range of 800 yards, it was reckoned to be most unlikely that without Gyp's acuity in this instance the man would have been found.

A number of the dogs that had seen service in Malaya were subsequently shipped to East Africa. In Kenya, dogs were used against the Mau Mau in the highlands, and there the troops and their dogs – the usual Alsatians and Labradors but here supplemented by the occasional bloodhound, Basset hound and Doberman Pinscher – worked as tracker dogs, guard dogs or infantry patrol dogs. The dogs, which were not only at risk from the Kĩkũyũ, but also from herds of wild rhino and buffalo, were highly regarded, generously rewarded for the numerous 'kills' and captures they effected, but 'although there is a deep bond of affection between each man and his dog, the animals are not treated as pets – they are soldiers of the Queen'.

During the Vietnam War, that lasted for 11 years from 1961–1972, in which as many as 3–4 million Vietnamese on both sides and 58,000 US service personnel were killed and

Rifleman Khan

On the cold, dark night of 2/3 November 1944 an Alsatian dog named Rifleman Khan crouched with his handler, Lance Corporal Muldoon of the 6th Cameronians, in a small assault craft crossing a channel that surrounded the low-lying Dutch island of Walcheren, near Antwerp. An artillery shell hit the small boat, nearly breaking it in half, and men and dog were thrown into the icy water. Rifleman Khan managed to swim ashore and struggle through the deep mud. But Lance Corporal Muldoon, unable to swim, was drowning. Somehow, the dog realised his master was in trouble and dashed back into the water, swimming until he reached his handler, grabbed his tunic in his teeth and battled back under heavy fire and piercing searchlights to dry land, pulling the exhausted soldier behind him. Although many of the Cameronians lost their lives that night – including the company commander – Rifleman Khan's steely determination saved his handler. For this the dog was awarded the Dickin Medal for valour: and Lance Corporal Muldoon was allowed to keep his saviour.

The Dickin Medal-winning Alsatian Rifleman Khan with his handler, Lance Corporal Muldoon, whom he rescued from drowning.

304,000 injured, dogs would work alongside the US troops in conditions of great danger and difficulty during guerrilla jungle warfare. An initial programme in which 300 dogs had been supplied from Germany via the US Defense Department to the South Vietnamese Army was not a success, due primarily to insurmountable cultural differences in the way the Vietnamese and the Americans viewed dogs, compounded by a lack of appropriate veterinary facilities in the country. But after the Gulf of Tonkin incident in August 1964 President Lyndon Johnson was faced with a stark choice: pull out or up the ante – he chose to escalate US involvement in Vietnam, and the dogs for war programme was reactivated and designated 'Project Top Dog'. By January 1970 there were approximately 300 dogs guarding US airbases in Vietnam. The dogs were subject to mortar attacks, including one on the Tan Son Nhut Base near Saigon on 4 December 1966 in which three airman and three dogs were killed. Nemo, a black and tan German shepherd dog was already a veteran sentry when he arrived in Vietnam. That day, Nemo and his handler, Airman 2nd Class Bob Thorneburg, had been assigned to guard duty near the runway. Hearing a noise, Nemo bounded after the intruder and was shot. Though in great pain, he crawled back and covered the wounded Thorneburg with his body and refused to leave until he was forcibly dragged away. Nemo lost an eye in the attack and had to undergo reconstructive facial surgery and could no longer act as a sentry. But he continued his war work by touring the US as an Air Force dog recruiter for a war that had by now deeply divided the nation.

In many ways, Vietnam was in terms of tactics and terrain a reprise of the Second World War in the Far East. To try to counter the guerrilla attacks of the Vietcong in a

ABOVE: ***Twelve years after the end of a brutal civil war, Mozambique was still dealing with a 'critical situation' from landmines in an area where more than a million people lived. A Belgian de-mining group trains rats there to detect mines since they have an acute sense of smell and apparently are easy to tame, train and maintain.***

ABOVE LEFT: ***Paul Hogarth (1917–2001):*** **'War Dog, Berlin. 1981'.** ***Hogarth, a distant relation of the 18th-century painter William Hogarth, was a youthful volunteer to the International Brigade during the Spanish Civil War, and worked for the Ministry of Information during the Second World War. He travelled widely in Eastern Europe, the location for this Cold War artwork.***

Rats on Alert

Rats was a mixed breed brown and white dog with quite a bit of corgi in him who was accustomed to scavenging around a small housing estate called Ardross on the outskirts of the frontier town of Crossmaglen in Northern Ireland. There he attached himself to the British Army in the mid-1970s. It was an unlikely embedding: South Armagh was 'bomb and booby trap country', a strongly Catholic and Republican area, with the British soldiers in constant danger of getting blasted to bits by an IRA-planted device. The continuous border patrols took their toll on the men and a tour of duty in Armagh only lasted four or five months. But Rats was welcome to stay. As Major Charles Woodrow explained: 'soldiers like having a dog – that's the first thing particularly in places like Armagh where the men felt isolated and unwanted' and in addition 'they are a good way of triggering a device. I would rather lose a dog than a soldier'.

Rats takes it easy in his retirement from the British Army.

Rats on patrol with his handler in Co Antrim, Northern Ireland.

Soon Rats (or Rat, short for Rations) was out on patrol with any patrol he could find – and one set off every 15 minutes around the clock. He rode in armoured cars, hitched lifts in helicopters that were combing the country for suspects – and jumped out without a parachute. As soldiers got injured, so did Rats. He lost half his tail in a fire bomb incident, was blown up by high explosives, singed by bullets and run over by a car – which was somewhat predictable since he was apt to give chase to any vehicle he did not recognise.

In time, Rats 'served' longer than any British soldier in Crossmaglen, and television made him a star. He was awarded a medal by an organisation concerned with animal welfare, and hundreds of people – mostly women and children – started to write to the dog and send toys and treats. The Army rewarded each correspondent with a paw-printed thank-you note.

Finally Rats had to be retired on grounds of ill health and sent to England. The searchlight of fame that settled on the feisty mongrel has a poignancy that perhaps surrounds all animals at war as they are a way of anaesthetising the complex, the unacceptable or the unbearable, a distraction certainly and a comfort, too. As Company Sergeant Major William Evans recalled, Rats was 'like an oasis of friendship in a desert of sadness' in those troubled years.

A tracker dog used to round up suspects is hauled into a helicopter after completing his task in the Malayan jungle during the Emergency, which lasted from 1948–60.

landscape they knew and understood, the US increased the number of scout dogs for their troops and by 1967, as the war dragged on, there were more than 1,000 scout dogs ranging over a territory roughly the size of Oklahoma. As Robert Lemish, the official historian for the Vietnam Dog Handler's Association observes, in unfamiliar, treacherous and remote conditions, men and dogs grew close. Such was this bond that some men were killed trying to save their dogs' lives and many dogs took the brunt of booby trap explosions, saving the life of their handlers. By the end of the war more than a hundred handlers had been killed and many more injured but Lemish is confident that 'more scout dog teams could have prevented even more casualties if they had been given a higher priority in the army'. As an instructor, Jesse Mendez, reflected, scout dogs 'are the only weapon system we ever devised to save lives'.

The conditions of the war in Vietnam meant that dogs were trained not only to search for mines and booby traps – which could be deadly punji pits studded with sharpened bamboo stakes capped with faeces so that any injury in the humid conditions of the jungle would turn gangrenous within short time – but also to look for the underground tunnels and rat holes with which the terrain was riddled, in which Viet Cong soldiers would hide. The dogs were trained to alert their handlers by stopping stock-still and sitting two feet from the trip wire that guarded the tunnel or its entrance. A specially trained armed volunteer known as a 'tunnel rat' would then enter the tunnel complex to flush out – or kill – its occupants.

A new arrival has its particulars taken in the records of a dog training school 'somewhere in the west of England', November 1944. The dogs were trained there to guard Allied airfields.

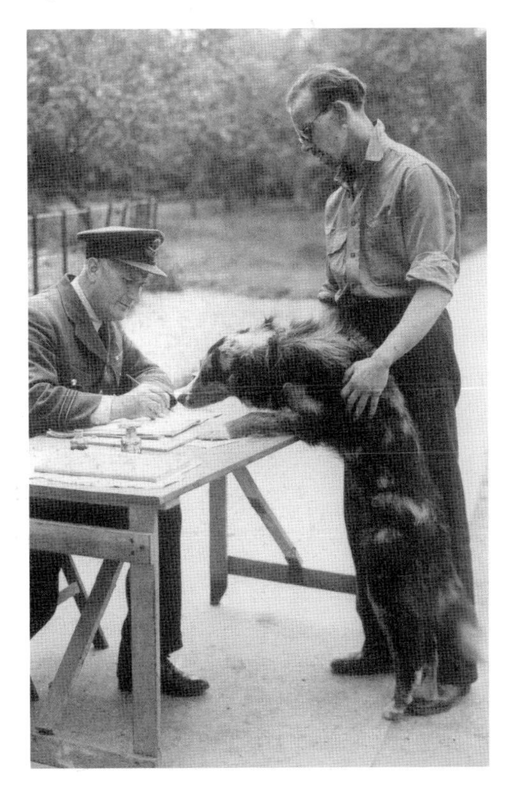

War dogs in training during the Second World War. Dogs that have been commanded to 'sit' are being trained to hold the position while their handlers walk away, and not to move until commanded to do so.

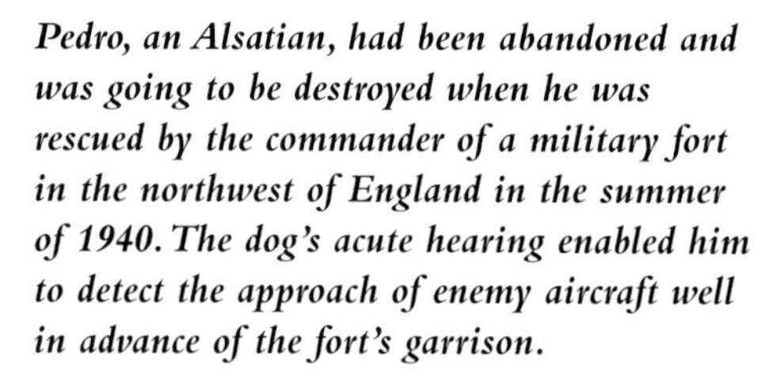

Pedro, an Alsatian, had been abandoned and was going to be destroyed when he was rescued by the commander of a military fort in the northwest of England in the summer of 1940. The dog's acute hearing enabled him to detect the approach of enemy aircraft well in advance of the fort's garrison.

Learning from the successful 'mopping-up' operations in the Pacific islands in the Second World War, the US Army, with British help, began in 1966 to train tracker dogs to supplement the teams of patrol or scout dogs in Vietnam. While German shepherd dogs continued to be preferred for scout duties, where their task was to pick up any unfamiliar scent, it was Labradors who could best follow a single scent. They were trained over several months, by being made to sniff an enemy footprint or a trail of blood, since every person has his or her own individual 'scent signature'. The bond between handler and dog was crucial: the dog had to learn what its handler expected, while the handler had to learn to read the dog's signals so he would know by a twitching ear or thumping tail that his canine partner had found what it had been detailed to search for. Increasingly, scout and tracker dogs would be used together, the former to sniff generalised danger, the latter to stay on the enemy trail.

Unsurprisingly, this led to the notion that it might be possible to breed a 'super

Arms Buster

Buster is the 60th recipient of the Dickin Medal – the 'animals' VC', and the Royal Army Veterinary Corps search dog received it in the 60th anniversary year of the medal's instigation, 2003.

A six-year-old springer spaniel specially trained to sniff out explosives, Buster unearthed a huge hidden cache of arms and bomb-making equipment in Iraq during a dawn raid in the southern village of Safwan. 'The rule is that the dog always goes first in case of booby traps and I was obviously concerned for him as he started his search,' explained Buster's handler, Sergeant Danny Morgan. 'Within minutes he became excited in a particular area and I knew he'd discovered something.'

The Iraqi insurgents denied having any weapons, 'but Buster found their arms even though they'd been hidden in a wall cavity, covered with a sheet of tin then with a wardrobe pushed in front of it ... We'd never have found the weapons without him and they would still be a threat to the troops and to the local population,' averred Morgan.

Buster, who is also the pet of the Morgan family, was recruited from Battersea Dogs Home, and Sergeant Morgan trained him 'by teaching him to fetch weapons like guns and ammunition instead of sticks and balls. He loves his job simply because he thinks it's a game and obviously has no idea he's going into dangerous situations.' But Morgan admitted to the journalist Nick Parker of the *Sun* that it is he who 'ends up worrying because [Buster] is not only doing a job out here [in Iraq] – he's my best friend.'

Buster with his handler, Sergeant Danny Morgan, in Iraq.

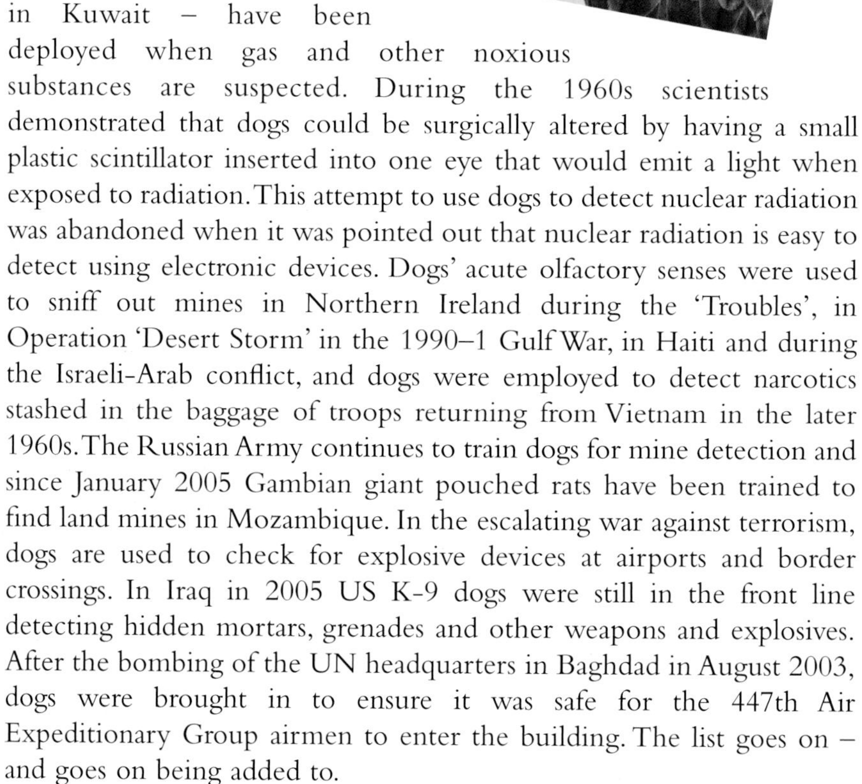

A hooded falcon with its Royal Naval handler. Falcons are sometimes used to clear military airfields of small birds that might interfere with an aircraft's landing or departure, but can be vicious predators to pigeons also bent on war work.

dog' combining the most useful characteristics of several varieties, while 'breeding out' their deficiencies. Though programmes for producing an 'Infantry Tactical Dog' died an early death, experiments on the ways that animals can be used to keep pace with the rapidly evolving technologies of warfare have been – and continue to be – an animal destiny, and it is not just dogs that are in the frame.

In the First World War canaries were used in the trenches to detect the presence of gas, goldfish were plunged into water containing respirators suspected of being contaminated with gas to establish which gas had been used, and in many areas of conflict subsequently fowl and birds – including chickens in Kuwait – have been deployed when gas and other noxious substances are suspected. During the 1960s scientists demonstrated that dogs could be surgically altered by having a small plastic scintillator inserted into one eye that would emit a light when exposed to radiation. This attempt to use dogs to detect nuclear radiation was abandoned when it was pointed out that nuclear radiation is easy to detect using electronic devices. Dogs' acute olfactory senses were used to sniff out mines in Northern Ireland during the 'Troubles', in Operation 'Desert Storm' in the 1990–1 Gulf War, in Haiti and during the Israeli-Arab conflict, and dogs were employed to detect narcotics stashed in the baggage of troops returning from Vietnam in the later 1960s. The Russian Army continues to train dogs for mine detection and since January 2005 Gambian giant pouched rats have been trained to find land mines in Mozambique. In the escalating war against terrorism, dogs are used to check for explosive devices at airports and border crossings. In Iraq in 2005 US K-9 dogs were still in the front line detecting hidden mortars, grenades and other weapons and explosives. After the bombing of the UN headquarters in Baghdad in August 2003, dogs were brought in to ensure it was safe for the 447th Air Expeditionary Group airmen to enter the building. The list goes on – and goes on being added to.

Simmi, a military police guard dog renowned for his viciousness, Second World War.

7

TO THE RESCUE

Carlo was a Belgian Malinois dog that was used in Kuwait to sniff out bombs, and during his 60-day tour of duty the dog managed to find 167 caches of explosives, some wired to explode on contact. One booby trap consisted of a pack of cluster bombs hidden underneath a box of American MRE (Meals-Ready-to-Eat) containers.

On his return to the US, Carlo's handler, Air Force Sergeant Christopher Batta, was awarded the Bronze Star for his efforts, but on learning that the US refused to bestow military honours on animals, the sergeant removed his medal after the ceremony and hung it round his dog's neck, insisting, 'Carlo worked harder than me. He was always in front of me.'

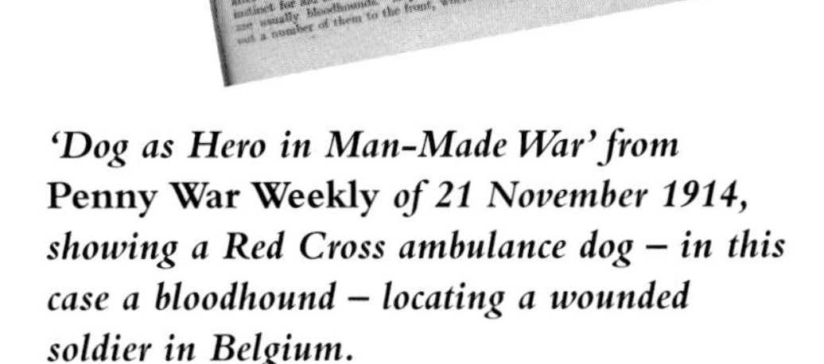

PENNY WAR WEEKLY

THE DOG AS HERO IN MAN-MADE WAR

Red Cross ambulance dog locating a wounded soldier after a battle in Belgium. These noble animals, whose instinct for aid is so sure, and whose intelligence is so great, are usually bloodhounds. Major Richardson recently took out a number of them to the front, where their services have been as valuable as those of the famous animals of St. Bernard. They carry a complete first-aid equipment and are taught to trace the wounded. Dogs trained by Major Richardson are also used by Russian soldiers for outpost and sentry work as well as with their ambulance corps.

'Dog as Hero in Man-Made War' from **Penny War Weekly** *of 21 November 1914, showing a Red Cross ambulance dog – in this case a bloodhound – locating a wounded soldier in Belgium.*

Winkie, the pigeon that alerted rescue services to the plight of the crew of an RAF aircraft that had crashed in the North Sea on 23 February 1943. She is shown with the crew whose lives she probably helped to save.

Rin Tin Tin

The dog as star. Rin Tin Tin Jnr in a 1936 film.

Along with Lassie and Old Yeller, Rin Tin Tin is probably the best-known dog in the West – thanks to the cinema. The original Rin Tin Tin was a German shepherd dog puppy, only a few days old when the kennel in which he was sleeping with his mother and rest of the litter was bombed on 15 September 1918.

An American Corporal, Lee Duncan, adopted two of the puppies, which he named after French puppets, Rin Tin Tin and Nanette.

Corporal Duncan had been so impressed by what he had seen of German war dogs that he visited a German kennel master who was now a POW to learn more about the breed of German shepherd dogs and their training.

Rin Tin Tin and Nanette were taken back to the US by Corporal Duncan who returned to his peacetime job in a Los Angeles hardware store. Sadly, Nanette died, but Rin Tin Tin was soon attracting attention at dog shows – including that of the film director Darryll Zanuck who offered Duncan $350 to film the dog in action.

Fired up with the prospect of stardom, Duncan touted his dog around the Hollywood film studios until one on the edge of bankruptcy, Warner Brothers Pictures, agreed to give the dog a chance. *Man From Hell's River* made Rin Tin Tin a star – and saved the fortunes of Warner Brothers. The dog made a total of 26 pictures for the studio and at the height of his fame he was receiving some 10,000 fan letters a week – right up there with the top Hollywood stars of the era such as Mary Pickford and Douglas Fairbanks, until his death on 10 August 1932.

But the line didn't die: Rin Tin Tin's son, Junior, assumed the film star mantle and when America joined the Second World War he and his offspring were volunteered for the US Army. With Corporal Duncan, they were involved in training more than 5,000 dogs and their handlers for the war effort. One of Rin Tin Tin's offspring was also involved in the notoriously brutal Cat Island 'attack and kill' training programme for dogs off the coast of Mississippi in 1942.

The Adventures of Rin Tin Tin, the popular television series aired in the 1950s, starred more of the family of the Second World War survivor, and a closely controlled breeding programme ensured that Rin Tin Tin's direct progeny are still being bred.

Dromedary camels fitted with cacolet panniers carry wounded men to safety on the North West Frontier of India in the First World War.

In Britain, those animals that have shown exceptional diligence and fortitude, and what many recognise as courage in wartime, are eligible to be awarded a Dickin Medal. The award, named after Mrs Maria Dickin, the founder of the People's Dispensary for Sick Animals (PDSA), was instituted in 1943. Between then and 1949 54 Dickin Medals were awarded to animals 'displaying conspicuous gallantry and devotion to duty while serving in the Armed Forces, or Civil Defence units during World War II and its aftermath'. One cat, three horses and 18 dogs have been so honoured, but by far the greatest number of recipients have been pigeons, 32 in total.

Despite the fact that aircraft could be tracked by radar and carried sophisticated wireless communication and location equipment during the Second World War, it was announced in 1939 that 'the RAF is to recruit 250,000 racing pigeons for use as messengers. In times of emergency, radio can easily be jammed, but trained birds "get through" nine times out of ten'. Soon almost every airfield had its own pigeon lofts and birds were carried on every bombing raid. Should a plane come down in the sea, the pigeon, carried in a special waterproof container, would be thrown clear. With any luck, it would bob about on the waves until the airmen in their inflated dinghy picked it up and scribbled a message with indelible pencil giving their position as well as they were able to ascertain it. The pigeon would then be despatched with its message and the men's fervent hopes and prayers that the bird would find its way home as quickly as possible, and that a search party would be alerted at the base.

Stanley Spencer RA (1891–1959): **'Travoys Arriving with the Wounded at a Dressing-Station at Smol, Macedonia, September 1916'.** *Travoys were two long poles slung on either side of a mule, either linked to another mule or trailing along the ground, and were used to transport the wounded. Spencer had volunteered as a medical orderly in spring 1915, and in September 1916 he was sent to the Macedonian Front, which is depicted in this painting. The dressing station had been set up in the 800-year-old village church, and Spencer gives a spiritual dimension to his painting of the aftermath of battle. 'In the midst of war there was a species of peace made and sustained by those in it but not of it ... I felt there was a grandeur about the scene.'*

The first recipient of the Dickin Medal was indeed such a pigeon. In February 1942 a Bristol Beaufort aircraft on its way back to RAF Leuchars in Scotland from a mission over Norway was hit by enemy fire and forced down in the icy North Sea. Parts of the wing and the fuselage broke on impact and the men were thrown into the sea. They managed to inflate their rubber dinghy and hoist themselves into it, but they were 120 miles from land and, with the weather deteriorating rapidly, their chances of survival looked slim. The airmen managed to locate the pigeon carrier and although the blue chequered hen pigeon had fallen out into an oil slick on the water, she managed to get free, shake her wings and fly off uncertainly into the murky afternoon.

Although the RAF base knew that the aircraft had ditched, it had lost radio contact with the men. An immediate air search was mounted but there was no indication of where the small dinghy might be. Shortly after dawn the next morning, the oil-bespattered, exhausted pigeon flew into her loft on the airbase. Although she carried no message the RAF Pigeon Service sergeant on duty was able to work out how long it would have taken the bird to get from the sunken boat to home, taking into account the wind direction. Based on his calculations another air search was launched and within a quarter of an hour the men had been located, their position radioed back, an air rescue team despatched and the men brought back to safety. This was the first time that a pigeon

Wounded Serbian troops being transported in cacolets carried by mules after the Monastir offensive in October 1916 when Allied troops advanced slowly along the Crno River in the face of Bulgarian resistance.

had saved the lives of an RAF crew in the Second World War and the pigeon, whose only designation was NEHU 40 NS1, was named Winkie on account of the way her eyelid drooped with sheer fatigue. In December 1943 she became the first recipient of the Dickin Medal.

There were 31 such plucky pigeons officially honoured. One such was GI Joe, a pigeon with the US forces in Italy, who was the first non-British recipient of the Dickin Medal. In October 1943 the British 56th Infantry Division sent a request for air support to help it break out of the heavily fortified German position at Colvi Vecchia and it was arranged that the Allied XII Air Support Command would bomb the town. Just as the aircraft were about to take off, GI Joe arrived with a message to say that the 169th Infantry Brigade had captured the village. The pigeon had flown the 20 miles in 20 minutes and had he arrived 10 minutes later it would have been too late to prevent the aircraft bombing their own men. Another was a blue cock, Billy, which was released with a message from the crew of a bomber that had been forced to come down in the German-occupied Netherlands. Eleven-month-old Billy flew 250 miles through atrocious wind and snow storms to deliver his message 26 hours later; there was another blue cock, Royal Blue, from King George VI's racing pigeon stable, which delivered a message from a bomber crew downed in the Netherlands by flying 120 miles back to the royal loft at Sandringham in less than

An appeal for funds from the Blue Cross, 1915.

Model of a horse-drawn ambulance from the First World War.

five hours. There was also George, a red chequer cock that alerted the RAF of a crew of four who had had to bail out in the Mediterranean 100 miles from land, and they too were rescued. There was White Vision, a hen, released with a message from a flying boat that was forced to ditch in rough sea with engine failure in October 1943. The radio had failed and no SOS was received back at base, and in such severe weather rescue searches were limited. After a nine-hour flight with hardly any visibility and with headwinds buffeting up to 25mph, a bedraggled and exhausted pigeon arrived to give the alert and the crew were saved. And there was Mary, decorated 'for outstanding endurance'. She served from 1940 right through to VE Day despite numerous casualties. She was attacked by a hawk when on a mission, returned from another mission with her wing broken and three pellets in her, and had a total of 22 stitches in her small, feathered body. Then, during the Baedeker raid on Exeter, she survived a 1,000lb bomb falling outside her loft and another crashing down near the garage to which the pigeons not killed by the first bomb had been moved. In addition, there were other pigeons that no doubt saved lives less directly, such as Gustav, who had flown back with the first news of the Normandy landings.

Were these decorated pigeons brave? They were certainly intrepid and single-minded and many persevered when they must have been exhausted, in the face of strong winds, sometimes hit by shrapnel or attacked by predatory hawks or falcons. But does this count as courage, or is it a hard-wired homing instinct that worked, as did so many other characteristics and abilities that animals possess, to man's advantage in war? Perhaps it would be easier to answer that question if scientists were able to tell us more about this remarkable homing instinct. How do pigeons find their way home? No one seems entirely sure. While the sun plays its part in setting the bird on course, when it comes to the 'map' a pigeon needs to find its loft, scientists are still divided. Two Oxford University zoologists are testing the hypothesis that the birds can use visual clues when flying over familiar features such as a railway line or road, and can even be observed flying 'up the Oxford by pass and turn[ing] off at particular junctions' to get home. Other scientists suggest that the birds' acute sense of smell or even their keen hearing orientate them, while others find the theory that the Earth's magnetic field provides pigeons with their compass the most promising explanation to explore, and others opt for a 'multifactoral system' combing subtle combinations of all mechanisms such as sun, smell and magnetism. Rupert Sheldrake brings his 'elastic band' theory into the equation, but concedes that he 'does not know how this interconnection might work …' and that at the moment 'appropriate explanations [of homing behaviour] may lie beyond the current limits of science.'

This homing instinct, however, is not limited to pigeons. During the Vietnam War US soldiers often transported their dogs by aeroplane or helicopter. If the men were suddenly ordered to evacuate an area, and the dogs were left behind, it was presumed that since a dog could have no idea of the route to where it had been left, it would not be able to get back to camp again. But this presumption was often confounded. Michael G. Lemish

OPPOSITE: ***A sergeant helps a wounded man from the mule that had carried him from the scene of battle during the Italian campaign, September 1943.***

Camouflage

A snowshoe hare merges into its white environment.

Camouflage (from a French word meaning to 'conceal' or 'disguise') is what allows otherwise visible things to remain indistinguishable from their surroundings. It is, in effect, a form of deception and as such the military has learned a great deal from nature.

In order to survive animals need to be able to fool their predators by blending into the environment or concealing their shape, and likewise predators need to be able to sneak up unaware on their prey. Evolutionary pressures lead some animals to use mimicry, seeming to be something else, a leaf maybe, or a twig or a stone, while others are adaptive, capable of what are known as 'chromatic responses', changing their colour as the environment changes, either with the seasons – ermine is an example – or far more rapidly, as chameleons do.

Ever since prehistoric hunters smeared themselves with mud, man has seen the value of concealment, but generally armies tended to prefer to demonstrate their power by wearing brightly coloured uniforms that might daunt the enemy as well as establishing their unit's cohesion and making the men easy to identify in the fog and smoke of battle.

However, casualties were so high among the British soldiers fighting in India in the mid-19th century that they were obliged to dye their bright red tunics a neutral, muddy colour they called khaki (from the Urdu word for dusty). But it was not until the Boer War that this murky green/brown became standard British Army issue and other European armies followed its lead in dressing their troops in muted shades. Except the French, that is, who stuck to their red trousers until high rates of casualties at the start of the First World War, and the fact that the red dye was manufactured in Germany, inclined them to conform to the dusty colours' initiative, choosing 'horizon blue' for their battle gear.

During the Second World War, a Camouflage Development and Training Centre was set up at Farnham in Surrey and among those who trained there were the surrealist artists Julian Trevelyan and Roland Penrose and the couturier Victor Stiebel. The distinguished Cambridge zoologist, Dr Hugh Cott, who had written the definitive study on *Adaptive Coloration in Animals*, attended too, and now 'applied the principles he had found in the animal kingdom to the disguise of guns and tanks'. The illusionist and magician Jasper Maskelyne (who would later claim to have managed to 'lose' the Suez Canal through the adroit use of lights) was another attendee, though he couldn't understand for the life of him why he was required to be there. At Farnham he 'learned how arctic rabbits suffer a

change of colour when snow falls and why tigers hang around tall grass ... Six weeks being told elementary things, almost drove me out of my mind ... A lifetime of hiding things on stage has taught me more about the subject than rabbits and tigers will ever know.'

ABOVE: ***Mule-drawn ambulance wagons disguised with camouflage paint transport the wounded on the Salonika Front in October 1916.***

LEFT: ***A pony disguised as a zebra: a camouflage presumably useful only in Africa where zebras are indigenous.***

An equine shield. A posed photograph of horses of the Russian Cossacks lying in the snow to afford cover from enemy fire,* circa *1941/2.

instances a scout dog named Trouble who had been airlifted with his handler to support a patrol. Its handler, Private First Class William Richardson, was injured and winched into a medical helicopter. Trouble was left behind. With no visual knowledge of the terrain covered and no scent to guide him, the emaciated dog arrived back at the air base after trekking through the dense jungle for three weeks. He wearily searched for his master's bed and fell asleep on it.

In the First World War, the Red Cross was able to supply motorised ambulances to transport the injured from the battlefield to medical posts and hospitals and these were found to be more satisfactory than the horse-drawn wagons of earlier wars. However, dogs continued to play a 'search and rescue' role in the Great War as in all earlier ones. Small two-wheeled ambulances that could accommodate one or two wounded soldiers and could be pulled by larger breeds of dog weighing over 80lb were used as Red Cross transport from battlefield to first aid station. Under cover of darkness, dogs would be sent out into the 'no man's land' that lay between the endless lines of opposing trenches to search for the wounded from the day's battle, since to send ambulances into this treacherous area would be to invite a fusillade of shells and bullets. The dogs would set out through the barbed wire, usually equipped with small canteens of water or spirits and

Nose Art

Should fighter and bomber aircraft not be sufficiently intimidating as they deliver death, injury and destruction from the skies, man has borrowed from the animal world to make them even more menacing. In a reverse of the principle of camouflage, by which military aircraft are usually painted grey or khaki in an attempt to disguise their presence, the snub-nosed design of aircraft seems to have been an invitation, even dating back to the First World War, to paint them to resemble fearsome predators – which of course they are.

No 112 Fighter Squadron of the Royal Air Force operating in the Western Desert in the Second World War painted its Curtiss P-40 fighters with a primitive – and, in fact, rather benign – shark's face. Subsequently, the squadron's Tomahawk or Kittyhawk and Mustang aircraft with their vicious-looking pointed noses acquired frighteningly sharp shark's teeth and mean shark's eyes and indeed No 112 became known – unofficially – as the 'Shark's Squadron'.

During the Second World War, in the USAAF, where air-brushed 'nose art' has become an esteemed art form, featuring beguiling scantily-clad blondes as well as fearsome beasts, the most famous of the shark's teeth aircraft was the Curtiss P-40 flown by the American Volunteer Group in China. It was alleged that as the entire Japanese race was short sighted, the teeth on aircraft operating against them should be painted a mammoth size so the unfortunate Japanese could get the message. 'Bats Outta Hell' were the eponymously-named aircraft of the US 499th Bomb Squadron operating against the Japanese, while aircraft of the 498th in the Philippines were painted to appear like fierce falcons about to swoop.

The German Luftwaffe discovered that its Messerschmitt Me110 fighter/bomber aircraft 'suited' shark's teeth particularly well, and they even adorned some gliders with drawn-back lips and little pointed teeth.

The trend has continued: in Vietnam the US F-4E Phantom of the 388th Tactical Fighter Wing and other aircraft of the 469th Fighter Squadron were decorated to look like sharks that had smelled blood, the Israeli Defence Force has customised some of its MD-450 Ouragans as sabre-toothed monsters, and air forces of the NATO alliance have tried to stress their pan-national unity in a number of ways including decorating the nose or tail of aircraft of several of the member nations with pouncing tigers or even painting the entire aircraft with tiger stripes.

TOP: *Royal Navy No 814 Squadron (Tiger Scheme), 1997.*

BELOW: *Curtiss Tomahawk P-40 fighter.*

The collar and lead of a German Red Cross rescue dog during the First World War.

medical supplies attached to a harness or saddlebag so if the man was conscious he could make use of these. If the soldier was unconscious or not able to move, the dog would run back to alert its handler with a cap, glove, badge or torn scrap from some item of clothing as evidence. This would also refresh the dog's memory when it was required to locate the victim again. The dog would then accompany the stretcher party, guiding them to where the victim lay, without barking or in any way alerting the enemy to the rescue party's presence. It would have been taught to 'freeze' on the ground if a volley of enemy fire illuminated the sky.

An American surgeon who served with Russian troops in the First World War recounted his work with Airedale terriers that were 'trained to locate the wounded in thickets and brushy places where they could not be seen by our searching parties, who, for obvious reasons, could not carry any light'. Surgeon Grow recounted one night when the dogs found 14 wounded men lying injured and each was brought back to the trenches and medical care. 'Do the dogs ever take you to dead bodies?' the surgeon was asked. 'No, never,' he replied. 'They sometimes lead us to bodies which we think have no life in them, but when we bring them back the doctors, by careful examination, always find a spark, though often very feeble. It is purely a matter of instinct, which, in this instance, is far more effective than man's reasoning powers.'

During the Second World War tracker dogs trained to follow a scent were again used to locate casualties in densely wooded or overgrown areas. In mountainous regions in Italy, the Middle East and the Far East horses, mules, donkeys and large dogs might be pressed into service to transport the injured carefully down steep narrow paths, along which no ambulance could venture. Likewise camels, which carried the fit, occasionally were loaded with the wounded if no other more suitable form of transport was available.

As the circumstances of war changed, so the tasks that animals were called upon to play expanded. The first 'civilian' recipient of the Dickin Medal was Sheila, a collie that led her master, a shepherd, John Dagg, to the rescue of some of the crew of a USAAF B-17 Flying Fortress bomber that had crashed on the remote Brayden Crags in the Cheviot Hills in Northumberland during a blizzard in December 1944. During the London blitz of 1940–1 it was discovered that dogs' keen sense of smell – and their ability to dig – could be put to use in locating civilians trapped under the debris after bombing raids. But Beauty, or Tipperary Beauty, to give the wire-haired terrier her pedigree name, was awarded a Dickin Medal for her work on the Home Front rescuing animals who were the victims of air raids, rather than people. This was a service for which the terrier had no training, but she first demonstrated her talent spontaneously one night in the East End when a cat was trapped under a splintered table beneath some fallen masonry and Beauty started scrabbling enthusiastically in the debris to get at it. By the end of the war, 62 other animals that might have died a lingering death from starvation or suffocation owed their lives to Beauty.

The four medals attached to the collar of Jet, one of London's 'rescue dogs'. Among his awards is the PDSA Dickin Medal 'for Gallantry' since it could be said of animals 'We Also Serve'.

Rip was a mongrel that had been found wandering the streets after a heavy raid on Poplar, East London, during the first weeks of the Blitz in September 1940. Homeless, the dog attached himself to an ARP warden and started to accompany him on his nightly patrols, and, like Beauty, whenever there was an 'incident' Rip would sniff around among

Rip, a mongrel winner of the Dickin Medal, was a stray when he was adopted by the Poplar ARP in East London. In this posed picture Rip shows how he would alert his handler to the fact that a person or animal might be buried below the rubble.

the debris and if he located someone trapped beneath the rubble would start to dig furiously, thus alerting the Civil Defence services. Rip kept up his war work for the duration and he, too, was awarded a Dickin Medal.

By 1944 it had been decided to regularise the organisation of dogs used in rescue work, rather than relying on a handful of enterprising canines. A number of dogs already trained in anti-sabotage and patrol work at the Ministry of Aircraft Production Dog School in Gloucestershire were selected for trial. After a brief spell of specialised training, the animals were taken to London where they were attached to Civil Defence rescue squads. The timing was fortunate for within a week of D-Day in June 1944 the first of the terrifying V1 flying bomb or doodlebug attacks started, followed in September by the arrival of the second of Hitler's 'secret weapons', the V2, which wreaked such havoc to property – and life. Under the command of Lieutenant-Colonel W. W. Dove, 14 dogs were made available to be sent to an 'incident' to see if they could help in rescuing people trapped after a raid. One was Jet, a black Alsatian from Liverpool, which, despite being sick all the way on the journey south, was at work in Edmonton in north London within a couple of hours of arrival in the capital.

In response to a call, a dog and its handler would report to the Incident Officer at the scene and would be directed to where it was thought people might be trapped. The

Blitz Heroines

When the call for 'dog power' came during the Second World War Mrs Margaret Griffin, a breeder and trainer of Alsatians, volunteered both herself and several of her dogs. Mrs Griffin became the chief trainer at the Ministry of Aircraft Production Dog School where dogs were trained for guard and patrol duties.

Two of the Alsatians, Crumstone Irma (known as Irma) and Psyche started their war service as emergency messengers for the ARP services carrying messages from the ARP Post to the Report Centre when telephone lines were out of action. But once the Civil Defence authorities had been shown how useful dogs could be in finding victims buried after an air raid 'incident', that is what the two Alsatian bitches spent many nights doing, often together, while other dogs such as Beauty, Peter, Rip, Thorn, Jet and Storm were busy at other incidents.

Mrs Griffin's diary, which she wrote most nights, paints an exhausting picture of hours spent with the dogs digging in dust and rubble to unearth victims – both human and animal. Irma's 'speciality was seeming to know whether the victim she was searching for was dead or alive and would indicate this clearly by her bark'. In total the Irma–Psyche team located 233 people; of these Irma on her own found 21 alive and 171 dead. Irma was one of two dogs chosen to represent all rescue dogs in the Civil Defence Stand-Down Parade in Hyde Park in 1946. Irma was also one of the 18 dogs nominated to receive the Dickin Medal for their work during the Second World War, and Mrs Griffin was awarded a British Empire Medal for her selfless service.

Two 'Blitz dogs', both awarded the Dickin Medal for their rescue work with the Civil Defence: Irma, left, with her handler, Mrs Margaret Griffin, and Beauty, the mascot of the PDSA (People's Dispensary for Sick Animals) Rescue Squad, with her handler, ARP warden Bill Barnett.

handler would work his dog carefully over every inch of the ground so that no rescue possibility was overlooked, and, should the dog pick up a scent, it would start digging, watched by other Civil Defence personnel who were on hand to help if an injured person, or a dead body, were found.

One of the hardest things that the ARP warden in charge of a bomb incident had to decide was when it was fruitless to continue digging since there were unlikely to be any more survivors, and the rescue team should be called off and moved onto another

ABOVE: ***Exhausted by days of fighting against Japanese forces on Peleliu Island in the Pacific, a US Marine sleeps in the sand. The dog, which had escaped from the Japanese lines and attached itself to the Marines soon after they landed on 14 September 1944, stands guard over its somnolent master.***

incident. It was in such cases that a dog's instinct and persistence could be literally life-saving. If an animal was reluctant to stop digging, and persisted in returning to the same spot, this was taken seriously and digging continued until the dog seemed satisfied that there was no one else to be found. Rex, an Alsatian, first earned his stripes in an incident in Lambeth when he refused to be distracted when called off and uncovered some bedding which he seized with his teeth and dragged clear. Further digging revealed some bodies underneath which none of the humans present had suspected. Later Rex was sent to a factory in Heston in Middlesex that had been bombed. It was still burning when dog and handler arrived, and even though the roof started to fall in the dog seemed reluctant to leave and had to be dragged away. When the fire abated, Rex padded over the still smouldering debris and within four minutes had indicated the presence of five bodies, which were recovered within the next quarter of an hour.

Fire is something that most animals find terrifying, yet during the Blitz there were occasions when a dog would have to enter a burning building in search of casualties. One such animal was another Dickin Medal winner, Thorn. In his recommendation for a medal, Sir Edward Warner, a Civil Defence Senior Regional Officer, commended Thorn's behaviour in entering a burning house. 'Thorn went slowly step-by-step into the thickest smoke. He repeatedly flinched but was encouraged forward until eventually he reached a spot approximately over the seat of the fire, and gave positive indication there. Casualties were subsequently recovered from this point. In my opinion the work of Thorn at this spot was the best I have yet seen from any Rescue Dog.'

In subsequent wars and disasters, wherever there has been the need to locate or dig out the dead and injured, dogs have often been in the front line alongside sophisticated heat-imaging equipment and other technological advances that keep threatening to make the role of animals redundant in such crises – but somehow never do.

Ground Zero

Michael Hingson with his guide dog Roselle that lead him to safety after the 9/11 attack on the World Trade Center in New York, 11 September 2001.

When the twin towers of the World Trade Center in New York were hit by terrorist aircraft on 11 September 2001, thousands of workers were trapped in their offices high above Manhattan. These included two men, Michael Hingson and Omar Rivera, who are both blind. In the darkness the golden Labrador retrievers Roselle and Salty led their owners down the crowded, debris-strewn, smoke-filled stairs to safety. In the case of Mr Rivera and Salty, this was from the 71st floor, while Roselle managed to escort both her master and a woman who had been blinded by the debris safely from the 78th floor to the ground floor.

In recognition of the dogs' devotion, the British Guide Dogs for the Blind made a special award of a trophy and thousands of people wrote in from all over the world praising the dogs' bravery and sending in gifts and donations that by early November had totalled more than $1 million.

Some dogs were trapped in apartments in the stricken building and over 150 had to be rescued by the American Society for the Prevention of Cruelty to Animals. Dozens of other dogs worked with their handlers in the heartbreaking search for survivors in the wreckage. And there were those dogs who assumed another traditional wartime role, that of comforter, to the victims at the Family Center. Here death certificates were provided and the bereaved relatives were taken by boat to Ground Zero to see for themselves where their loved ones had perished.

8 Mascots and Other Animals

The root of the word 'mascot' comes from the Provençal French word meaning 'witch' and signifies something that brings good luck. In war a mascot takes on a special poignancy and urgency when the odds are seemingly stacked against survival. Pilots have been known to refuse to fly without their 'lucky' sprig of heather or such like; civilians refuse to go into the shelter during an air raid until they find a particular cushion or whatever they half believe may have 'protected' them in earlier bombing raids.

In war, the good-luck aspect of a mascot is compounded by the need for a boost to morale, for comfort, for an outlet for the sentimentality that is the inevitable companion to danger, for a focus and a distraction in difficult – and often intensely boring – times. So not only do regiments select animals or birds for their mascots but often groups of individual servicemen or women adopt an animal that then accompanies them throughout their campaigns – no matter how inappropriate the circumstances might be.

Prince Rupert, who led King Charles I's cavalry into battle during the English Civil War, was always accompanied by his small white dog, Boye, until it was killed at the battle of Marston Moor on 2 July 1644. Indeed, after that fatal encounter, the Royalist cause in the north was lost, and ultimately the victory of the Parliamentary forces assured.

During the Crimean War of 1854–6, mascots played a rather less bellicose role: Russian soldiers would button up their greatcoats over their regiments' fluffy kittens to keep themselves warm with this living 'comforter'.

However, it is the goat of the Royal Welch Fusiliers, which was present at the Battle of Bunker Hill on 17 June 1775 during the American War of Independence, that provides the first record of a British regimental mascot. Gradually since then, the practice spread. In the USA an eagle, Old Abe, was named after President Abraham Lincoln. The bird had been acquired from a native American in exchange for a bushel of corn and it was clearly a good bargain. Old Abe joined his Volunteer Infantry Regiment, the Wisconsin 8th, in some 36 battles during the course of the Civil War, and was a fearsome fighter, flapping its wings and screaming in battle.

During the First World War, the popularity of mascots burgeoned with goats, dogs and birds being the most popular. Over the years a veritable menagerie of animals has been

Poster designed by Mabel Lucie Atwell 1879–1964 for Our Dumb Friends' League.

An antelope named Bobbie, the regimental mascot of the 2nd Battalion, Royal Warwickshire, with the Warwickshire Commander Lieutenant-Colonel R. C. MacDonald and Field Marshal Montgomery (right).

adopted as mascots in Britain and all over the world, from the domestic – rabbits, dogs, cats, horses, mules, donkeys, goats, bulls and pigs – to the more zoological – bears, deer, birds, monkeys, alligators and even a lion. Nowadays the mascot of the 1st Battalion of the Prince of Wales Own Regiment of Yorkshire is a ferret with its own cap and ceremonial jacket.

The bulldog spirit of the Royal Navy: Joey, the mascot of* HMS Queen Elizabeth *during the Second World War.

Military mascots are a regimental concern, and if the mascot is given a rank, and a number, and awarded a medal for exceptional service – as many are – these are regimental initiatives that don't have any official sanction. Although transporting mascots and paying for their quarantine when necessary comes out of the public purse, it is the regiment that pays for the animal's food and care.

Sometimes the choice of animal or bird is associated with a unit's regimental badge. The Royal Warwickshire Regiment has an antelope as its badge, and its mascot is an antelope, too. Subsequently, some antelopes have been acquired from Indian maharajahs, others from the London Zoo, and one, 'liberated' from Hamburg Zoo as the Allied troops advanced through Germany in 1945, accompanied the regiment to the Middle East. The Parachute Regiment has chosen a Shetland pony (sadly without the wings) to vivify its regimental badge which shows the mythic winged horse, Pegasus. A Canadian unit, the 49th Battalion of the Canadian Expeditionary Force, the Loyal Edmonton Regiment, did things

The kitten mascot of the aircraft carrier HMS Eagle *stretches out in the hammock made for it by the ship's sail maker, 1945.*

the other way round. It had a favourite mascot, Lestock, a coyote, and, when in 1916 the regiment was fighting in France and was to receive a new cap badge, the soldiers pressed that their emblem should be the coyote's head. The Canadian authorities demurred since the coyote had 'no heraldic standing' but finally acquiesced – though the official blazon called Lestock a wolf.

In other instances the mascot might be chosen to represent the place of origin of a military unit – and remind the men of home. For example, Australian regiments have kangaroos, and Canadian regiments often favour black bears, while the US forces tend to go for eagles, raccoons and coyotes above other animals. The Irish Guards has an Irish wolf hound as its official mascot. The first of the line was named in 1902 after the famous King of Ireland Brian Boru (AD975–1014) – though he was always called Paddy to his face – and his direct descendents have served as mascots ever since.

The Royal Welch Fusiliers have had goats as their mascot since Bunker Hill. In 1844 Queen Victoria presented each of the two regular battalions with a goat and ever since then replacements have come from the royal herd at Windsor, and the goats are always named Billy. In February 2002, the existing two Billies were retired after long and honourable service to be replaced by six-month-old twins which also came from the royal herd, now kept at Whipsnade, the country establishment of London's Regent's Park Zoo. They are direct descendents of the goats Queen Victoria presented over 150 years ago. On ceremonial occasions the goats march at the front of the parade led by a Goat Major and their horns are gilded for special parades and ceremonies.

A grey mule was the mascot of the Queen's Own Madras Sappers and Miners from 1891 until he was pensioned off in 1922. During his tenure the mule served in seven campaigns, including Egypt (1915–17) and Palestine (1917–18), and when he finally died in 1933 aged around 47 one of his little grey hooves was made into 'an artistic ink pot stand' which stood in the officers' mess in Bangalore.

Since the Second World War mascots owned by British forces have had their own 'club'. The People's Dispensary for Sick Animals (PDSA), treated a number of animals and

Sammy, the mascot of the Northumberland Fusiliers, accompanied the regiment to France. He was wounded in the Second Battle of Ypres, was gassed on Whit Monday 1915 and was present during the Battle of the Somme, as well as being injured by shell fire on several occasions.

RIGHT: ***Jumbo, the three-month-old puppy mascot of an artillery battery stationed in a 'south eastern coastal town' during the Second World War. The puppy had been born on the gun emplacement.***

OPPOSITE: ***Artillery officers relax with a piano and a dog outside their billets near St Floris during a lull in the Lys offensive on 2 May 1918.***

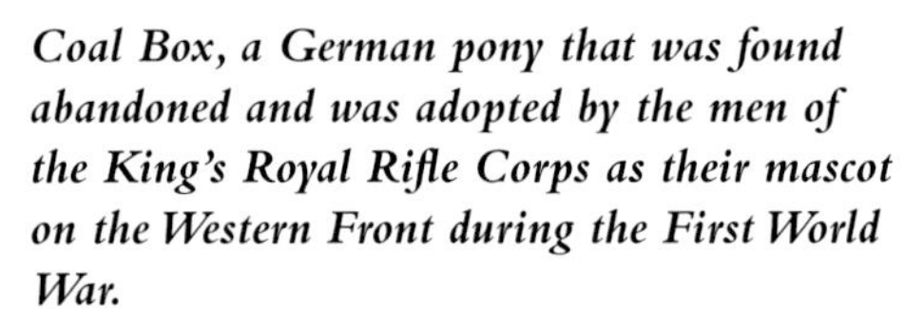

Coal Box, a German pony that was found abandoned and was adopted by the men of the King's Royal Rifle Corps as their mascot on the Western Front during the First World War.

bird mascots brought into its various hospitals and dispensaries at home and abroad. They realised what an important part such creatures played in the lives of the troops, and also how generous people were in donating these animals to the services. Consultations were held with Mrs Maria Dickin, who had opened the first dispensary for sick animals during the First World War in the face of considerable opposition. It was arranged that the PDSA would log all animal mascots 'with a good war record' and enrol them in what was to become the Allied Forces Mascot Club.

According to the club's wartime secretary, Miss Dorothea St Hill Bourne, there were three distinct categories of animal enrolled: the mascots which represented those thousands of animals that were taken into the Forces by their owners, or those adopted by soldiers or service units abroad; animals and birds conscripted into the services to act as messengers, guards, trackers and other military functions; and third came some

Soldier Bear

After the invasion of Poland, and its defeat by German forces, Polish soldiers, sailors and airmen joined the Allied forces and fought and died in almost every major battlefront in Europe during the Second World War. In the battle of Monte Cassino, the Poles – many of them released from Soviet prisoner-of-war camps – suffered appalling losses. Among the fighting troops was an unusual recruit – a brown bear. Wojtek ('little one'), known as Voytek, was a Syrian bear that had been bought as a tiny cub by a group of Polish soldiers as they passed through the mountains of Iran on their way to a posting in Palestine. Adopted by the 22nd Artillery Supply Company of the Polish II Corps, the appealing bundle of light brown fur soon grew to weigh 250lb and to stand more than six feet tall with paws capable of inflicting mortal damage. But Voytek was a tame ursine who enjoyed human company, raided the cookhouse and wrestled affectionately with the men.

In March 1944 the Polish II Corps arrived with its *grande orso* in Italy to supply British and Polish front-line troops with ammunition, artillery shells and food. Despite the fact that the Corps was invariably under fire, Voytek opted to hitch a lift in the munitions trucks, his head hanging out of the window. But despite his initial apprehension, the bear was more than a passenger: he joined the supply side, cradling 25lb shells or boxes of ammunition in his massive arms and passing them carefully along the line.

The Polish soldiers dreamed of returning to their homeland at the end of the war, and of taking Voytek with them. But this was not to be: most were left with no homes to go back to with their country devastated and under Soviet domination. Polish troops were displaced all over the world, and the bear mascot that had become something of a symbol of Polish courage ended his days as a popular visitor attraction at Edinburgh Zoo.

ABOVE: ***A ceramic plaque showing Voytek carrying a shell. This became part of the insignia of the Polish 22nd Company, of the Polish II Corps in Italy.***

RIGHT: ***A bear mascot belonging to HMS*** **Royal Oak,** ***circa 1918.***

Philip Connard RA (1875–1958): **'St George's Day, 1918: Bridge of HMS Canterbury'.** *The Canterbury was on patrol on 23 April when the naval raid on Zeebrugge and Ostend, the main bases for the German Navy's light vessels and U-boats, took place. A small black dog (left) watched the action.*

'honorary members' that represented, in St Hill Bourne's words, 'the countless "faithful beasts" who were called to no spectacular point of danger nor were they required to endure the harsh tedium of life on the Home Front, but who were capable when the testing time came of reaching the heights of courage and endurance.' Much like the entire civilian population of Britain.

The first enrolee was a donkey, Barney, which as a foal had been the prize in a pub darts match between teams from the Royal Navy and the RAF, which the RAF won. His new owners decided that if the donkey was going to be one of them, he had better learn to fly, so they bundled him in a jeep to take him to Hendon airfield. On the way, the nervous donkey struggled out and injured his leg. He was taken to the PDSA sanatorium in Ilford, where his leg was set in a plaster of Paris cast, and Barney was then installed in a kennel to recover since he was so small that he would have rattled around a loosebox. The donkey became something of a favourite among the PDSA staff caring for him and when he was fully recovered he was enrolled as the founder member of the Allied Forces Mascot Club in July 1943.

Minnie was a mascot born on active service. In March 1944 the 1st Battalion, Lancashire Fusiliers was posted to Burma. During a fierce Japanese mortar attack one of the battalion's pack ponies went into labour and the foal was called Minnie, after a mortar post near the spot where she was born. In those difficult days Minnie brought a great deal of pleasure to the troops, who fed her titbits and taught her to drink tea from a pint pot. When the troops were ordered to evacuate, Minnie was too young to be able to march very far with the other pack animals so she was flown by transport aircraft to India to await their arrival. She was soon ensconced as the battalion's mascot, marching in parades, gracing important events with her presence and taking liberties in the mess. In December 1945 the battalion became fully mechanised and so Minnie could no longer be fed from food pinched from the regular transport mules. A special 'Minnie Fund' was set up by the men to pay for her keep, and when the fusiliers returned to Britain, Minnie came too.

A book about military mascots and pets concludes with what amounts to a child's alphabet of exotic mascots. There was an alligator, Spike, mascot of the US Atlantic Fleet Amphibious Force. There were various varieties of bear including Cuddles, which the US 390th Bomb Group stationed in the UK adopted as its mascot, and when the King's Own Yorkshire Light Infantry was stationed in Penang in Malaya in 1950 it was presented with a short-sighted honey bear (which liked condensed milk, too) called Isau (Malay for 'girl friend'). An Australian field artillery unit appropriately chose a koala bear that it named 'Butch'. Again, appropriately, a falcon named Fred was adopted as the mascot of the RAF (Parachute Training School) at Abingdon in Berkshire, and a duck went to Korea with the US 187th Regimental Combat

CERTIFICATES OF QUALIFICATION AS FIRST PILOT

[K.R. & A.C.I., para. 805]

Name SAMMY OLIVE PHILPOT Rank ACTING DOG PILOT

(i) Certified that the above named has qualified as a first pilot (day) on BEAUFORT BEAUFIGHTER ALBACORE WELLINGTON landplanes w.e.f.

Unit T.D.U. GOSPORT. Signature

Date 1ST JANUARY 42. Rank F/LT.

(ii) Certified that the above named has qualified as a first pilot (night) on ..... landplanes w.e.f. .....

Unit ..... Signature .....

Date ..... Rank .....

(iii) Certified that the above named has qualified as a first pilot (day) on ..... seaplanes w.e.f. .....

Unit ..... Signature .....

Date ..... Rank .....

(iv) Certified that the above named has qualified as a first pilot (night) on ..... seaplanes w.e.f. .....

Unit ..... Signature .....

Date ..... Rank .....

LEFT: ***Sammy Philpot was a dog belonging to Flight Lieutenant Oliver Philpot, one of the three courageous men who took part in the famous 'Wooden Horse' escape from Stalag Luft III POW camp in October 1943, where Philpot had been imprisoned after being shot down off the Norwegian coast in April 1942. Sammy accompanied his master on non-operational flights and the 'Acting Dog Pilot' was issued with its own 'Pilot's Flying Log Book' which recorded his flights with some often acerbic comments about Sammy's human co-pilots.***

OPPOSITE: 'Bulldog Rescued' ***1916 by Cyrus Cuneo (1879–1916). Cuneo, an Italian born in the US, came to Britain and worked as an artist on the*** **Illustrated London News.** ***His war paintings, including this one of the rescue of Norah, the mascot of the HMS*** **King Edward VII,** ***after the ship was hit by a mine, proved very popular and one raised enough money at auction for two ambulances, named after Cuneo, to be sent to France.***

BELOW: ***'War Dog, 1939–1945'. A red, white and blue collar issued to all British dogs that had been officially involved in war service during the Second World War.***

A photograph sent home to England probably in May 1917 by Lieutenant Lance Bettison, serving with the A Company, No.2 Platoon, Honourable Artillery Company in France. On the reverse of the card he wrote 'Don't think this is good enough for the* Daily Mirror*! Note the cockerel with the bow and the old cook holding the cat. The cockerel usually shares a kennel with my dog.'

Team in 1950. A goose, Jacob, had been rescued from the pot and adopted as the Royal Dragoons mascot in the 1920s, and a jackdaw, 'that most intelligent of birds', according to its fans, was the mascot of an 8th Air Force fighter squadron. A falcon named Cressida became the mascot of the Sherwood Foresters and was smuggled to North Africa with the soldiers. Fighting in Tunisia, her keeper, Lieutenant Summers, was injured by a shell burst that also caught the falcon's wing. Man and mascot were captured by the Germans and spent the rest of the war in a German POW camp where Cressida earned her keep by catching rats and mice and keeping up the spirits of the POWs.

A buffalo was the choice of the US 510th Tank Regiment stationed in Germany as part of the Allied occupation after the Second World War. An ant eater that refused to eat ants appealed to a company of US Marines in the First World War, while a baby elephant was kitted up in the colours of the 27th Squadron of RAF Strike Command stationed in Lincolnshire. It, again, was an appropriate choice: the squadron had an elephant on its crest and was known as the 'Flying Elephants' because in 1915 it had been equipped with the Martinsyde Scout, an aircraft nicknamed 'the elephant' because of its cumbersome appearance. Gorilla, which was actually a baboon, was adopted by a South African regiment in 1918, and was twice injured in battle. A racoon known as Willie flew with the US 6th Air Force, while the seafaring Coast Guards chose a seal, and in Guadalcanal the US Marine Corps wound a 5ft 8in snake, Zombie, round its guns as its mascot, and a US motor pool adopted what appears from the photographs to be a cobra while it was in Vietnam. Parrots, turtles and a wallaby complete the list, and then there was Poilu, the mascot of the 19th Division during the First World War: Poilu was a lion.

The regimental goat mascot of the Royal Inniskilling Fusiliers, 36th (Ulster) Division. Like the men, it is wearing a steel helmet, or 'tin hat' as the troops called it.

Although he had been acquired as a cub, Poilu soon grew to such a size, with a corresponding appetite, that a young aide-de-camp was detailed to provide food for the beast. Most mornings he would telephone around: 'Anyone got a dead horse this morning?' Poilu might have entertained the men in the trenches near the Ypres salient, but the top brass were less amused and intimated that he should be removed, to which the response was, in effect, 'fine: come and get him'. But when the division's commander, General Bridges, was wounded, his successor did not share his tolerance of the leonine mascot, and Poilu was finally crated back to Britain – though he managed to escape during the rough Channel crossing – and was settled in a private zoo where he died aged 19 in 1935.

Most mascots, however, fell somewhat short of the 'exotic' category. There was at least one mouse, there were pigs and pigeons and deer, mules, donkeys, Shetland ponies and rabbits with names like Smudge, Quanto (which was exceptionally fierce and rumoured to have been sired by a kangaroo though he had been born in Italy) and Muncher (the name is self-explanatory). As well as peacocks and pelicans and parrots and parakeets, there were several canaries, one of which, Jib, was a well-travelled troop ship's mascot that accompanied the men from North Africa to India, Italy, Canada and Singapore, and then back home from Rangoon with the men of the 14th Army. Jib could always be relied on to sing so exceptionally sweetly whenever a concert was organised on board that she was affectionately dubbed 'Old Nellie Wallace', after the music hall entertainer. There were a number of sheep, rams and goats, a fox, and several rabbits, and had all the dogs and cats been mustered together they would have probably formed a platoon or two of their own.

Cats were considered to be a useful addition to a ship's crew: some served as simple mousers, others had a more elevated status as mascots. There was Minnie, the mascot of HMS *Argonaut*, which was on board as troops stormed the Normandy beaches on D-Day, and who travelled the world until she went AWOL in Singapore in 1946 and the *Argonaut* had to return sadly without its mascot. There was Beauty, the cat mascot of HMS *Black*

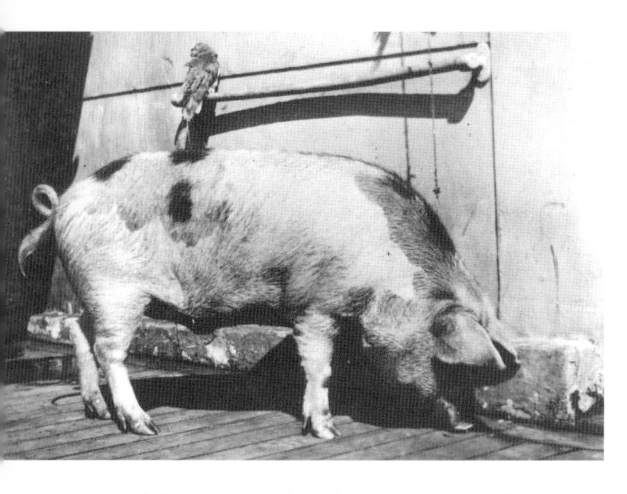

Tirpitz was aboard the German light cruiser Dresden when it was sunk by the Royal Navy on 14 May 1915. A sailor from HMS **Glasgow** *noticed the pig swimming in the sea and managed to rescue it. Tirpitz, named after Admiral Alfred von Tirpitz, Prussian Naval Minister and advocate of unrestricted submarine warfare, served as the mascot of the Glasgow for a year until being retired to the Whale Island Gunnery School in Portsmouth.*

A soldier plays with a kitten in the snow at Neulette on the Western Front on 17 December 1917.

Prince that actually gave birth to a litter of three kittens as her ship's guns pounded the beaches of Normandy prior to the D-Day landings. Whiskey, a tabby cat, managed to sleep through one of the naval triumphs of the Second World War when the guns of HMS *Duke of York* sunk the German battle cruiser *Scharnhorst*. Wren Figaro was a small black and white cat, adopted by a company of Wrens, that really understood the privations of war and preferred dried milk to the fresh variety. Rum and Coke were the mascots of the US 7th Anti Aircraft Artillery base on Okinawa. Murphy, a cat, survived the sinking of the US destroyer *Blue* in the Solomon Islands, and the mascot of the US 104th Infantry Division was a tiny kitten when he was adopted and given the wannabe name, Butch. And there was Preddy, a cat that was a co-mascot with a rabbit, Bofor, of the RAF regiment, and was reputed to be frustrated that she could never teach the rabbit to be a mouser. Also Andrew, a stray that had been taken in by a member of the Mascot Club's staff, was 'appointed' its mascot – possibly because he had an inverted white 'V' for victory on the bridge of his nose.

Ben, soon known as 'Benghazi Ben', was found abandoned by the 8th Army as it advanced towards El Alamein and was adopted as the 523rd Company Royal Army Service Corps' mascot. He travelled with them everywhere until he was run over by an army lorry in December 1943 in Syria and buried in the desert by his grieving company under a headstone that referred to the dog as 'one of us'. Sam started his career as a military mascot in the desert, too, this time with the 572nd Field Company, Royal Engineers. When his company was among the first troops to enter Naples, Sam went along too, and was present at the battle of Monte Cassino and the advance on Rome. When the Italian front had finally been mopped up, Sam, often sitting on the bonnet of an armoured car, was part of the advance into Austria.

Flash was a 'cross whippet Irish terrier bitch' enlisted at only six weeks old as the mascot of the 443rd Battery, 61st Field Regiment, Royal Artillery and she accompanied her master, Gunner Duffield, to Normandy in June 1944. According to Dorothea St Hill Bourne, as the gun tractor was going ashore the sea rushed in and the crew found themselves waist-deep in water. Flash had to be held aloft as the men scrambled ashore. From that inauspicious start, the dog followed Gunner Duffield from Caen to Emden and proved her worth by diving into a slit trench every time she sensed a shell was coming over as early warning for the soldiers. When the battery found itself short of rations, Flash supplemented supplies by bringing back hares and rabbits that she had caught, which were cooked up in an old petrol can with any vegetables that could be scavenged.

The Army did not enjoy a monopoly of mascot dogs – 'trade: mascot' read the WAAF (Women's Auxiliary Air Force) service document of Bungie, a liver and white springer spaniel, and his official rank was Flight Sergeant. Although Bungie adored flying and sat on the pilot's knee (though this was not permitted on operational flights), his main wartime task was as a recruiter, sitting in a van while his owner, Flight Officer B.W. Lecky signed up recruits for the RAF. When Lecky was posted to Berlin after the war to work with the British Control Commission, she decided to cut through bureaucratic red tape and list her dog as 'Welfare Equipment and Props', which was not at all a bad description for a lot of mascots.

Wimpy, a collie mascot of the WAAF band at RAF Hereford, was promoted to rank of Warrant Officer for 'good conduct and rat catching'. The stray collie also earned his stripes by parading at numerous 'Wings for Victory' events and 'Salute the Soldier'

Sir William Orpen RA (1878–1931): **'The Mascot of the Coldstream Guards'**, *1917, showing a small white goat. Orpen was an established portrait painter when war broke out in 1914 and was recruited as an official war artist at the end of 1916. Promoted to major, he was despatched to France where he painted portraits of a number of generals, privates and other war scenes. Following the armistice, he was appointed the official war artist at the Paris Peace Conference, but also registered his protest at the conduct of the political elite at the expense of the common soldiers in his controversial painting* **'To the Unknown British Soldier in France'.**

parades. Dinghy, the mascot of Royal Canadian Air Force (RCAF) squadron on Islay earned his accolades for being a performing dog, being 'shot' for a newsreel and entertaining the troops by doing tricks and barking out not only the number of days in the week but also the number of 'kills' achieved by his squadron. Blitz, a black and tan terrier that had lost an eye in an air raid (hence the name), was co-mascot with Group Captain Goat of 609 Squadron, and no pilot cared to set off on a mission unless he was certain that the two mascots were present at the base to 'guarantee' his safe return. A number of dogs – no doubt strictly against regulations – flew on 'ops', including Anthony, a mascot of the WAAFs at Kingsbridge in Devon. He was a seasoned flyer over France and Germany, while Stuka was the mascot of the famous US Flying Fortress bomber *Memphis Belle* and a veteran of 25 bombing raids over occupied France and Germany.

Rover, on the other hand, a rather elderly mongrel mascot, earned *his* spurs by keeping 'his' Staffordshire air base and the nearby Ministry of Supply dump free of rats that had previously constituted an infestation. Beauty, a large black Alsatian bitch, operated on the ground, too. She was the mascot of various WAAF balloon site operatives, moving round the country to help guard sites.

As did cats, so some dogs served as mascots on board ship. There was Pluto who served on HMS *Cossack*, which captured the German prison ship *Altmark*, was present at the second battle of Narvik, saw the *Bismarck* sunk in 1941 and then went down with his ship in the Mediterranean in 1942.

RIGHT: ***The draped coffin of Flight Sergeant Lewis, a goat that was the mascot of the RAF Association, is solemnly borne to its final resting place. Lewis was named after the 'goat' in the BBC comedy programme* Band Waggon *with Arthur Askey and Richard 'Stinker' Murdoch, which was hugely popular in 1938–9.***

OPPOSITE: ***An ATS girl and her pet dog wait at a London terminus in the early spring of 1944.***

A passer-by putting a donation in a collection box strapped to a poodle's back raising funds for the Royal Navy charities during the Second World War.

Bamsie, a huge St Bernard, was the mascot of a Norwegian warship, the *Thorod*, and he took his duties very seriously. Whenever the ship was in port and the sailors went ashore Bamsie would act as an anxious guardian, touring the local bars and rounding up 'his' charges to make sure they were back on ship in time and in reasonable shape. H. E. ('High Explosive') Kelly was a US Coast Guard mascot, born at sea – on an 83-footer in the Atlantic. He spent the war there and in the Pacific, hardly ever setting foot on dry land.

It was reckoned that Pepsie, a small brown terrier bitch, had travelled over 33,000 miles on board ship in less than two years when she became a member of the Mascot Club in January 1945. During one of her many trips across the Channel to Normandy, she had given birth to a litter of four puppies on board. Susanna, a small brown and white terrier, had been evacuated with her owner when Jersey was occupied by German troops in July 1940. Susie's owner settled in Britain, but the dog returned to sea as a mascot on the ship that had evacuated her, SS *Whitstable*. The dog would take her watch along with the sailors and went below to wake up the relief watch when it ended. When the ship was in port Susie would stand guard at the top of the gangplank and proved as good a rat catcher as any living creature.

Adelbert was the first ex-Nazi mascot to fill the same position for the Royal Navy. The wire-haired terrier was rescued from a U-boat sunk by HMS *Orwell* in August 1943, and according to his master 'quickly became English in outlook and mentality'. When HMS *Falmouth* sank five German trawlers in the North Sea, one of the survivors was a fox terrier found floating on a piece of wood. The dog was hauled aboard and adopted as mascot by the crew who, however, changed the name on his tag, Fritz, to Fred. Another Fritz acquired by the British was a St Bernard German police dog found roaming around

POW

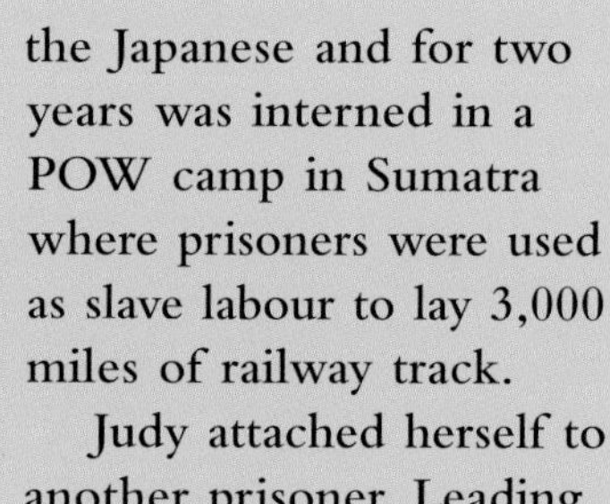

ABOVE: ***Judy, whose bark was heard on the BBC, wearing her medal.***

RIGHT: ***The Dickin Medal awarded to Judy, the only animal officially to have been a POW of the Japanese during the Second World War.***

'For magnificent courage and endurance in Japanese prison camps, thus helping to maintain morale among her fellow prisoners and for saving many lives by her intelligence and watchfulness,' ran the citation for an award to Judy. Judy was a pure-bred English pointer, born in Shanghai, who had been adopted as a mascot by the Royal Navy and served on a number of naval vessels.

When one was torpedoed, Judy, along with the crew, was captured by the Japanese and for two years was interned in a POW camp in Sumatra where prisoners were used as slave labour to lay 3,000 miles of railway track.

Judy attached herself to another prisoner, Leading Aircraftsman Frank Williams, and went everywhere with him. She threatened and distracted the guards on numerous occasions when they were brutalising prisoners. The dog was liberated in 1945 along with the POWs – and was an obvious candidate for the Dickin Medal.

during the battle for Arromanches on 7 June 1944. Later the dog arrived with a batch of German POWs in Britain. His death sentence was reprieved when a Leading Wren offered to pay his quarantine fee, and presented the dog to the Royal Hampshire Regiment, which adopted Fritz as its mascot, resplendent in a ceremonial coat embroidered with the names of the countries where the Hampshires had served.

But as the Mascot Club had always made clear, animal mascots were not the only animals that 'served' in wartime. Mascots were representatives of the thousands of animals that in various ways aided, comforted and cheered the troops, dogs like the 'one-eyed bitch wire-haired terrier' given to an ambulance driver, Albert Lowy, a private in the Royal Army Service Corps, who got permission to take her overseas with him when he was sent to Italy. 'X' (as Lowy refers to the dog in his memoirs) 'lived on bully beef and biscuits and never minded if I used her as a pillow at night'. In Italy Lowy 'was taken off my ambulance to be a despatch rider … I obtained an extra large rucksack and carried 'X' on my back wherever I had to go. She would sit in it with her head poking out and often resting on my shoulder, enjoying the rush of air: my back seat driver.' Problems came, however, when it was time to return to England. 'There is a strict law that any animal from abroad must spend four months in quarantine [in fact six] to ensure that it is not carrying rabies.' This had been a problem in the First World War, too. As the historian of the RSPCA said: 'British soldiers have a habit of collecting dogs wherever they may be stationed and the 1914–18 war was no exception to this trait.' To deal with the problem of soldiers at the front going home on leave, the society established some temporary kennels at Boulogne

The RAF makes friends with the jackdaw mascot of the troopship bringing the men back to Britain from France after Dunkirk in June 1940.

where the dogs could be housed and collected again when the men returned to war. When hostilities ceased the RSPCA stepped in again, starting the Soldiers' Dogs Fund to meet the cost of bringing the animals home and keeping them until their demobilised masters could take them. Five hundred kennels were specially built at Hackbridge in Surrey to accommodate the animals.

After the Second World War the War Office instigated a similar scheme. Quarantine kennels were set up for the animals of fighting men, who were charged on a sliding scale according to their rank. A corporal would pay £5 for the six-month period, while officers above the rank of captain would pay £20. The RSPCA had inspectors on hand at the various ports where men and their animals (usually dogs) would arrive and special wooden box kennels to be used in transporting the animals by train to the various quarantine kennels, would be standing ready.

As well as helping to reunite dogs with their masters, the RSPCA took a very

Peter, the mascot of a submarine depot ship, leaves one of the submarines after a visit. The dog was on board a German-manned ship from Vichy, France which was intercepted and sunk by a British submarine, and was rescued by a Royal Navy boarding party.

Able Seaman Simon

Featured in the film *The Yangtse Incident*, Simon is the only cat to be awarded the Dickin Medal.

The frigate HMS *Amethyst* was sailing up the Yangtse with supplies for the British Embassy in Nanking in April 1949, taking advantage of a temporary truce between the warring Chinese Communists under Mao Zedong and Chiang Kai-shek's Nationalists. Suddenly a salvo of shells rained onto the ship, killing 25 crew members and wounding many more, including the captain who died later. The ship then ran aground under Communist fire.

Simon, the *Amethyst's* mascot was badly injured in the incident, suffering burns and a punctured lung, but he recovered and became a focus and a distraction for his fellow ships mates during the 101 days they spent as the enforced 'guests' of the Communists. The black and white cat also kept the ship's rat and mouse population under control and for feline 'behaviour of the highest order' was nominated for a Dickin Medal. Sadly, his glory was short lived for Simon died in quarantine and the medal had to be awarded posthumously.

The plaque commemorating the role Simon played during the 'Yangtse Incident' in 1949.

A puppy abandoned by one of the 605 German soldiers who surrendered to the Allied troops in the battered citadel of St Mâlo, Brittany, in August 1944.

active role in animal welfare in the field. In the first four months of the Great War 90 of the Society's 230 employees enlisted in the Armed Forces, most joining the Army Veterinary Corps. The RSPCA sent out two horse ambulances for the use of the AVC, sheepskins and waterproof rugs for the horses, and 50,000 books on lameness and equine first aid. It began to train men to enlist in the AVC and its staff gave talks to hundreds of soldiers on the care and management of horses. The RSPCA Sick and Wounded Horse Fund raised over a quarter of a million pounds which was spent on building 13 hospitals, each with its own operating theatre, forage barns and dressing sheds. One hundred and eighty horse-drawn ambulances and 26 motorised ones were acquired and crates of bandages and medications despatched.

Lord Kitchener turned down the suggestion of the Blue Cross to provide veterinary care for animals at the front, but the French took up the offer and hospitals were set up at each of the four French depots under British control, and kennels were established to care for injured and sick dogs that had been working as messengers, guard dogs and on patrol.

On the outbreak of the Second World War the RSPCA offered the £20,000 balance of the Sick and Wounded Horse Fund to the government, and set up the War Animals (Allies) Fund. Help was also sent to the Finnish Army which, during its Winter War with Russia, was reported to have 12,000 sick horses. The RSPCA despatched thousands of blankets and hundreds of veterinary chests to the Middle East and then to Greece. After the German invasion of the Soviet Union in June 1941, sympathy for the Russians and the desire to aid (and keep on side) what was at last a major ally for Britain led to the setting up of the War Aid to Russia Fund. Winston Churchill's wife, Clementine, was its President, and 'since our

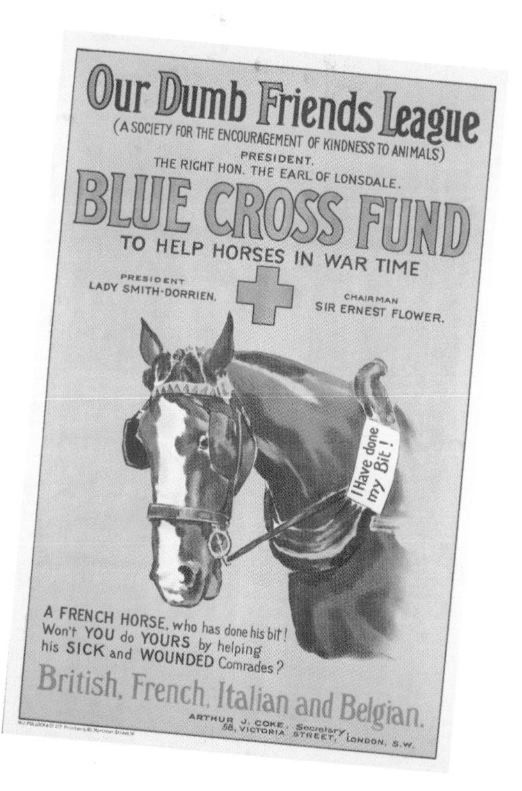

Demob

'Horses know not the stakes of war
Or why their riders fight;
They seek the haynet and the straw,
The ease and still of night.

'Yet, understanding naught, they stood
And held the line all day.
Ah! When the fire brake from the wood
They suffered where they lay…

'… Few lads enough returned to dance
In Bristol or in Bath,
But not one charger came to prance
Anew on English path.

'So beasts that bear and beasts that mount
Are mingled in the earth,
And those who run and ride may count
The beasts of equal worth.'

Thus wrote Laurence Cotterell, a trooper with the Middlesex and then the North Somerset Yeomanry who had fought with the cavalry against Vichy French forces in Syria during the Second World War, as a tribute to the horses that died in the service of their country. But what of those that did not perish? How was their service rewarded? The official history of the Veterinary Services in the Great War makes bleak reading. In a chapter headed 'Disposal of Animals' a table details the number of horses sold at auction to farmers and breeders (7,775), those sold to Paris horse butchers (28,384) and those to local horse butchers (16,578). In addition, some 11,000 horses were 'dealt with by butchery detachments or departments and sold as carcasses or issued to prisoners of war or dealt with by horse carcass economizer plants by conversion into by-products' and the 'approximate amount realized' by these means was £858,377.

After the Second World War the problem of what to do with the animals was again acute: an example was the surrender of the enemy forces in Austria on 8 May 1945, which left a small area 'about the size of Wales ... suddenly swamped with an influx of over 58,000 hungry, fatigued horses. The country had no forage stocks to speak of, either military or civil, so that all these animals had to be fed entirely from the immediate countryside ... animals in a concentration of 10,000 or more consume the countryside at an amazing rate, and, what is more, they consume crops destined for human consumption.' Fortunately, the surrender had come in the spring when the countryside was verdant, but nevertheless 700 horses a day were eventually dispatched for agricultural work, which 'did something towards getting Europe busy on the production of its own food'. Others were 'at first regarded as the spoils of war, as one might acquire a car, motor-cycle or even a motor-boat. First come, first served was the natural rule, and flushed with victory, the British soldier was not slow to enjoy the fruits thereof. It was no unusual sight to see Tommy Atkins going full tilt down the tarmac road hanging onto the front arch of a heavy German saddle and, ignorance being bliss, thoroughly enjoying himself and not realising for a moment that his horse was not equally enthralled,' according to a member of the Royal Army Veterinary Corps.

Nevertheless, of those horses that could not be dispersed for agricultural purposes as soon as possible before they became 'useless from emaciation', thousands were slaughtered for food for near starving displaced persons, although the RAVC made 'every effort to avoid the slaughter of any young or potentially useful animal.'

However, for thousands of horses requisitioned by the Army for the

Dorothy Brooke with some of the 5,000 ex-British Army horses which were rescued by the hospital she established in Cairo.

campaigns in the Near East and Palestine during the First World War there was, if not a reward, at least a sanctuary, thanks to the efforts of an Englishwoman, Dorothy Brooke. Living in Cairo, where her husband, a Brigadier-General, had been posted, Mrs Brooke was horrified to discover that at the end of the war some 2,000 British and Australian cavalry horses had been sold to gharry drivers. Old, exhausted and decrepit as the animals might be after wartime service, they were still trudging round the dusty streets pulling carts and even working in the stone quarries of Egypt. 'Always hungry, weak, overloaded to a degree, lame, crippled, galled, ill-shod, frequently blind, suffering from perpetual thirst, tormented by flies ... straining under the whip,' they laboured on.

Determined to secure a better retirement for these veterans, Mrs Brooke wrote a letter to the press about the horses' plight and was rewarded with an avalanche of cheques and postal orders. The first Brooke Hospital for Animals was established in 1934, vets were appointed and some 5,000 ex-Army horses were rescued and given food and comfortable stables, while those that were old and ill were humanely destroyed.

Over 70 years later, the charity still operates hospitals in Egypt, Pakistan, India and Jordan and also works in Afghanistan, South America and Africa helping animals afflicted by war. It also helps the owners – war victims, too – because in many cases 'they have nothing but their horse to rely on and if you take that away, they'll be left with nothing at all.'

RIGHT: ***'... Republican leaders have not been content with attacks on me, or my wife or sons,' complained President Roosevelt in a speech during the 1944 presidential election campaign. 'They now include my little dog, Fala*** **[pictured right]** ***... he resents this. Being a Scottie, as soon as he learned that the Republican fiction-writers had concocted a story that I had left him behind on an Aleutian island and had sent a destroyer back to find him at a cost to the tax payers of two or three or twenty million dollars – his Scottish soul was furious. He has not been the same dog since. I am accustomed to hearing malicious falsehoods about myself ... But I think I have the right to object to libellous statements about my dog.' A statue of Fala stands at the Franklin D. Roosevelt Memorial in Washington DC.***

struggle and Russia's are indissolubly linked' the RSPCA set up a specific organisation to raise money to aid to Russian horses. By August 1943, the fund had raised over £40,000, and vast quantities of drugs and hospital equipment were despatched to Russia.

Notwithstanding these larger concerns, the problem of getting his mutt home continued to exercise Private Lowy. He had written 'to the proper authority for papers, but perhaps due to my being a mere private, I got no reply. I therefore determined to try to smuggle my darling "X" back to England.'

All the way to Cherbourg, Lowy kept 'X' quiet but when he arrived at the camp to await embarkation he found officers patrolling the tents, looking for dogs. '"X" had to spend quite a lot of time in my bag, lying quite still and no one suspected that an animal was hidden.' He somehow managed to stagger aboard with 'X' (who was no light weight) concealed in his kit bag. When they arrived in Britain, it was to find that there was a train strike and Lowy was wracked with anxiety that, with all the waiting around, 'X' might still be discovered and sent back to France. Finally, Lowy and 'X' got on a train in which they travelled like sardines to Wimbledon, where, in a crush of marching soldiers, 'X' got separated from Lowy. It wasn't until an hour and a half later that the two were joyfully reunited at the demobilisation camp.

Finally Private Lowy was issued with his demob suit, signed his discharge papers, and the pair set off for home, the war truly over at last for man and dog.

RIGHT: ***'I love animals, and especially dogs,' proclaimed Hitler in one of his 'table talks' on the night of 25–26 January 1942. In the First World War he owned a dog called Foxl. 'It was crazy how fond I was of that beast ... I used to share everything with him ... when I had to go into the line, and there was a lot of shelling, I used to tie him up in the trench. My comrades told me that he took no interest in anyone during my absence.' In the Second World War the Führer's favourite dog was Blondi, a grey German shepherd given to him by Martin Bormann. According to his secretary, Hitler had trained it to be 'one of the cleverest, most agile dogs I ever saw ... [Hitler] said he relaxed best in the dog's company.' But on the final days in the Berlin bunker at the end of April 1945, Hitler's near vegetarian, herb-eating dog was taken into the toilet and an ampoule of cyanide was forced down her throat. 'Soon after, Hitler showed up and went into the toilet to make sure Blondi was dead. He did not say a word nor betray any emotion.'***

Churchill's Pets

'This cat,' said Winston Churchill to R. A. Butler, then President of the Board of Education, pointing to his black cat Nelson who inhabited No 10 Downing Street, 'does more for the war effort than you do. He acts as a hot water bottle and saves fuel and power.' The wartime Prime Minister was very fond of animals: as a young man he had dogs that went by such names as Pinky Poo and Peas, each of his children owned a dog and from the 1950s he had a succession of chocolate-coloured poodles. He owned racehorses, became sentimental about some goats in Marrakech, took a great delight in the white and black swans that swam on the lake at Chartwell, his house in the Kent countryside, developed a penchant for tropical fish, frequently dictated letters and memoranda with a cigar clamped in his mouth and a budgerigar perched on his head, and was once reported as saying 'the world would be better off if it were only inhabited by animals' – though that was after a fox had killed one of his beloved black swans, and it presumably excluded the fox.

Winston Churchill is introduced to General Bernard Montgomery's spaniel in Normandy. The dog was named Rommel, after the man whose forces Montgomery had triumphed over in the Western Desert.

9 The Home Front

In 1939 Britain had a human population of about 48 million. Its animal population was estimated to be between six and seven million dogs and cats, more than 56 million poultry and some 37.5 million farm animals. That is, there were nearly twice as many domestic animals in Britain as there were human beings. So, what, a leaflet issued published under the auspices of the Home Office asked pertinently, 'is to be done about animals in wartime?'

Wartime demands would be made of all in what became known as the 'people's war', equality of sacrifice would be called on from all, danger would be shared by all. And animals would be right there on the front line, too. On the one hand, many would be valued for their wartime roles, some even decorated for their wartime bravery. On the other, there would be periodic disquisitions as to whether, when the nation was at war, animals were a distraction, a luxury even, that it could ill afford.

A government leaflet pointed out that 'animals, like human beings, will be exposed to the risks of air attack in a modern war, and everyone will wish, both from practical and humane motives, to do what is possible to protect them and relieve their suffering.' But it went on to caution that 'dogs and cats and other pets must be considered the responsibility of their owners'.

RSPCA poster showing a lithograph by Leonard Raven Hill reminding owners that horses on the Home Front had suffered by having their feed rationed during the First World War.

Winston Churchill metamorphoses into a British bulldog in a cartoon by Wells, **circa** *1941.*

A mobile PDSA (People's Dispensary for Sick Animals) clinic set up in front of its bombed premises, giving medical aid to Londoners' pets during the Second World War.

People fleeing the cities crammed the family pets into their cars – muzzles were recommended for dogs but probably few took this advice. One man, who intended to leave London, walked into the foyer of the Rialto cinema in Enfield and enquired whether his six goldfish could be accommodated in the ornamental pool in the foyer for the duration. The Home Office had warned that 'school pets such as rabbits, guinea-pigs etc, housed on school premises for the primary training of children in the care of and kindliness to animals will have to be destroyed unless they have been evacuated in advance or satisfactory arrangements have been made to leave them in charge of the caretakers.' The RSPCA stepped in and when London schools were evacuated, on 1 September 1939, over 500 animals from some 69 schools were taken to Homes of Rest in Surrey and Hertfordshire and 'every animal was carefully labelled'. The Society also volunteered to take care of any guide dogs if their blind owners were not able to take the animals with them when they were evacuated, and two owners took up their offer. One man pleaded: 'Please see that "Boy" is well looked after, for … he is my eyes and I now feel that I am blinded all over again. You will find him gentle and without a single vice. Please, please see that he comes back to me all right when all this trouble is over …'

The Duchess of Hamilton appealed for country dwellers to offer wartime homes for unaccompanied pets living in towns and cities where bombs were expected to fall. Advertisements appeared in *The Times*, the *Lady*, and other publications offering temporary billets for animals. Prior to the outbreak of war on 3 September 1939, a firm in Donegal had suggested 'Evacuate dogs for a holiday to neutral territory. Ten shillings a week, gun dogs £1', while budgerigars could be evacuated for as little as a penny a day.

An advertisement in the RSPCA magazine **Animal World** *for a stun gun. It appeared in the autumn of 1944 during the V1 and V2 attacks.*

But for a distressingly large number of animals it was less a case of relocation than of termination. Anxious that the bombs would terrify if not kill or maim their animals, unsure how to protect them and worried about how to feed them, euthanasia seemed the only option – indeed, some pet owners seem to have been convinced that it was a government wartime regulation like putting up black out. No official figures exist as to how many animals were slaughtered in those first few weeks of what turned out to be a 'phoney war', with no major air raids for a further year. Vets would find their surgeries crammed with people demanding to have their pets put down. Some found this so distressing that they moved their practices to the country, while others stoically administered the lethal dose and left the animal corpses piled outside under tarpaulins, awaiting collection by overworked firms that specialised in such grisly disposal.

The RSPCA had given an assurance that all its clinics in the Metropolitan Police area would 'be open day and night for the euthanasia of small animals. Large supplies of chloroform, ammunition, drugs and dressings were secured, and arrangements were made by which double staff was available at every clinic.' It was just as well. 'From [1 September] onwards all the Society's clinics in the London area were working at high pressure, day and night. The clinics of other welfare societies were employed in the same way, so the work of destroying animals was continued, day and night, during the first week of the war.' The society did advise, however, that it might be better to wait before taking such a final step.

A Sunday newspaper reported that the dead animals were being taken by vans from all over London to a secret burial ground in East London and that, on one night alone, 80,000 carcasses had been tipped in. Questions were asked in the House about exactly what local authorities were doing about the disposal of these animals. The response was non-committal. The PDSA, which believed that animals should not be needlessly destroyed, 'for our many years of experience in dealing with animals has proved that they possess an inhuman sense of escape', nevertheless had to bow to the pressure, and offered 'the use of a meadow in the grounds of our Sanatorium' as a mass burial pit which 'necessitated finding transport, procuring 40 tons of lime, and extra labour'. Some estimates put the death toll in those first few weeks of war at over two million, but the RSPCA thought it was more likely that around 200,000 dogs had been put down. There were fears that the cull of cats would lead to a plague of vermin, as had been the case in Spain during the Civil War.

By no means all city pets had such a gruesome – and, it has to be said, largely unnecessary – end and many owners were conscientious in planning how to look after their animals in wartime. There was plenty of advice. One good thing was that in the Second World War dogs of clearly Germanic descent were not vilified as they had been in the First. Dachshunds, for example, could waddle around the city pavements with no fear of being stoned or spat upon. Indeed, when it was discovered that in his haste to leave his embassy and return to the Fatherland, the German Chargé d'Affaires, Theo

A cow on an Essex farm is painted with white stripes in September 1939 so that it will be visible in the black out.

Kordt, had abandoned the Embassy dog, 200 people came forward offering to give the Chow a home.

Pets were not allowed in public shelters since no one quite knew how they might react when the bombs began to fall – and there was the question of hygiene. It was suggested that a dog could be secured outside the shelter - which must have been terrifying – and the National Air Raid Precautions for Animals Committee (NARPAC), set up by the Home Office, studded white posts all over Hyde Park with chains and leads attached so that dogs could be tethered. An air raid shelter exclusively for dogs was built in Kensington Gardens in 1940. It accommodated 36 animals, cost over £100 to build, and was intended to be 'blast-proof and splinter-proof'. There were criticisms in the press that 'to build a shelter for dogs is a disgraceful display of maudlin sentimentality – until every woman and child in this country has been properly provided with safe and healthy shelters' which, when the article appeared, they certainly had not. However, the Anti-Vivisection Society countered: 'having accepted the responsibility of domesticating dogs, it is the bounden duty of their owners to provide them with adequate protection against physical injury'.

Alternatively, when the air raid siren sounded, a dog or cat could be left in the house as the family set off for the public shelter. The RSPCA advised that, if this was the case, the animal should not be shut in one room, but given the run of the house. Or the pet could be taken into the Anderson shelter in the garden, if there was one. The RSPCA's

Poster by S. R. Chilvers urging the British to save their waste for the war effort, following the example of a dog.

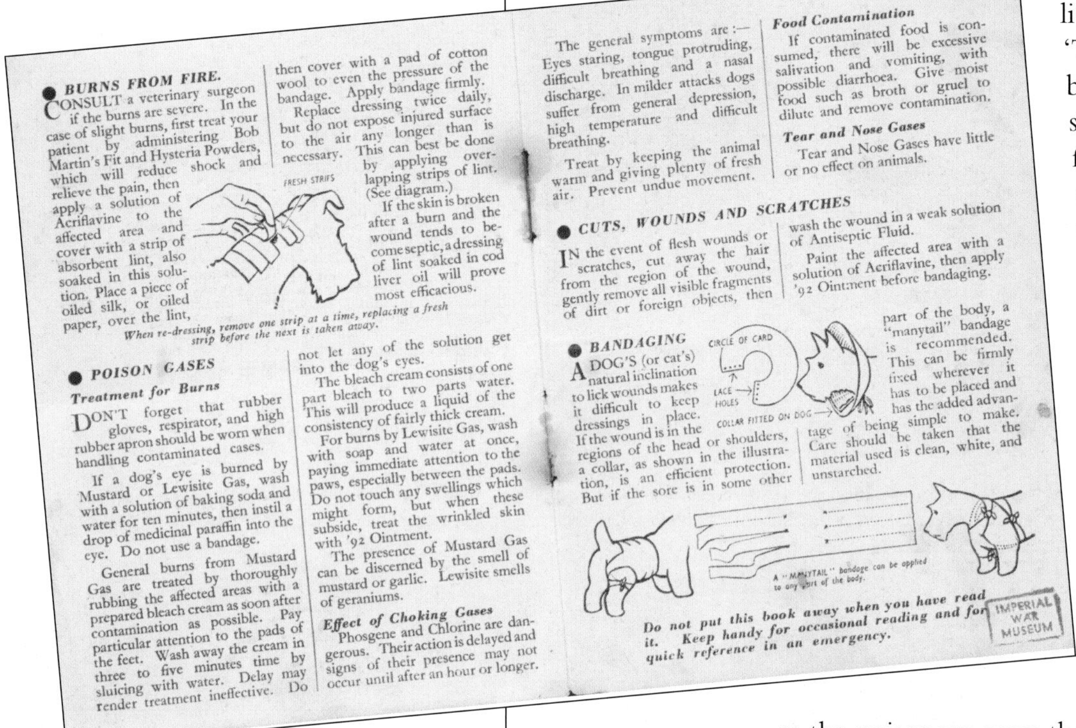

● BURNS FROM FIRE.

CONSULT a veterinary surgeon if the burns are severe. In the case of slight burns, first treat your patient by administering Bob Martin's Fit and Hysteria Powders, which will reduce shock and relieve the pain, then apply a solution of Acriflavine to the affected area and cover with a strip of absorbent lint, also soaked in this solution. Place a piece of oiled silk, or oiled paper, over the lint, then cover with a pad of cotton wool to even the pressure of the bandage. Apply bandage firmly.

Replace dressing twice daily, but do not expose injured surface to the air any longer than is necessary. This can best be done by applying overlapping strips of lint. (See diagram.)

If the skin is broken after a burn and the wound tends to become septic, a dressing of lint soaked in cod liver oil will prove most efficacious.

When re-dressing, remove one strip at a time, replacing a fresh strip before the next is taken away.

● POISON GASES

Treatment for Burns

DON'T forget that rubber gloves, respirator, and high rubber apron should be worn when handling contaminated cases.

If a dog's eye is burned by Mustard or Lewisite Gas, wash with a solution of baking soda and water for ten minutes, then instil a drop of medicinal paraffin into the eye. Do not use a bandage.

General burns from Mustard Gas are treated by thoroughly rubbing the affected areas with a prepared bleach cream as soon after contamination as possible. Pay particular attention to the pads of the feet. Wash away the cream in three to five minutes time by sluicing with water. Delay may render treatment ineffective. Do not let any of the solution get into the dog's eyes.

The bleach cream consists of one part bleach to two parts water. This will produce a liquid of the consistency of fairly thick cream.

For burns by Lewisite Gas, wash with soap and water at once, paying immediate attention to the paws, especially between the pads. Do not touch any swellings which might form, but when these subside, treat the wrinkled skin with '92 Ointment.

The presence of Mustard Gas can be discerned by the smell of mustard or garlic. Lewisite smells of geraniums.

Effect of Choking Gases

Phosgene and Chlorine are dangerous. Their action is delayed and signs of their presence may not occur until after an hour or longer.

The general symptoms are:— Eyes staring, tongue protruding, difficult breathing and a nasal discharge. In milder attacks dogs suffer from general depression, high temperature and difficult breathing.

Treat by keeping the animal warm and giving plenty of fresh air. Prevent undue movement.

Food Contamination

If contaminated food is consumed, there will be excessive salivation and vomiting, with possible diarrhoea. Give moist food such as broth or gruel to dilute and remove contamination.

Tear and Nose Gases

Tear and Nose Gases have little or no effect on animals.

● CUTS, WOUNDS AND SCRATCHES

IN the event of flesh wounds or scratches, cut away the hair from the region of the wound, gently remove all visible fragments of dirt or foreign objects, then wash the wound in a weak solution of Antiseptic Fluid.

Paint the affected area with a solution of Acriflavine, then apply '92 Ointment before bandaging.

● BANDAGING

A DOG'S (or cat's) natural inclination to lick wounds makes it difficult to keep dressings in place. If the wound is in the regions of the head or shoulders, a collar, as shown in the illustration, is an efficient protection. But if the sore is in some other part of the body, a "manytail" bandage is recommended. This can be firmly fixed wherever it has to be placed and has the added advantage of being simple to make. Care should be taken that the material used is clean, white, and unstarched.

Do not put this book away when you have read it. Keep handy for occasional reading and for quick reference in an emergency.

IMPERIAL WAR MUSEUM

Advice to dog owners about how to treat a pet suffering a war injury or from the effects of gas, from* Your Dog and Cat in Wartime*, 1939.

OPPOSITE: ***This elderly man had taken his dog for a walk in Norwood before his Saturday midday meal on 1 July 1944. While out, a V1 flying bomb landed, completely destroying his house and killing his wife.***

suggestion of a dustbin dug out for dogs, its lid perforated with holes, got short shift. 'The proper place for a dog when bombs begin to fall is with his human friends … shutting him up in a dustbin may save him from the physical impact of high explosives, but the subsequent opening of the "chamber of horrors" is likely to discover a completely mad dog.' What *was* recommended was that dogs of a nervous disposition could be dosed with bromide – two tablets for a terrier-sized dog crushed and put on the tongue – or, if bromide was hard to find, aspirin would do: half a tablet for a Pekinese and two for an Alsatian. Soon the pet food manufacturer, Bob Martin, was promoting its 'Fit and Hysteria (ARP) Powders' for the purpose.

Householders had been warned to prepare a gas-proof room in their home as the poisonous gases that had been released in the trenches in the First World War were feared on the Home Front in the Second. The human population had all been issued with gas masks – and it was advised that 'you should get your dog accustomed to seeing you in a gas mask for your appearance and the sound of your voice will be unfamiliar.' Although messenger dogs had been fitted with masks in the First World War, their use was not generally recommended. The RSPCA ventured that '*some* dogs will submit … to having a wad of cotton wool placed under its ear flaps tied on with a sort of surgical mask' but warned that '*few cats will tolerate anything of the kind*'. A better solution was to place a cloth soaked in water or a solution of permanganate of potash or a glycerine and washing soda solution over the kennel or basket, or invest in one of the gas-proof kennels. In these the bellows attached to the floor were operated by the animal's breathing and they were offered for sale by the PDSA at £4 each – though the RSPCA was 'against these' since if the animal's owner became a casualty of a raid 'the animal may be overlooked and die of starvation'. Birds, of course, were also vulnerable to gas and similarly soaked cloths should be hung over their cages, too. Government leaflets were issued advising treatments for the effects of a gas attack on animals as on humans – with terrifying scenarios involving burning gas, blistering gas, choking gas, tear gas or mustard gas. In the case of animals it was advised that a contaminated cat or dog would need to be shot and special stun guns were sold for the purpose. Thankfully, gas attacks were never launched against Britain.

The NARPAC instigated a scheme by which dogs and cats could be registered. They would be issued with a numbered disc to be attached to an elastic collar and then if they were found wandering after a raid they could be traced back to their owner. It was,

Evacuees from the Chapman LCC school, Whitechapel, in London's East End, feed the pigs on a farm in Pembrokeshire, Wales, in 1940.

however, strongly urged that dogs should not be let out during the black out as they could be a danger to cyclists and to pedestrians liable to trip over them in the stygian gloom. The dogs would themselves be at risk from motorists whose dimmed headlights could not easily pick out a canine form.

Another scheme involved people putting a card in the window of their house specifying what animals were present – and how many – so that, again, in the event of a raid, wardens would know the extent of those who might lie buried under the debris. First aid posts for animals comparable to those for humans were set up and as ARP wardens rushed to their posts when the alert went, so PDSA staff manned theirs, and stayed in post until an hour after the 'All Clear' sounded so anyone could bring in an injured animal for treatment.

Squadrons of animal first-aid ambulances operated in London and other major cities, and staff wearing protective tin hats would go out in search of injured animals. This often involved climbing into bombed and sometimes still burning buildings where there was believed to be a trapped animal. The RSPCA had developed a 'cat and dog grasper' during the First World War when there had been a massive explosion at a TNT processing works in Silvertown in London's East End and it had been necessary to extract hundreds of cats and dogs that were so terrified that they would not let anyone rescue them. This was found to be extremely useful in the Blitz when animals were wedged under debris. Rescue dogs might join in the search, sniffing out the victims. When the bricks and rubble had been painstakingly cleared away and the victim extracted, the animal would be taken to a first-aid post, a mobile surgery equipped with medicines, bandages, splints

Cat in a bombed out building. Cats would often return and live in the wreckage of their former homes.

and an operating table, or by animal ambulance to a dispensary. Delayed-action bombs brought particular problems: the area would have to be evacuated speedily and animals might be left behind in unoccupied premises, sometimes for days. RSPCA inspectors were intrepid in venturing in to such buildings to rescue animals – sometimes at considerable peril to their own lives. In one incident some pigs were trapped but as the authorities feared that the vibrations of a motor vehicle might detonate the unexploded bomb, the pigs had to be brought out individually in large sacks slung over the inspectors' shoulders.

When the V1 'flying bombs' started to fall on Britain in June 1944, the work of animal rescue accelerated: between June and September 16,265 animal victims were dealt with. In towns and cities these tended to be dogs and cats though according to the RSPCA 'one peculiar feature of the bombing was the number of fowl killed outright' and many chickens and bantams, which householders had started to keep during the war, might be liberated by the blast and found wandering the streets.

Some animals stood up to raids better than others. Dogs could be traumatised even if not actually injured, canaries were particularly resilient while budgerigars often ingested dust and expired. Goldfish hardly stood much of a chance if a piece of masonry fell in their bowl and shattered it. The aftermath of any major raid left animals dead, wounded, homeless or abandoned, and soon colonies of near feral stray cats could be found scavenging on the bomb sites of most cities.

Dogs – and occasionally cats – were often credited with animal intuition, and superior hearing, so they would act as a customised alert system. Hearing the approach of enemy

Faith, the tabby cat belonging to the vicar of St Augustine's Church, Watling Street, near the Mansion House in the City of London. Faith normally slept with her kitten in an upstairs room at the vicarage, but one day she insisted on carrying it three floors downstairs to lodge it in a cubby hole where music was stored. The vicar kept carrying the kitten upstairs, Faith kept bringing it down until the vicar gave in and moved Faith's basket to the cubby hole. Three days later the vicarage was badly bombed, the roof fell in and fire raged, but Faith and her kitten were safe.

Zoos at War

'The first thing I did ... was to see that the black widow spiders and the poisonous snakes were killed, sad though it was,' wrote Julian Huxley, Director of the London Zoo on the outbreak of the Second World War. 'I closed the aquarium and had its tanks emptied; and arranged that the elephants, who might well have run amok if frightened by the expected bombing (elephants are very nervous creatures) be moved to Whipsnade.' Huxley had previously set up an air squad of keepers, allowed by special dispensation to carry rifles, to be on guard during the night, and the head keeper was instructed to shoot any dangerous animal that might escape during a raid. The director also organised an Animal Adoption scheme under which individuals and organisations could pay for the upkeep of any animal they chose and in return have their name put on its cage – which proved a canny move when so many of the Zoo's potential visitors were evacuated to the country. There were other minor problems to be overcome, including the need for the Zoo to breed its own mealworms to feed insectivorous birds and mammals rather than importing them from Germany.

A bomb did hit the Zoo on 26 September 1940, and though the camel house was badly damaged the camels were unhurt and unperturbed, and firemen managed to contain the blaze by siphoning water from the sea lion pond as the water mains had been hit.

The Berlin Zoo was bombed several times, with the worst raid coming in November 1943 when scores of animals were killed, and soon afterwards many of those remaining were evacuated to other zoos. In 1939 there had been 14,000 animals, birds, reptiles and fish; by early 1945 there were around 1,600 and these were becoming increasingly difficult to feed as Allied attacks grew fiercer and Allied troops drew nearer. Only one out of the original nine elephants remained, the huge 530lb gorilla Pongo had lost weight and Rosa the hippo was wasting away. The lions, bears, zebras, monkeys and rare wild horses were all suffering from vitamin deficiencies and the keeper of rare cattle suspected that some of his missing animals had been stolen by Berliners, desperate for food.

As the end of Hitler's Third Reich drew close, the Zoo was devastated again. Rosa was killed in her pool by a shell, the lions had been shot, birds flew around in terror and finally the Zoo's director decided he would have to shoot the rare baboon that he had personally brought from the Cameroons.

In Baghdad in May 2003 a sign reading 'No Alibaba' hung outside the Zoo. It meant 'no thieving'. But it was too late. Only a small number of animals – lions, cheetahs, brown bears, wild pigs, ostriches and a porcupine – were left: 650 had been slaughtered or looted for sale or possibly consumption in the bitter fight for the capital of Iraq. In Afghanistan, Marjan, the blind lion found in Kabul Zoo after the overthrow of the Taliban, became a symbol of animals injured in modern-day warfare and in Iraq, US soldiers were unsure what to do with those the animals that were left there – many of them dangerous carnivores – too dangerous to steal. 'We didn't really know too much about lions and tigers,' admitted a young soldier from Illinois to a journalist from *The Times*. 'We would find dead birds and ducks and put them in the cages ... and we gave them dates and MREs (meals ready to eat) that the guys didn't like. They ate everything we gave them.'

A rare 14-year-old Bengal tiger – an endangered species – suffered even more in this 'war of liberation' in September 2003 when he mauled the arm and bit off the finger of a US soldier who allegedly climbed into the beast's outer cage when drunk. The tiger was then shot dead by another US soldier.

ABOVE: *Mandor, a Siberian tiger belonging to Saddam Hussein's son, Uday, in his enclosure at Baghdad's zoo on 23 April 2003. The tiger was left starving and neglected after the zoo had been attacked and looted.*

OPPOSITE: *Carel Weight (1908–97):* **'Escape of the Zebra from the Zoo during an Air Raid'.** *After London Zoo was bombed, a zebra escaped and was seen cantering through Regent's Park. The Zoo's director, Julian Huxley, and its air-raid squad set out in pursuit and managed to head the stallion back, but it took a great deal of persuasion to coax him back into a shed. Weight was commissioned by the War Artists' Advisory Committee to recapture the scene.*

Rip, accompanying his Civil Defence warden master on his nightly rounds, pays a morale-boosting visit to children taking refuge in a London street shelter.

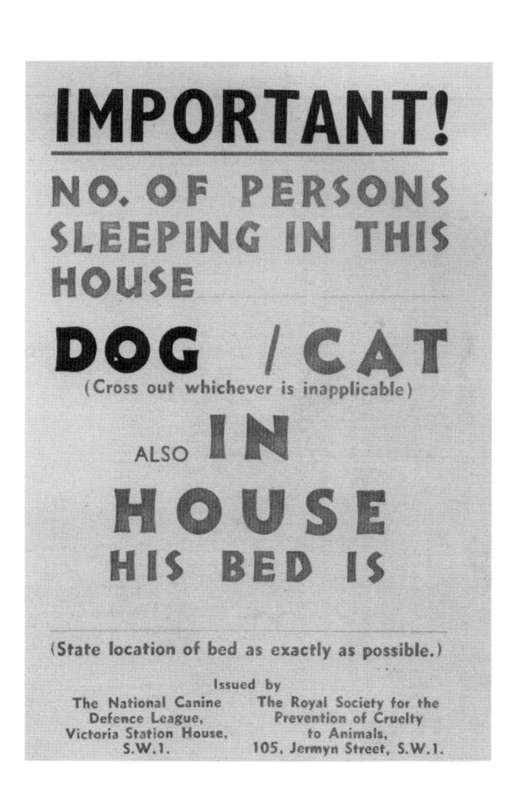

IMPORTANT!

NO. OF PERSONS SLEEPING IN THIS HOUSE

DOG / CAT

(Cross out whichever is inapplicable)

ALSO IN HOUSE

HIS BED IS

(State location of bed as exactly as possible.)

Issued by

The National Canine Defence League, Victoria Station House, S.W.1.

The Royal Society for the Prevention of Cruelty to Animals, 105, Jermyn Street, S.W.1.

raiders even before the siren went they would take refuge themselves or round up the family and nudge its members into the Anderson shelter or wherever they customarily took shelter during a raid. But even those pets that provided no such useful service were often particularly valued in wartime for the amusement, companionship and comfort they gave in disturbing and often frightening times.

Keeping pets in wartime was not easy. The Waste of Food Order, 1940, was translated by some to mean that it was illegal to feed animals with food that could have been consumed by human beings, but the RSPCA was quick to point out that was not actually the case even though a woman was reported to have been prosecuted for putting out breadcrumbs on her bird table. The point was to avoid profligate waste in time of war when it was hazardous to import food and shipping space was needed for troops, the matériel of war and essential food for the population. Since food was rationed, pet owners had to be scrupulously careful to feed their animals only food that was a) plentiful, b) grown in the UK or c) not suitable for human beings. Although it might be acceptable to feed the scraps off your plate to your pet, food shortages and rationing which bit harder as the war progressed ensured that there were unlikely to be many such titbits any more. Meat was rationed, as were a number of other commodities, but fish wasn't, though it was

ABOVE: ***'All that is left'. Civil Defence workers carry a pet bird in its cage after a V1 'incident' on 1 July 1944 in Norwood, London SE19.***

LEFT: ***Two London cats join the other shelterers in a West End shelter during an air raid*** **circa** ***November 1940.***

often hard to obtain and, if a harassed housewife did manage to procure it, it would be served to the family not the family pet. But fish still had heads and tails and these could be fed to animals. Offal was never 'on the ration' and though a dog would be unlikely to be fed liver in wartime, tripe, testicles, lungs and windpipes and the like might come its way. Horsemeat could also be used, though it had to be cut in strips and boiled first then mixed with stale bread, boiled rice, oatmeal, haricot beans or whatever was available to give bulk. Vegetables were never rationed either and it was suggested that dogs could be fed things like turnip tops and cabbage stalks. Although potatoes were not normally recommended, on account of their high starch content, it made sense to 'put in a few extra tubers when digging for Victory' which could be mixed with the gravy obtained from boiling up bones (though the bones themselves were needed for salvage). Cats could 'enjoy' a similar diet, particularly if a little sardine oil or stock made from fish trimmings was stirred in and both would benefit from bones from game, poultry or rabbits crushed by a hammer 'and reduced to fragments not larger than a split pea' which would provide essential calcium.

There were periodic calls for food for animals to be rationed to ensure fair shares, but the additional bureaucracy involved was a disincentive. As the Parliamentary Secretary to

PRIVATE AND CONFIDENTIAL

NATIONAL A.R.P. FOR ANIMALS COMMITTEE

REPORT ON CASUALTIES

Date.	Number and Class of Animal Involved.	Approx. Age.	Cause. (State Numbers.)				Nature of Injury.	Action Taken. State Numbers.)			Approx. Value. £	Remarks.
			H.E.	I.	M.G.	G.		T.	S.	D.		
23 Jan 1941.	1 Pony.	9	Yes.	—	—	—	Puncture wounds due to splinters	Yes.	—	—	£12	Splinters extracted, treatment successful.

H.E. = High Explosive
I. = Incendiary Bomb
M.G. = Machine Gunned
G. = Gassed

T. = Treated
~~S. = Salvaged~~
~~D. = Destroyed~~

Owner's Name Miss Arran
Address [illegible]
Berden Essex

Report made by [illegible] M.R.C.V.S
Address 14 Rye Street
Bp's Stortford Herts.

Valuation assessed by * Veterinary Surgeon.
~~Auctioneer.~~
~~Slaughterhouse Agent.~~
~~Parish Animal Steward.~~

Please delete designations which do not apply.

Original report to be retained by owner.
Duplicate copy to be sent to :
CHIEF EXECUTIVE OFFICER, N.A.R.P.A.C.,
36, GORDON SQUARE, LONDON, W.C.1.

ABOVE: ***A National ARP for Animals Committee report on injuries sustained by a nine-year-old pony as a result of high-explosive bombs during a raid on 23 January 1941.***

the Ministry of Food explained in answer to a question about rationing horsemeat: 'this would mean setting up more machinery. It would, for instance, be rather difficult to try to make a census of cats.'

Since imported seeds for canaries, budgerigars and parrots had been cut right back to save on shipping space, owners had to grow their own and were encouraged to plant teasel, hemp, linseed and sunflower, and even to have a go with millet (hard to grow in Britain's chilly climate). However, much could be garnered in the hedgerows and those who kept goats were encouraged to mow roadside verges for their sustenance. An anxious enquiry elicited the information that though the cost of lettuces was prohibitive by August 1940, tortoises 'will thrive quite well on oranges and bananas and if placed on a lawn will find additional food in mixed grasses'. In fact, oranges and bananas were a

LEFT: ***A bomb which failed to explode landed near the stable of this donkey in January 1941. The police had the difficult task of persuading the animal to leave its home while the bomb was made safe.***

On Guard. Farmer Cook, an early member of Britain's Home Guard, took his dog, Lady, with him on his lonely vigils in the summer of 1940, and used her as a messenger if he observed anything untoward.

luxury by this time and a tortoise might be more likely to be offered an apple, though unfortunately 'many do not seem to appreciate this'.

Wartime concerns were not just about food *for* animals, but also about animals *as* food. Many an urban householder became enthusiastic about a few chickens scratching about in the back yard that would supplement the family's rations with fresh eggs. 'Hey! Little hen/When, when, when will you lay me an egg for my tea?' was the refrain of a popular wartime song and by the end of the war it was reckoned that 11.5 million hens were being kept by 'back yarders' – more than double the pre-war figure. Poultry feed was rationed and could be procured only in exchange for a family's egg ration entitlement. Once the hen was no longer a good layer, it was usually destined for the pot, its feathers sold off for war purposes.

Rabbits were another likely source of food – and warm gloves – and the fancier's magazine *Fur and Feather* printed an exhortation to 'every rabbit breeder in the country [who] should now be making plans to produce rabbit flesh'. It pointed out that for a

AIR RAID SHELTER

modest expenditure of a few pence on feedstuff, they would get two and a half pounds of meat. There were no rations for rabbits unless they were being bred to provide meat for a hospital, for example, so the animals existed on whatever vegetable trimmings came from the kitchen – and would even eat tea leaves in moderation. Advice was given on the most humane way to kill a rabbit – strike it at the base of the skull with a piece of blunt wood rather than attempting to wring its neck unless you were an expert – but many wartime rabbit owners found that when it came to it they just couldn't bring themselves to kill the appealing bundle of fur in the back garden that the whole family had grown so fond of.

Families were, perhaps, rather less likely to feel sentimental towards a pig: they were, however, likely to feel grateful for the bacon, brawn, chops, faggots, joints, sausages, savouries, trotters and lard its slaughter could provide. In the anti-waste wartime campaign, the Small Pig Keepers' Council had been set up to encourage people to keep pigs, which would eat kitchen and garden waste. A Middle White was recommended as a suitable garden pig: it was of a quiet disposition and weighed around 13 stone on average when fully grown – though some grew to nearer twice that. Not very many town dwellers had the space – or the inclination – to keep a pig in their own back yard, so a First World War idea, the pig club, was revived. Workmates or neighbours would club together to buy a pig and contribute their kitchen leavings. Some pig clubs were modest affairs with just a few co-owners saving scraps for their porker, while in Tottenham in north-east London 68 refuse collectors ran what almost amounted to a small holding. Starting with 100 pigs, bins were attached to their refuse lorries for vegetable scraps that had to be boiled for an hour, according to Ministry of Agriculture regulations before being fed to the pigs. Soon local authorities set up pig bins in the street where households could throw their vegetable waste: it was then collected and turned into swill. Pig clubs were advised to seek professional help when it came to killing the fatted pig, though not all did, and the Ministry of Agriculture employed instructors to visit clubs to show the members how to slaughter humanely – and how to maximise every scrap of meat.

These attempts at urban animal husbandry along with 'digging for victory', growing vegetables anywhere they could be fitted in, from herbaceous borders to railway embankments, were all part of the government policy to make Britain self-sufficient in food production in wartime. To this end permanent pasture land was ploughed up so it could be used for growing food crops: the target was two million acres of newly ploughed arable land before the 1940 harvest. As a result of this, and the reduction of imported livestock feed, the number of farm animals in Britain was drastically reduced: the number of pigs fell by a half, sheep by a fifth and farmed poultry (as opposed to those in the back garden) by a quarter. Indeed, so thoroughgoing was this livestock slaughter towards the end of 1940 that

OPPOSITE: ***Animal ARP volunteers find a cat in a bombed-out building in November 1940.***

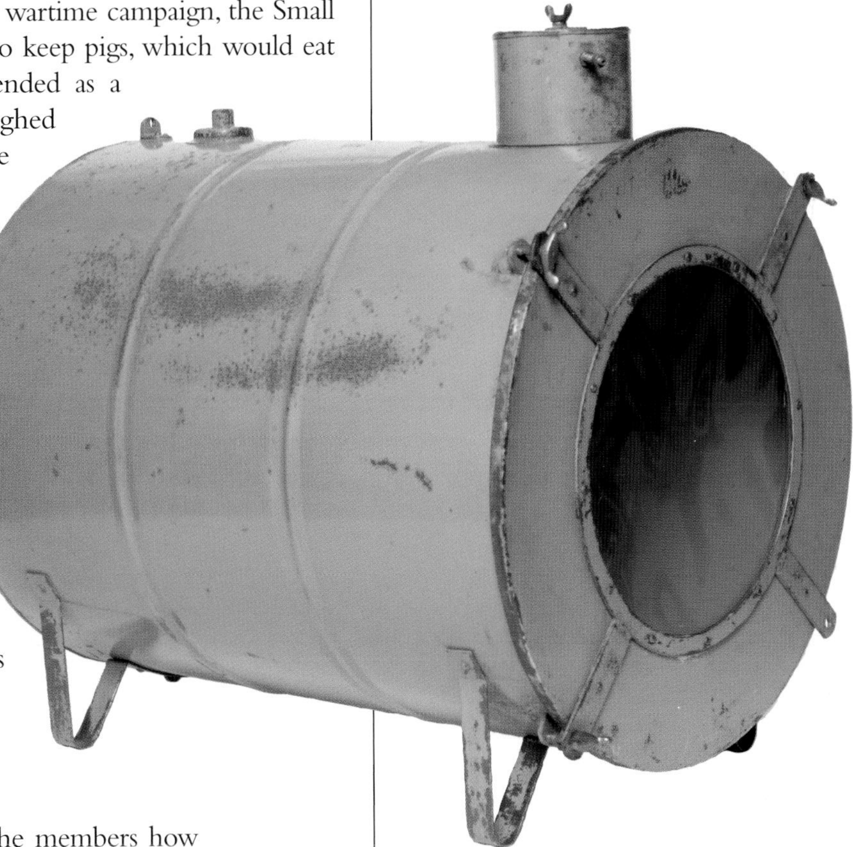

A domestic gas-proof dog kennel from the Second World War.

Back to the Land

'Women can look after chickens, but they cannot ditch. They can feed the pigs, but they cannot look after the boar. They can milk cows, and if they have enough experience, which is not very often, they can attend to their calving, but they cannot look after a bull ... In fact they cannot do any heavy work on the farm, and there is not a great deal of light work; the idea of substituting women for men on the farm is absurd' opined a farming commentator when the Women's Land Army (WLA) was revived on 1 June 1939. But he was wrong.

By June 1940 8,800 women – many of them confirmed 'townees' – had volunteered to work on the land to improve Britain's agricultural production and make the nation as self-sufficient as possible in wartime.

Paid less than the men for equivalent work, often lonely, cold and very tired, and initially the butt of farmers' prejudice and derision, the women, wearing a uniform of fawn corduroy breeches or khaki dungarees, learned to do almost all the jobs men did with animals – including in some cases becoming super efficient rat catchers. Some 5,000 of more than 80,000 who served in the WLA grew to like farm work so much that when the war was over they stayed on the land.

LEFT: ***Women's Land Army. Iris Joyce, who worked as a typist before volunteering for the WLA in the Second World War. She received four weeks' training at the Northampton Institute of Agriculture before going to work on the farm where she is pictured leading a bull.***

BELOW: ***Cecil Aldin (1870–1935):*** **'A Land Girl Ploughing'**, ***in the First World War. Aldin enjoyed a considerable reputation as a painter of the countryside, of animal life, and particularly of hunting scenes.***

so much meat flooded onto the market that the ration had to be raised temporarily.

Life could be perilous for those animals left alive in wartime: for a start many were at the mercy of members of the Women's Land Army who had been recruited to fill the gaps in manpower caused by wartime conscription. However, these women usually proved a great success, being willing, hard working and competent additions to the rural labour force – despite initial prejudice of a number of farmers. The black out could be hazardous for stock being driven along pitch-black country lanes, but, much more seriously, farm animals, since they were often unprotected in open fields or flimsy sheds, were very vulnerable to bombs – many of which did fall in open country. Cattle in Kent, Sussex and Surrey were sometimes hit by shrapnel or machine gun fire as the Battle of Britain was fought in the skies overhead, the first V1 flying bomb landed on a farm in Kent, and in Kent alone 100 horses, 500 cattle and 1,000 sheep were killed by bombs or fragments of shells from the defending guns. Around Dover, a port that was in the frontline of bombing and shelling throughout the war, 3,046 animals were dealt with by the RSPCA during these attacks, the majority of which were farm animals. Throughout the country Luftwaffe aircraft returning from bombing raids would release the last of their deadly load as they flew over the countryside, rather than take the risk of landing with bombs still on board. Furthermore, the deep craters caused by such bombs presented a considerable danger to livestock, resulting in broken legs or even drowning.

Working horses stabled in city centres were at risk. Biddy was trapped in her stable for over nine hours after a raid: eight other horses were also rescued but three were killed.

Nobody would have doubted that there were a large number of cats and dogs in London. A census of Greater London taken in 1937 showed 400,000 dog licences had been issued that year but, since that did not include puppies under six months, the real total was higher; it was thought impossible to know how many cats there were, but an estimate was over a million and a half. What seems surprising now is the number of farm animals that were resident in the capital. There were some 9,000 cattle, approximately 6,000 sheep, 18,000 pigs (and this was more than three years before the pig club initiative) and 40,000 horses, and the situation was not far different in other large cities throughout Britain. Cows were housed in inner cities to bring the supply of milk as close as possible to the consumer. Horses became of increasing importance during the war. With the introduction of petrol rationing and the difficulty of getting tyres and replacement parts for delivery vans and other forms of motorised transport, horses were again put between the shafts to deliver milk, post, bread and other necessities. Railway horses alone moved nine million tons of freight and 26 million parcels each year between 1939 and 1945.

During the Second World War petrol rationing and other shortages meant that many horses were re-employed for transport. Here, horse-drawn carts mingle with London buses at Ludgate Circus,* circa *March 1944.

The danger to horses on the street during the black out was great and once the raids started it multiplied many fold. An appeal was broadcast to the public for the loan of sheds and garages so that horses going about their business could be sheltered when the air raid siren ululated. So many cars had been requisitioned for war work that offers of garages poured in, and King George VI offered part of the Royal Mews to be set aside for horses that had been bombed out of their stables. Soon dray horses from a destroyed London brewery were ensconced in the regal apartments. If no shelter was available during a daytime raid, drivers were advised to tether their horse to a stout tree or a heavy stationary vehicle but 'never to lamp posts, traffic beacons, or area railings'.

After a raid on Southport in Lancashire, in which four horses were killed outright, others were found tied firm by their harness rope an`d unable to be helped to escape. A quick-release device was developed to enable horses (and cattle and other tethered animals) to be released quickly from their stables in the event of fire, rather than securing them with a thick rope or chain. So effective was this shackle that it was adopted by airborne troops needing to disengage quickly from their parachute harness. However, rescuers found it almost impossible to persuade a terrified horse to leave its burning stable and various tricks were tried including putting a sack over its head or having a goat lead it through the flames, which finally seemed somehow to calm by example.

Underground rather than at the Front, nevertheless some 25,000 pit ponies played an essential part in war production, working down coal mines such as this one at Crofton Mill, Northumberland.

On the outbreak of war, the mounts of the Metropolitan Police were evacuated to Surrey, but they were soon brought back to patrol the London streets and were trained to become accustomed to the terrors of the wail of the siren, the crump of bombs, the whine of shells and the crackle and smoke of fire. Only one police horse lost its life in an air raid, and in fact Regent was on a 'refresher course' in Surrey when he had to be destroyed after a flying bomb hit the stables. Three of the Met's horses were awarded Dickin Medals for outstanding bravery. Regal was twice trapped by fire in his stables in separate incidents, but, although he received minor injuries and was showered with debris, he 'showed no sign of panic' according to his citation. Olga was on duty when a flying bomb demolished four houses in Tooting, South London, and a plate glass window crashed immediately in front of her. Although she initially bolted, Olga allowed herself to be ridden back to the scene of the incident and remained on duty with her handler, controlling traffic and assisting rescue operations. Upstart was on duty in Bethnal Green when a flying bomb exploded 75 yards away, showering both horse and rider with glass and debris. Upstart was unperturbed and continued with his duties as his rider controlled the traffic. Stalwart horses all, and among those many, many animals in wars throughout the centuries that have saved lives, given succour, comfort, encouragement and companionship in wars not of their making, as they continue to do today – regrettably.

Postwar reconstruction. Kiri, a circus elephant, helps clear the streets of Dresden, Germany, which had been devastated by US/British bombing raids on 13–15 February 1945.

That men may fight...

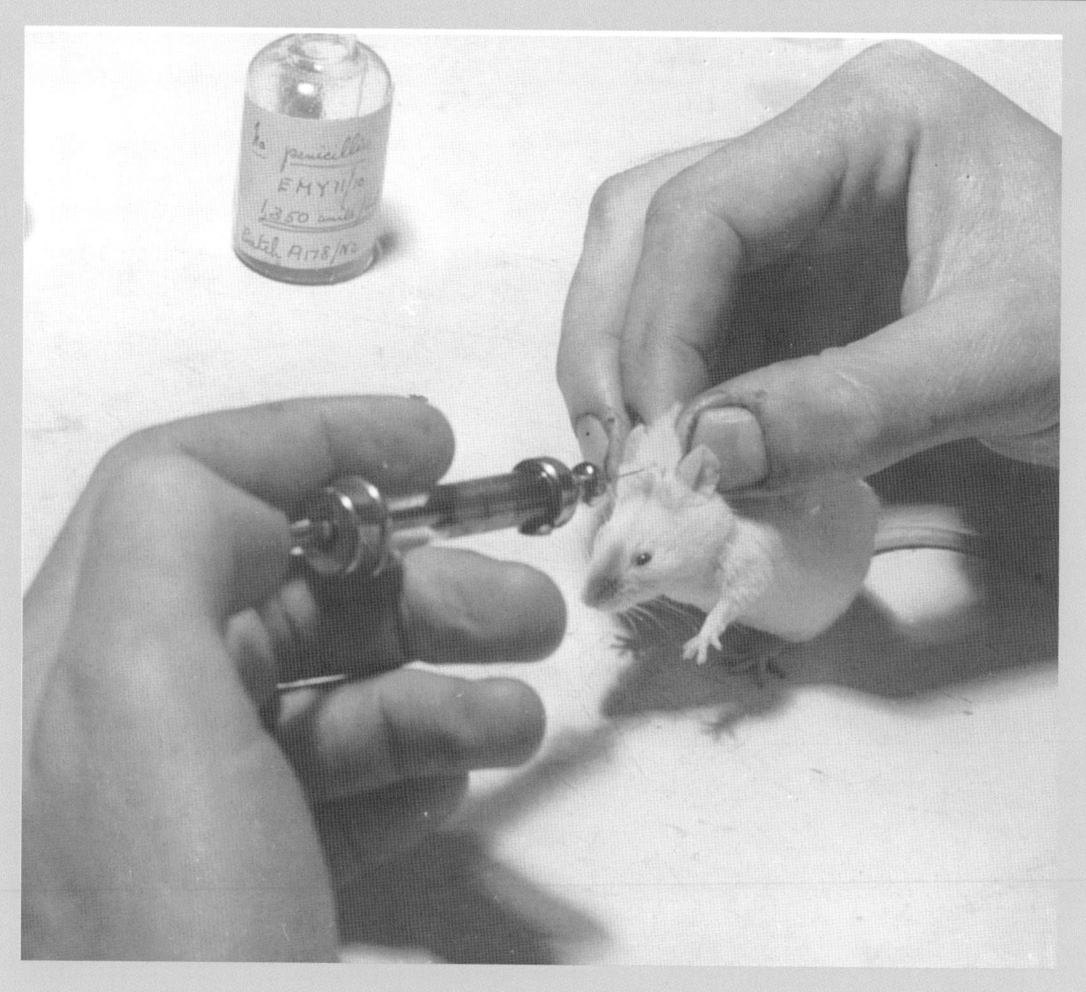

'I am in favour of animal rights as well as human rights. That is the way of a whole human being' wrote the US President Abraham Lincoln.

The Animals' War has detailed and described the many and various ways that animals have been used in men's wars. Their role has been decided, so what then of their rights? The first sentence in the preamble of the Universal Declaration of Human Rights adopted by the General Assembly of the United Nations on 10 December 1948 declares that 'the recognition of the inherent dignity and of equal and inalienable rights of all members of the human family is the foundation of freedom, justice and peace.' But when peace is violated so are all human rights. The Geneva Convention may lay down rules applicable in all conflicts but these include a protocol that civilians are not to be subject to attack, that there is to be no destruction of property unless justified by military necessity, that warring parties must not use or develop biological or chemical weapons. All these things have happened in almost all wars in the 20th and now the 21st century. So if human rights are set at naught in times of armed conflict, how is it possible to argue the case for animal rights in wartime?

The usual response is that animals cannot give their consent to take part in military exercises, they do not volunteer to fight, nor do they know what danger they might be putting themselves in when they do what they have been trained to do such as sniffing out mines, entering burning buildings, or attacking armed men.

But of course most men and women who go to war are not volunteers, they are conscripted by law, or their political, social or economic circumstances in practice render their consent nugatory. And although by the Second World War, a number of countries had allowed the principle that a person could object to taking part in wars on religious or ethical grounds, this was by no means a universal right then, nor is it today.

Yet a consideration of animal rights strikes right to the heart of issues of war. The canine research scientist Caroline Hebard found in her studies of the Mexican earthquake in 1985 that dogs became depressed and demotivated when their tasks were concerned entirely with finding corpses, but that their enthusiasm revived when they 'saved' an injured person. If one accepts that animals are sentient, possess considerable cognitive powers, can feel pain, experience loss and anxiety, demonstrate loyalty and generally act altruistically, then animals must surely deserve to be treated on a continuum with human beings.

The same objections to the use of gas and chemical warfare, the same arguments against the deployment of nuclear weapons, the same demand to avoid escalation to war, the same insistence on as many safeguards and restraints as possible should war come, the same concern at experiments designed to perfect better ways of killing one another, pertain for beast as for man. Mankind's duty of care for animals will always be tested in extremis in times of war – and will, no doubt in the nature of such conflict, often be found wanting.

'Unless he extends the circle of his compassion to all living things, man will not himself find peace', wrote Albert Schweitzer.

OPPOSITE: *A mouse inoculated with penicillin as part of ongoing research into its uses in Britain, the USA and Canada, probably in 1943/4.*

BELOW LEFT: *A report of gas trials involving goats, rats and cats carried out at the Royal Engineers Experimental Station, Porton Down, Wiltshire, during the First World War.*

BELOW: *A four-and-a-half-year-old Himalayan hornless mountain goat, known as Lord Nelson, being put into a pressure chamber to test its reaction. Goats were used in such wartime experiments because their bodies reacted in similar ways to humans.*

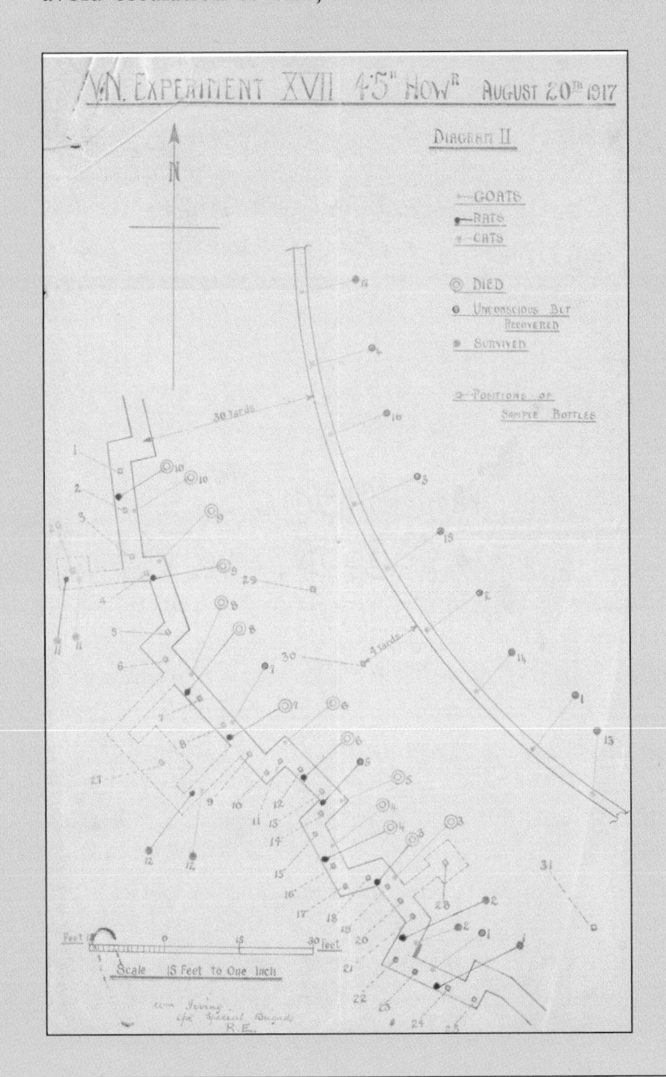

In Memoriam

The Animals' Memorial, Brook Gate, Hyde Park, London.

In 1931, writing of the part that horses had played in the Great War, Major-General Sir John Moore, who had been the director of Veterinary Services with the BEF, in France, mused that 'it seems strange that in this country where animals under domestication are held in such affectionate esteem, and where their value is so highly appraised in commercial life and for our pleasures, there should not have been some thoughtful recognition of the great services rendered by them during the late war, of the hardships they endured, of the sacrifices they made, and of the share which is due to them in victory.'

Animals that fought in war have had their 'thoughtful recognition' in the improvements in care, in animal management, and in medical treatment. And in many countries they have their monuments that concretise this recognition and pay permanent respect to the part animals played in combat. There are memorials to US Army dogs in Fort Benning, Georgia, and Riverside, California, and statues of Kurt, a Doberman Pinscher that served in Guam, stand both on Guam and in Tennessee. In Maryland there is a plaque to the horse, First Flight, 'for his vital role in Operation Desert Storm', since he was used by the US military to test vaccines against botulinum toxins for military and civilian personnel, and his ashes were scattered nearby. In Port Elizabeth, South Africa, a memorial to the 326,073 horses that died in the Boer War also embraces all those animals killed in human conflicts. The inscription reads: 'The greatness of a nation consists not so much in the numbers of its people, or the extent of its territory – as in the extent and justice of its compassion.'

Scotland has a cemetery for soldiers' dogs of the garrison in the courtyard of Edinburgh Castle. There is a monument to the horses requisitioned during the First World War at the church of St Jude on the Hill in Hampstead, north London, inscribed with the words 'most obediently and often most painfully they died – faithful unto death'. On the wall of a building which was used as an RSPCA dispensary in Kilburn, north London, there is a plaque that records 'the deaths by enemy action, disease or accident of 484,143 horses, mules, camels and bullocks and of many hundreds of dogs, carrier pigeons and other creatures, on the various fronts during the Great War'. It also records the fact that, in France alone, 725,216 sick and wounded animals were treated in veterinary hospitals provided by the RSPCA. Above it a plaque dedicates the building 'as a memorial to the countless thousands of God's humble creatures who suffered and perished in the Great War of 1914–18. Knowing nothing of the cause, looking forward to no final victory, filled only with love, faith and loyalty, they endured much and died for us. May we all remember them with gratitude and, in the future, commemorate their suffering and death by showing kindness and consideration to living animals.'

Rough wooden crosses fashioned from twigs or bits of firewood or small pebble cairns probably still mark shoebox graves in gardens and fields all over Britain, homely remembrances of pets that served and came home, or were killed on the home front. On battlefields all over the world, where men fell in combat and lie buried, unknown soldiers in unmarked graves, the same is true of their horses, mules, dogs … Yet all over Britain are unconscious, unacknowledged memorials to animals. Generals and brigadiers, field marshals and commanders-in-chief sit forever immortalised in bronze or stone astride their horse, as sculpted medieval knights lie in churches and cathedrals with their faithful hounds at their feet for eternity.

Frederic Henri Kay Henrion (1914–1990): **'Dove of Peace', circa** *1944. Born in Nuremberg in Germany, Henrion took British nationality in 1936 and during the Second World War worked as a graphic designer for the Ministry of Information. The dove has been a symbol of peace and innocence for thousands of years in many different cultures. In Christian art the dove was used to symbolise the Holy Ghost and was often painted above Christ's head. But it was Pablo Picasso who made the dove a modern symbol of peace when he used it on a poster for the World Peace Congress in 1949.*

In 2005, 60 years after its end, a memorial to the part that women played in the Second World War was finally unveiled in Whitehall, not far from the Cenotaph. Since November 2004 there has also been a fitting tribute to 'Animals in War' in Hyde Park – a link both to the women's memorial and to the 37,500 war memorials to the dead of both world wars that stand sentinel throughout the country. This memorial is due to the efforts of the novelist Jilly Cooper, author of the inspirational *Animals in War*, who was saddened and incensed by the lack of official recognition, and who, with two other trustees, became the moving spirit behind an appeal to the public to fund such a monument. The memorial, designed by the sculptor David Backhouse and built in Portland Stone, commemorates *all* animals caught up in the wars that ravaged the 20th century. It is rich in meaning. On the inner wall there are profiles in bas-relief of horses, dogs, camels, monkeys, goats, bears, elephants and even the glow worms that allowed troops to read their maps in the trenches during the First World War. Ghostly silhouettes of animals representing those that were lost in wars steal wraith-like along the outer wall. The carved inscription reads 'They Had No Choice'.

Approaching this daunting wall of war trudge two heavily-laded bronze pack mules and through a small gap in its forbidding mass can be seen a bronze horse and a dog pointing north. They are bearing witness to the loss of their colleagues but also representing hope for the future, the possibility of an end to wars and conflict, to endless slaughter and dispossession, in which man and beast have been caught up since the beginning of time.

> 'And some there be which have no memorial:
> Who perished as though they had not been.'
>
> (Ecclesiastes 44.9)

Bibliography

Blenkinsep, Major-General Sir L. J. and Rainey, Lt-Col. J. W. (eds.), *Official History of the War Veterinary Service* (HMSO, 1925)

Bourne, Dorothea St Hill, *They Also Serve* (Winchester Publications, 1947)

Brereton, J. M., *The Horse in War* (David & Charles, 1976)

Brown, Malcolm, *Tommy Goes to War* (Dent, 1978)

The Imperial War Museum Book of 1914: the men who went to war (Sidgwick & Jackson, revised ed 2004)

Lawrence: the Life, the Legend (Thames & Hudson, 2005)

Calvert, Michael, *Fighting Mad* (Jarrolds, 1964)

Clabby, Brigadier J., *The History of the Royal Army Veterinary Corps 1919–1961* (J. A. Allen & Co, 1963)

Cooper, Jilly, *Animals in War* (Wm Heinemann 1983; new ed Corgi, 2000)

Davies, Jennifer, *The Wartime Kitchen and Garden: The Home Front, 1939–45* (BBC Books, 1993)

De Grazia, David, *Animal Rights. A Very Short Introduction* (Oxford University Press, 2002)

De Waal, Frans, *The Ape and the Sushi Master: Cultural Reflections by a Primatologist* (Penguin, 2002)

Edwards, Major T. J., *Mascots and Pets of the Service* (Gale & Polden, 1953)

Fergusson, Bernard, *The Wild Green Earth* (Collins, 1946)

Fudge, Erica, *Animal* (Reaktion Books, 2002)

Galtrey, Captain Sidney, *The Horse and the War* (Country Life Publications, 1918)

Gardiner, Juliet, *Wartime: Britain 1939–1945* (Headline, 2004) *The Children's War* (Portrait in Association with the Imperial War Museum, 2005)

Going, Clayton G., *Dogs at War* (Macmillan, 1945)

Gray, Ernest A., *Dogs of War* (Robert Hale, 1989)

Greenwood, Jeremy, *Sefton 'The Horse of Any Year'* (Quiller Press, 1983)

Grow, Malcolm C., *Surgeon Grow: An American in the Russian Fighting, etc* (William Briggs, 1918)

Hall, Major R. J. G., *The Australian Light Horse* (The Dominion Press, 1966)

Halstock, M., *Rats: The Story of a Dog Soldier* (Gollancz, 1981)

Hamer, Blythe, *Dogs at War: True Stories of Canine Courage Under Fire* (Carlton Books, 2001)

Hammerton, Sir John (ed.), *A Popular History of the Great War. Volume VI: Armistice and After* (The Fleetway House, 1934)

Harfield, Alan, *Pigeon to Packhorse. The Illustrated Story of Animals in Army Communications* (Picton Publishing, 1989)

Hogue, Oliver, *The Cameliers* (Andrew Melrose, 1919)

Huxley, Julian, *Memories* (George Allen & Unwin, 2 vols., 1970–73)

Inchbald, Geoffrey, *Camels and Others* (Johnson, 1968)

Imperial Camel Corps (Johnson, 1970)

Kramer, J. J., *Animal Heroes. Military Mascots and Pets* (Leo Cooper/Secker & Warburg, 1982)

Le Chêne, Evelyn, *Silent Heroes: The Bravery and Devotion of Animals in War* (Souvenir Press, 1994)

Lemish, Michael G., *War Dogs: The First Comprehensive History of the Military Dog* (Brassey's Inc, 1996)

Longmate, Norman, *How We Lived Then: a history of everyday life during the Second World War* (Hutchinson, 1971)

Lubow, R. E., *The War Animals. The Training and Use of Animals as Weapons of War* (Doubleday, 1977)

Lunt, James, *Charge to Glory! A Garland of Cavalry Exploits* (Heinemann 1961)

McCafferty, Garry, *They Had No Choice: Racing Pigeons at War* (Tempus, 2000)

MacFetridge, C. H. T., and Warren, J. P. (eds.), *Tales of the Mountain Gunners* (William Blackwood, 1974)

Midgley, Mary, *Animals and Why They Matter* (University of Georgia Press, 1983)

Mitchell, E., *Light Horse. The Story of Australia's Mounted Troops* (Macmillan, 1978)

Moore, Major-General Sir John, *Army Veterinary Services in War* (H&W Brown, 1921)

Morgan, Geoffrey and Lasocki, Wieslaw A., *Soldier Bear* (Collins, 1972)

Moss, Arthur W., *Valiant Crusade: The History of the RSPCA* (Cassell, 1961)

Moss, Arthur and Kirby, Elizabeth, *Animals Were There. A record of the work of the RSPCA during the war of 1939–1945* (Hutchinson, 1947)

Osman, Lt.-Col A. H., and Major W. H., *Pigeons in Two World Wars* (The Racing Pigeon Publishing Company, 1976)

Piekalkiewicz, Janusz, *The Cavalry of World War II* (Orbis Publishing, 1979)

Richardson, Lt.-Col. E. H., *British War Dogs: their training and psychology* (Skeffington, 1920)

Rogers, Col H. C. B., *The Mounted Troops of the British Army, 1066–1945, Vol. III* (Seely, Service & Co., 1959)

Sheldrake, Rupert, *Dogs That Know When Their Masters Are Coming Home and other unexplained powers of animals* (Hutchinson, 1999)

The Story of the Royal Army Service Corps, 1939–1945 (The Institution of the Royal Army Service Corps and G. Bell and Sons, 1955)

Tamblyn, Lt-Col. D. S., *The Horse in War* (Country Life, 1918)

Terraine, John, *The Smoke and the Fire. Myths and Anti-Myths of war, 1861–1945* (Sidgwick & Jackson, 1980)

Turner, E. S., *The Phoney War* (Michael Joseph, 1961)

Ward, Sadie, *War in the Countryside, 1939–45* (Cameron Books, 1988)

Williams, J. H., *Elephant Bill* (Rupert Hart Davis, 1950)

Bandoola (Rupert Hart Davis, 1953)

Articles

Corvi, Steven J., 'Men of Mercy: the Evolution of the Royal Army Veterinary Corps and the Soldier-Horse Bond during the Great War', *Journal of the Society for Army Historical Research* 76 (1998)

Phayre, Ignatius, 'War Duties for the Dogs', *The Windsor Magazine* (June 1916)

Wilson, David A. H., 'Sea Lions, Greasepaint and the U-Boat Threat: Admiralty Scientists Turn to the Music Hall in 1916', *Notes and Records. Royal Society of London* 55(3) (2001)

Givenson, Irene M., 'Man's Loyal Friend, the Dog in Time of War', *The Red Cross Courier*, 1926.

Hipgrave, D., 'The Hook, Northaw, 1942-5. The Army Dogs' Training Schoool', *Journal of the Potters Bar and District Historical Association* no. 8, 1995

Illifff, Susan A., 'An Additional "R": Remembering the Animmals', *Institute for Laboratory Animal Research* vol. 43 (1), 2002.

Marren, Peter 'Dolphins Go to War', *Independent*, 5 October 2005.

More, Cordula V., Davison, Michael, Wild, and Walker, Michael M., 'Magnettoreception and its trigeminal mediation in the homing pigeon', *Nature*, vol. 432, 25 November 2004

National Defense Magazine February 2002

Steele, Garrison 'The British Army Veterinary Corps and National Humane Organization in the Present European War', *American Journal of Veterinary Medicine*, February 1915.

The Animals' Defender September and November, 1940

The Animal World May, September, November 1917, October1939, August 1940, November 1940, January, 1941, November 1944, November 1945

The Journal of the Royal Army Veterinary Corps November 1943, February 1944, May 1945, February 1946, May 1946, February 1947, March 1950, June 1949, June, 1954, March 1955, Spring, 1958.

Web sites

http://news.bbc.co.uk/1/hi/middle_east

http://linasog.com/military

http://old.handzon.com

http://sheldrake.org/experiments/pigeons

http://usmiliitary.about.com/cs/airforce

www.armedforces.co/uk/army

www.army.mod.uk/Irishguards

www.cordis.lu/express/archive

www.geocities.com

www.news.mod.uk

www.uk.diving.co.uk

Acknowledgements and Permissions

Writing *The Animal's War* has been a journey of discovery for me. I have learned a great deal both about the enormous contributions that animals have made to the prosecution of wars, and the terrible experiences many suffered in wartime. I am extremely grateful to the people who have helped me with these discoveries. My thanks first to the staff of the Imperial War Museum: to Angela Godwin and Penny Ritchie Calder who planned the exhibition which this book accompanies; to Elizabeth Bowers and Gemma Maclagan who were so helpful in acting as my link with the Museum; to Roderick Suddaby and his colleagues in the Department of Documents for the unfailing helpfulness, knowledge and ingenuity on which I have come to rely, and above all to Terry Charman without whose expertise, advice, scrutiny, and sheer hard work this book simply could not have been written.

I also owe a great debt to Jilly Cooper whose path-breaking work in retrieving so many stories about animals in wartime in her own book, *Animals in War* (which accompanied another IWM exhibition over 20 years ago), has been an inspiration to me. I am particularly grateful for the way she shared her passion for the subject with me, encouraged me in my writing, and generously lent me material she has assiduously collected over the years.

At Piatkus my thanks go to Alan Brooke who again has shown great enthusiasm for the project and a steely determination to bring it to fruition, and to Alison Sturgeon who has again proved an exemplary editor in every possible way. At Compendium Simon Forty and Frank Ainscough have made the process efficient and painless.

My thanks, as usual, go to my agent Deborah Rogers for her help and encouragement.

I am also greatly indebted to Dr Jacky Turner whose wisdom in the field of animal science and animal welfare saved me from both errors and, I hope, misjudgements; to Malcolm Brown whose deep knowledge of the First World War and of T. E. Lawrence was most generously shared; and to Professor Henry Horwitz whose rigorous yet encouraging support proved, as so often, invaluable.

I am also grateful both to the Trustees of the Imperial War Museum and to the individual copyright holders for allowing me access to the collections of papers held by the IWM and for permission to publish extracts from them.

Department of Documents
Item 912; K709002; Misc.60: Misc. 98 (1502); Misc. 225 (3227); Mrs E. M. Bilbrough (90/10/1); J. T. Capron (87/33/1); Captain J. I. Cohen (85/77/1); A. Cornfoot (97/37/1); Lieutenant E. W. Cotton (P262); Miss M. Coules (97/25/1); Captain J. B. Foulis (85/15/1); Captain J. S. D.Hardy (93/19/1); A. Lowy (60/78/1); R. M. Luther (87/8/1); Lieutenant J. W. McPherson (80/25/1); Major D. G. Pearman (78/21/1); Captain E. R. Pennell (P427); R. I. Smith (86/36/1).

The debt I owe to writers who have traversed this territory before me is acknowledged in the Bibliography. Any errors or omissions remain, of course, my sole responsibility.

Image permissions
Image references listed from top to bottom and left to right as they appear on the page

© Imperial War Museum, London:
p.8 PST 6189; p.10 Mary Kessell *A Dying Horse Pulling Chattels*; p.11 PST 0408; p.12 PST 7675; p.17 Q 2032; p.19 John Singer Sargent RA *Scots Greys*; p.21 Q 60706; p.22 Q 10876; p.23 Q 2213; p.24 Feliks Topolski *A Russian Cavalry Horse-drawn Machine-gun*, Q 4687; p.25 RR 705; p.26 James Prinsep Barnes Beadle *The Breaking of the Hindenberg Line*; p.27 Q 8446; p.29 Q 13301; p.30 Edwin Noble *An Injured Horse being loaded into a Motor Ambulance*; p.31 Q 1424, MOD 120; p.32 EA 31; p.33 EA 30, HU 2618; p.34 Darsie Japp MC *Regimental Band*; p.35 Stuart Reid *Bombing of the Wadi Fara, 20th September*; p.38 Q 1565; p. 39 Q 5198; p.42 Q 5943; p.43 Edwin Noble *A Horse Ambulance Pulling a Sick Horse out of a Field*, MOD 257; p.44 Q 4599, Q 5717; p.46 Q 24556, MOD 560; p.49 Q 1425, PST 6185; p.50 Q 54993, Q 10957; p.51 H 1050; Q 10603; p.54 Q 50845; p.55 James McBey *The Camel Corps: A Night March to Beersheba*; LN 534913; p.57 MOD 001054; p.58 Q 012578, MOD 001048; p.60 James McBey *Water Transport*, MOD 1052; p.61 Q 15697, Q 58754; p.63 Q 58863, James McBey *Camel Transport Corps*; p65 Q 12513; p.67 Q 12518; p.68 Q 8531; p.69 Q 5766; p.70 Q 5941; p.71 Q 16176, Q 4855; p.72 Q 31581; p.73 EQU 28, E AUS 91; p.74 Q 24505; p.75 NA 9358; p.76 MOD 103, Q 31581; p.77 NYF 31412, Q 32469; p.79 A 24292A; p.80 SE 3199, HU 67371; p.82 Q 114807; p.83 Q 48445; p.84 NY 3815, TR 1496; p.85 H 12985, NYP 14111; p.88 Q 9276, Q 6475; p.90 Q 11305; p.93 Q 50649; p.94 Q 50671; p.95 MOD 310; p.97 CO 1414; p.98 Q 6230; p.100 MOD 307; p.101 Q 9247, PO 868; p.102 COM 000928; p.103 D 442, Q 8870; p.104 H 11281; p.105 H 11281; p.108 B 6501; p.109 B 6506; p.112 James McBey *The Long Patrol: Tracks Discovered*; p.113 HU 2624; p.114 Q 53539; p.116 E (AUS) 1683; p.118 HU 2616; p.119 ART 1S307; p.120 HU 48650, HU 48647; p.121 A 32632; p.122 NY 8994, HU 93693; p.124 HU 41992; p.125 HU 45623; p.127 Q 54973; p.128 Stanley Spencer RA *Travoys Arriving with Wounded at a Dressing-Station at Smol, Macedonia, September 1916*; p.129 Q 32471, PST 10968; p.130 MOD 559; p.131 TR 1376; p.133 Q 32433, Q 45738; p.134 HU 49315; p.136 EPH 007673, EPH 4540; p.137 D 5945; p.138 HU 2625; p.139 NYF 41515; p.142 BU 8177, EPH 007630; p.143 A 33564, Q 1451; p.144 H13193, Q4328; p.145 Q 6586; p.146 LD 006502, Q 017983; p.147 Philip Connard *RA St George's Day 1918: Bridge of HMS Canterbury*; p.150; p.151 Q 10654; p.152 Q 47559, Q 6400; p.153 Sir William Orpen *The Mascot of the Coldstream Guards*; p.154 HU 43624; p.155 D 18961; p.156 HU 2621, EPH 007779; p.157 C 1746, A 15996; p.158 HU 43657; p.159 EA 34600; PST 6190; p.161 HU 44288; p.162 HU 49658; p.163 B 8766 (XF); p.165 HU 43577; p.166 *Animal World*; p.167 PP00358; p.168 *Your Dog and Cat in Wartime*; p.169 D 21224; p.170 D 984; p.171 D 24212, HU 44469; p.174 D 5953; p.174; p.175 D 1639, D 21220; p.176 Misc 2381 1064 1; p.179 EPH 7658; p.180 D 8839, Cecil Aldin *A Land Girl Ploughing*; p.182 D 16835; p.183 BU 11451; p.184 D 16967; p.185 Misc3227 11989 1, A 29530; p.187 Frederic Henri Kay *Dove of Peace*

© The Artist's Estate From IWM collection: p.37 © William Roberts Society. William Roberts RA *'Feeds Round!' Stable-time in the Wagon-lines, France*; H R Cooke *Saving the Horses*; p.45 Lucy Kemp-Welch *The Straw Ride*; Haydn Reynold Mackey *Epéhy, 1918*; p.86 George Soper *'Cheerio! I've joined up!'*, p.105; p. 111 Colin Self *Guard Dog on Missile Site 1966*;

© Other copyrights From the IWM collection: p.13 90/10/1; p.14 Misc 274; p.18 Misc 912 49/20/1; p.41 Captain J.B. Foulis (85/15/1); p.57 J.W. McPherson (80/25/1); p.59 Misc1502 (9964); p.64 BuchananA_4429 1; p.65 Major D.G. Pearman (78/21/2); p.91 Misc2490 2158 1p. 92 Q 7346, COM 1068; p.93 Q 23697; p.96 Misc1430 8687; p.117 Misc2529 2383 1; PL 15225; PhilpotOLS 13456 1, EPH 4618

Other copyrights
p.4, 41, 47, 125 From the private collection of Anthony Langley. *War Illustrated* images by Stanley Wood; p.7, 9, 66, 186 © **Edifice**; p.16 used with permission from **Egmont UK Ltd;** p.20 from the Marshall family; p.28 Artist's copyright Sir Alfred Munnings *Charge of Flowerdew's Squadron, c.1918*; p.47, 87, 148 © **Mary Evans;** p.53 The Home of Rest for Horses; p.62 From the Marist Collection; p.99,140 **Rex Features**; p. 105 Guy Burn *Divisional Pigeon Loft, Italy 1944*. © The artist; p. 106, p.110; p.132 Rod Planck **NHPA**; p.107, p.112, p.115, p.119, p.183 **Getty**; p.123 **Corbis;** p.124, p.135 **Austin J. Brown Aviation Picture Library**; p.126, p.154, p.173 **Corbis**; p.162 **AP**; p.172 **Manchester Art Gallery**

Every effort has been made to identify and acknowledge copyright holders of the following material. Any errors or omissions will be rectified in future editions, provided that written notification is made to the publisher.
From the IWM Collection: p.21 PST 12472; p.36 PST 2750; p.81 Rupert Hart-Davies; p.74 E Zimmerman *Hark! Hark! The Dogs Do Bark!*; p.78 PST 10972; p.83 PST 13398; p.89; p.94 PST 6184; PST 10976; PST 10977 IWM; p.164; p.167 PST 13422; p.177 HU 93694, HU 93696; p.178 HU 93145; p.181 HU 93695
Other: p.15, 69 Country Life

INDEX

NB: page numbers in italic indicate paintings, photographs or illustrations; page numbers in bold indicate artistss